NBCOT® Study Guide

for the OTR® Certification Examination

Occupational Therapist Registered

Mission

Serving the public interest by advancing client care and professional practice through evidence-based certification standards and the validation of knowledge essential for effective practice in occupational therapy.

Vision

Certified occupational therapy professionals providing effective evidence-based services across all areas of practice worldwide.

Accreditation

NBCOT certification programs have received and maintained accreditation from the American National Standards Institute (ANSI) and the National Commission for Certifying Agencies (NCCA).
All rights reserved. No part of this publication may be reproduced, stored in a retrieval system, or transmitted in any form or by any means (electronic, mechanical, photocopying, recording, or otherwise) without prior written permission of the copyright owners.

This study guide is one of a number of official NBCOT study tools designed to assist candidates with their exam preparation. NBCOT does not guarantee enhanced performance on the NBCOT certification examinations for those using these products.

Foreward

Letter From the President

Like many candidates, as you aspire to reach your certification goal, you probably wonder, "How can I best prepare for the NBCOT Certification Exam?" With the numerous options available, deciding which study tools to use can be a challenge.

Well, there is no magic answer. You are the only person who can make that decision by considering your personal learning style, current academic strengths and weaknesses, fieldwork experiences, and resources. However, one thing is certain: following a realistic and well-planned study schedule can help you feel more prepared for the certification exam.

This study guide provides an overview of what to expect on the Occupational Therapist Registered® (OTR) exam, options on how to prepare, and practice-focused sample items grouped under the major domain areas of the certification exam content outline. Feedback, answer keys, and references are provided to enhance test preparation strategies.

We hope the information in this guide supports and augments your overall exam preparation activities. We know the practice of occupational therapy is constantly evolving. The National Board for Certification in Occupational Therapy, Inc. NBCOT® includes only current information in examination items used for certification purposes. Although the information contained in this guide is current at the time of publication, you should refer to the most recent editions of references when studying for the NBCOT OTR® Certification Exam. The information and sample items in this guide can assist your overall study efforts, however they will not ensure or guarantee a passing score on the certification exam.

Best of luck as you pursue your professional career as an OTR.

Paul Grace, MS, CAE
President/CEO

i

NBCOT® Study Guide for the OTR Certification Examination

Introduction

How to Use This Guide

Historically, regulation of the health professions in the United States began with a necessity to protect the public from the under-educated and under-trained professional. Over time, licensure, credentialing, and certification have continued the tradition of protecting the public; they have also increased their scope of activity to continuously improve the quality of practice in the profession.

NBCOT® uses a formal process to grant the certification credential to an individual who:

1. Meets academic and fieldwork experience requirements,

2. Successfully completes a comprehensive examination to assess knowledge and skills for practice, and

3. Agrees to adhere to the NBCOT Candidate/Certificant Code of Conduct.

How This Study Guide Is Organized

SECTIONS

We have divided the study guide into sections to make it easier for you to find the information you are looking for. There are three sections:

Section 1
NBCOT OTR® Examination

In this section, we discuss the specifics of the NBCOT OTR exam and provide information and resources for you to be informed as you prepare for the exam. You will find an overview of the format of the Clinical Simulation Test (CST) problems and multiple choice questions used on the OTR exam, and a summary of what happens after you have completed the exam. In addition, the NBCOT Navigator®

ii

Competency Assessment Platform and other benefits of earning and maintaining your OTR credential are outlined for you.

Section 2
Preparing for the Exam

Here, we provide you with tools and methods to self-reflect on your perception of your test readiness and to develop a personalized study plan that you feel will work for you. We have included multiple resources, including the *NBCOT Illustrated Description of Entry-Level OTR® Practice*, the *OTR® Entry-Level Self-Assessment* tool, and a worksheet for you to develop your own personalized study plan. We hope you take the time to review the *NBCOT Exam StudyPack* and NBCOT Aspire exam prep tools to determine if you think these tools fit into your overall study plan.

Section 3
Time to Practice

In the *Time to Practice* section, we provide you with multiple choice practice test questions organized by the domains of the *OTR Exam Content Outline*.

OTR DOMAIN DESCRIPTIONS

DOMAIN 01	EVALUATION AND ASSESSMENT
	Acquire information regarding factors that influence occupational performance on an ongoing basis throughout the occupational therapy process.
DOMAIN 02	**ANALYSIS AND INTERPRETATION**
	Formulate conclusions regarding client needs and priorities to develop and monitor an intervention plan throughout the occupational therapy process.
DOMAIN 03	**INTERVENTION MANAGEMENT**
	Select interventions for managing a client-centered plan throughout the occupational therapy process.
DOMAIN 04	**COMPETENCY AND PRACTICE MANAGEMENT**
	Manage professional activities of self and relevant others as guided by evidence, regulatory compliance, and standards of practice to promote quality care.

Clinical Simulation Test Problems

The sample Clinical Simulation Test (CST) problem presented in this study guide closely mimics the format of the computer-delivered CST problems on the exam. However, this sample is not interactive. There are several options to experience interactive, computer-delivered CST problems:

- The Full Practice Exam in the *NBCOT Exam StudyPack* has 170 multiple- choice items and 3 CST problems.

- The Clinical Simulation Practice Test has 3 CST problems.

- There are practice CST problems available at: https://secure.nbcot. org/CSTDemo

Multiple Choice Items

Each chapter in this section of the study guide starts with a multiple choice practice test. An answer key is provided after each practice test—one option is to answer all the questions, then use the answer key to determine your total score on the practice test. Or, you may decide you want to answer each item one at a time and use the answer key as a reference to learn the correct response. How you approach using these practice tests to study is up to you! After the answer key in each chapter are the rationales for the correct answers and the references for each multiple choice question.

Appendices

To help streamline the information in the study guide, the following supporting documents and information are included in the Appendices:

APPENDIX A
2017 Content Outline for the OTR® Examination

APPENDIX B
An Illustrated Description of Entry-Level OTR® Practice

APPENDIX C
Worksheet: *Illustrated Guide*

APPENDIX D
OTR® Entry-Level Self-Assessment tool

APPENDIX E
References used during the development of this OTR Study Guide

Callout Boxes Used in This Study Guide

We have used distinct callout boxes throughout the study guide to make different types of content stand out. Callout boxes used in this study guide are as follows:

> **ⓘ Tips**
>
> These are ideas or suggestions for you to consider and think about when you are preparing for the NBCOT exam.

🔑 Key Points

A summary of information that is presented in a list.

> **❗ Important**
>
> Important information that you will want to repeat to yourself a few times.

⊕ Learn More

These callout boxes will provide you with the location of additional information in case you want to access and learn more about the topic.

> **📄 Note**
>
> Provides you with new information to clarify a particular topic.

> **👍 Remember**
>
> This is information that may be repeated a couple of time to draw attention to it.

Important Information for You to Know

This study guide is one of a number of NBCOT Aspire study tools designed to assist candidates with their exam preparation. NBCOT does not guarantee enhanced performance on the NBCOT certification examinations for those using these products. **NBCOT does not administer, approve, endorse, or review preparatory courses relating to the NBCOT certification examinations or study materials produced by other vendors.**

Table of Contents

Section 1
NBCOT OTR Examination

2 Chapter 1
Where to Start
Being informed.

5 Chapter 2
All About the Exam
The development and the format of the OTR exam.

10 Chapter 3
Format of the Test Items
Clinical simulation test (CST) problems and multiple choice questions

15 Chapter 4
After the Exam
Scoring, score reports and more

18 Chapter 5
Certification Renewal
Your OTR® credential and benefits of maintaining certification

Section 2
Preparing For The Exam

24 Chapter 6
NBCOT Illustrated Description to Entry-Level OTR® Practice
Critical thinking and Self-reflection

28 Chapter 7
NBCOT OTR® Entry-Level Self-Assessment Tool
Identifying your strengths and learning needs

32 Chapter 8
Personalized Study Plan
A method for developing a study plan that works for you.

37 Chapter 9
Exam Day
Planning for Exam Day and Test-taking tips

Section 3

Time to Practice

42 Chapter 10
Sample CST Problem
Sample CST problem with answer key
and references

52 Chapter 11
Domain 1: Multiple Choice
Sample Questions
Practice questions with answer key
and references

114 Chapter 12
Domain 2: Multiple Choice
Sample Questions
Practice questions with answer key
and references

186 Chapter 13
Domain 3: Multiple Choice
Sample Questions
Practice questions with answer key
and references

258 Chapter 14
Domain 4: Multiple Choice
Sample Questions
Practice questions with answer key
and references

Section 4

Appendices

332 Appendix A
Content Outline for the
OTR Examination

344 Appendix B
An Illustrated Description
of Entry-Level OTR® Practice

380 Appendix C
Worksheet: Illustrated Guide

382 Appendix D
NBCOT OTR® Entry-Level
Self-Assessment Tool

393 Appendix E
References

Section 1
NBCOT OTR Exam

Chapter 1

Where to Start

Being informed

Earning a passing score on the NBCOT OTR® Certification Exam is an important milestone in your certification journey. The OTR credential is representative of practitioners who have satisfied national standards in education, experience, and professional conduct. Certification as an OTR indicates to the public that you have demonstrated the knowledge and skills necessary to provide occupational therapy services. Currently, all 50 states, the District of Columbia, Guam, and Puerto Rico require NBCOT certification as an OTR as a component for becoming licensed to practice.

🔍 Learn More

As you prepare for the certification exam, review the *NBCOT Certification Exam Handbook* available at www.nbcot.org/Students/get-certified.

Being Informed

As you embark on the journey to certification, it is important to be informed about the resources available to you. Information about the NBCOT OTR® Certification Exam, initial certification, and certification renewal as an OTR is available to you at www.nbcot.org.

NBCOT Certification Exam Handbook

The *NBCOT Certification Exam Handbook* is an important resource to refer to on your journey to certification. The Handbook was developed to provide information on how to complete and successfully submit a certification exam application. Be sure to locate the Exam Application Procedures Checklist in the Handbook, which can guide you through the exam application process.

📄 Note

The *NBCOT Certification Exam Handbook* is your go-to resource for information on how to successfully submit a certification exam application.

MyNBCOT Account

A required step to register for the NBCOT OTR® Certification Exam is to create a MyNBCOT account. This is a necessary step in the exam application process, and also allows you to access the Aspire study tools. When you log in to your MyNBCOT account, you will be able to view details about the status of your application on your personalized Student Dashboard. You will continue to use your MyNBCOT account after you earn your certification to view information related to your certification status and to access many benefits provided to you by NBCOT for use throughout your certification journey.

⊕ Learn More

Register for a MyNBCOT account at
www.nbcot.org/Students/get-certified

Begin your certification journey by creating a MyNBCOT account. With an account you can:

Apply for the Exam

Apply for the exam and track your application status and service order status.

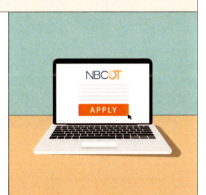

Use Aspire Study Tools

Access and use your Aspire study tools to prepare for the exam.

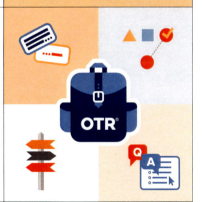

⊕ Learn More

Access Aspire study tools at
www.nbcot.org/Students/Study-Tools.

Stay Informed

Receive notifications on the latest NBCOT news and update your information.

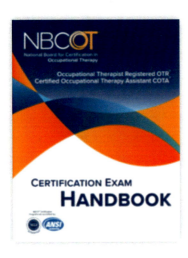

Staying Informed

This study guide provides information about the NBCOT OTR® Certification Exam and strategies for developing a personalized study plan. Answers to many of the questions you may have about the exam are available in the *NBCOT Certification Exam Handbook*, on the NBCOT website (www.nbcot.org), and on your personalized dashboard in your MyNBCOT account.

⚘ Key Points

- Explore the NBCOT website: www.nbcot.org
- Read the *NBCOT Certification Exam Handbook*.
- Register for a MyNBCOT account.

Chapter 2

All About the Exam

The development and the format of the OTR exam

NBCOT OTR Certification Exam

The primary purpose of the exam is to protect the public interest by certifying only those candidates who have the necessary knowledge of occupational therapy to practice as an OTR.

The current OTR certification exam is constructed from a content outline that will be described in this chapter.

NBCOT conducted an OTR practice analysis study in 2017. The results from this study were used to revalidate the exam content outline for the OTR exams that will be administered from January 2019 onward. In line with certification industry standards, NBCOT certification exams are constructed based on the results of practice analysis studies. A practice analysis study is a large-scale survey administered to entry-level OTR practitioners who are asked to evaluate job requirements on criticality and frequency rating scales. The results of the practice analysis study are used to:

- understand and classify the job requirements as the domains, tasks, and knowledge required for current occupational therapy practice

- develop a valid and defensible content outline for the exam

- determine content for the OTR certification exam

- ensure that there is a representative linkage of the test content to practice

⊕ Learn More

To learn more about this important study, view the *Practice Analysis of the Occupational Therapist Registered— Executive Summary*: www.nbcot.org/en/Students/Study-Tools/Exam-Outline.

NBCOT OTR Exam Development at a Glance

A practice analysis study validates the domain, task, and knowledge areas that are critical to and frequently used in occupational therapy practice.

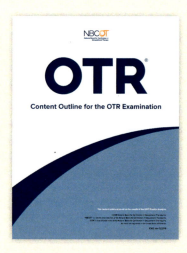

Items on the exam are based on the validated domain, task, and knowledge statements from the practice analysis study.

All OTR exam items meet:

- ✓ **BLUEPRINT SPECIFICATIONS**

- ✓ **CERTIFICATION INDUSTRY STANDARDS**

- ✓ **PSYCHOMETRIC AND SCORING STANDARDS**

Validated Domain, Task, and Knowledge Statements

From the results of this practice analysis study, the content outline for the OTR exam is developed. The results from the practice analysis identified four major domain areas for OTR practice. Within each of the four domain areas, there are a number of tasks and accompanying knowledge statements that were defined from the study results.

All items on the NBCOT exams are classified according to these domain, task, and knowledge statements.

Domains
Broadly define the major job components of the profession.

🔍 Learn More

To learn more about the development and construction of the OTR exam, review the Foundations of the NBCOT Certification Examinations at www.nbcot.org/Educators/Foundations.

DOMAIN 01	EVALUATION AND ASSESSMENT
	Acquire information regarding factors that influence occupational performance on an ongoing basis throughout the occupational therapy process.

Task 0101	Identify the influence of development; body functions and body structures; and values, beliefs, and spirituality on a client's occupational performance.

KNOWLEDGE OF:	
010101	Impact of typical development and aging on occupational performance, health, and wellness across the life span
010102	Expected patterns, progressions, and prognoses associated with conditions that limit occupational performance
010103	Impact of body functions, body structures, and values, beliefs, and spirituality on occupational performance

Tasks
Describe activities that are performed in each domain (i.e., things that practitioners do).

Knowledge Statements
Describe the information required to perform each task competently.

See Appendix A to read the Content Outline for the OTR Examination.

NBCOT® Study Guide for the OTR Certification Examination

OTR Exam Specifications

From the results of the practice analysis study, the OTR exam specifications were developed. The exam specification table shows the percentage of exam items that appear in each domain area of the exam. The percentage of items in each domain area is shown in **Table 2.1**. The percentage of items in each domain area remain constant on each OTR exam form.

Table 2.1:
OTR content outline specifications based on the *2017 Practice Analysis Study* (effective for OTR exams administered January 2019 onward)

OTR DOMAIN DESCRIPTIONS		% OF EXAM
DOMAIN 01	**EVALUATION AND ASSESSMENT** Acquire information regarding factors that influence occupational performance on an ongoing basis throughout the occupational therapy process.	25%
DOMAIN 02	**ANALYSIS AND INTERPRETATION** Formulate conclusions regarding client needs and priorities to develop and monitor an intervention plan throughout the occupational therapy process.	23%
DOMAIN 03	**INTERVENTION MANAGEMENT** Select interventions for managing a client-centered plan throughout the occupational therapy process.	37%
DOMAIN 04	**COMPETENCY AND PRACTICE MANAGEMENT** Manage professional activities of self and relevant others as guided by evidence, regulatory compliance, and standards of practice to promote quality care.	15%

Percentage of items in each domain area

All About the Exam

Format of the OTR Exam

The OTR exams are delivered by computers at testing centers located throughout the United States and internationally. You can schedule to take the exam during the business hours of the testing center at a time that is optimal for you. Scheduling instructions are provided in your Authorization to Test letter that is sent to you after your exam application is complete.

Candidates taking the OTR exam are allotted 4 hours to complete the exam. The OTR exam contains two sections: one section has three clinical simulation test (CST) problems and the other section has 170 single-response multiple choice items.

You may take an optional tutorial about the functionality of the test screens at the beginning of each section of the exam. These tutorials demonstrate the functionality of the exams in the computer-based testing environment. The tutorials do not count against the overall time you are allotted for the exam. Time spent using a tutorial is NOT deducted from the 4-hour testing time.

> ### 👍 Remember
>
> You are given 4 hours to complete the NBCOT OTR® Certification Exam.

🔍 Key Points

All OTR exams:

- Are computer-delivered
- Have a 4-hour time limit
- Contain scored & unscored items

The OTR exam is a computer-based exam that has 2 distinct sections:	
3 clinical simulation test (CST) items	**170** single-response multiple choice items

9

NBCOT® Study Guide for the OTR Certification Examination

Chapter 3

Format of the Test Items

Clinical simulation test (CST) problems and multiple choice questions

Clinical Simulation Test Problems

Clinical simulation testing (CST) is a format of assessment designed to replicate the types of situations OTR practitioners encounter in their everyday practice. The OTR exam consists of three CST problems. Each simulation problem consists of three main parts:

1. **An opening scene.**
   This includes general background information about a practice-based situation that sets the scene for the entire CST problem.

2. **A series of four accompanying sections, each with section headers.**
   Each section header provides information specific to the OT process that is addressed within the section.

3. **A list of response options.**
   This is a list of potential options the OTR may consider when responding to the question posed in the section header.

The list of response options in the CST problem consists of positive and negative responses. You must respond to all options in the CST sections by selecting either "Yes" or "No" for EACH option.

When responding to CST problems, you should select "Yes" for the optimal response options provided. Options given a "Yes" response will cause a feedback box (see **Figure 3.1**) to appear to the right of the response option. You can use this feedback information to supplement the decisions you make in other sections of the CST problem. You should select "No" for options that are not optimal. Feedback is not provided when a "No" response is selected. After answer choices have been selected for each response option within a section, you should select the "Next" button at the bottom of the screen to proceed to the next section.

> ### 🗋 Note
>
> The feedback box does NOT provide information about your score on the CST problem or indicate if you have selected the correct or incorrect response option.

10

Format of the Test Items

Figure 3.1: Example CST section header, partial list of options, and feedback box (Note: This image is for illustrative purposes only.)

Section A: Which actions are appropriate for the OTR to take during the screening process to determine the appropriateness of occupational therapy services for this student?

Select "Yes" next to those options that are appropriate at this time. Select "No" if the option is not appropriate at this time. You must select either "Yes" or "No" for every option.

	Yes	No		
A.	☑	☐	Ask the teacher to identify the student's favorite storybook.	The student's favorite book is The Cat in the Hat.
B.	☐	☑	Observe the student participating in classroom activities.	
C.	☐	☑	Complete a review of the student's school health record.	
D.	☑	☐	Confirm the allocation of COTA hours to the school.	The school is allocated 15 hours each week.

👆 **Remember**

To progress through the CST problems, all options must be given a "Yes" or "No" response.

Navigating the CST Problems

Only one CST problem is presented at a time. Although you will be able to scroll back and forth between sections within a single CST problem, you will not be able to return to completed CST problems. Once you have submitted your responses for all four sections of a single CST problem, that CST problem will close and another will appear. This will continue until you have completed all three CST problems.

While working on a single CST problem, you can scroll back through the simulation problem to view the:

- opening scene

- section headers

- response options selected

- feedback associated with options where a "Yes" response was selected

You can navigate back to previous sections of a CST problem; however, your responses cannot be changed once you have progressed to a new section within the problem.

Highlight and Strike Out Features

During the exam, you will be able to highlight text in the opening scene, section header, and/or outcome that you deem is important. A strike out feature is also available to aid you in determining the appropriate response options during your decision-making process.

CST Scoring

Your score for these items is based on correctly indicating "Yes" for the positive options and "No" for the negative options in each section of each problem. One point is awarded each time you correctly select a "Yes" or "No" response. Zero points are awarded or deducted if you incorrectly select a "Yes" or "No" response.

📄 Note

Do NOT hover the mouse cursor over a decision/action statement as this may accidentally select an undesired statement option.

Format of the Test Items

🔑 Key Points

- A CST problem consists of an opening scene with accompanying linked sections and lists of options.

- Remember, once a response option of "Yes" or "No" has been selected, it cannot be deselected.

- You can proceed to the next CST problem only if a "Yes" or "No" response is selected for all options in a section.

- As you progress through a CST problem, you can scroll back to previous sections within a CST problem to review them.

Multiple Choice Test Items

Multiple choice items contain a stem and three or four possible response options. Of the response options presented, there is only one correct or best answer. You earn a point if the correct response is selected. There is only ONE correct response in the multiple choice test items. The other options are incorrect responses or distractors. Distractors typically represent common fallacies or misconceptions about the item topic.

Each multiple choice item starts with a stem or premise. This is usually in the form of a written statement or question. Stems always relate to tasks and knowledge required for entry-level OTR practice.

The following is an example of a multiple choice test item:

ITEM STEM:

1. A client has left hemiparesis secondary to having a CVA one week ago. Results from a motor evaluation indicate mild upper extremity weakness and decreased fine motor coordination of the affected upper extremity. The client's primary goal is to resume playing the piano to perform at an upcoming family reunion. Which activity would be **MOST BENEFICIAL** to include as part of the initial intervention to support progress toward the client's goal?

RESPONSE OPTIONS:

A. Turning pages in a music book to select a song for a former colleague to perform at the event

B. Bearing weight through the right arm on the piano stool while using the left hand to play a tune on the piano

C. **Integrating piano keyboard drills into a repetitive therapeutic upper extremity exercise program**

D. Listening to favorite piano music while completing dominance retraining activities

> 🗅 **Note**
>
> For this sample question, the correct answer is C.
>
> To assist in your studies, the correct answers are bolded and highlighted in the Answers and Rationales section in Section 3 of this guide.

Chapter 4

After the Exam

Scoring, score reports, and more

Scoring

All NBCOT certification exams are criterion-referenced. In order to pass the exam, you must obtain a score equal to or higher than the minimum passing score. The minimum passing score represents an absolute standard and does not depend on the performance of other candidates taking the same exam. The minimum passing score for the OTR exam is set by content experts using widely recognized standard setting methodologies.

NBCOT uses a scaled scoring procedure to determine a candidate's final score. The scaled score is not a "number correct" or "percent correct" score. Raw scores are converted to scaled scores that represent equivalent levels of achievement regardless of test form. The passing point for the OTR exam is set at 450 points, with the lowest possible score set at 300 points and the highest possible score set at 600 points.

Score Reports

After you complete and submit your exam, it will be scored by NBCOT. Exam scores are released on a predetermined schedule indicated on the scoring calendar. Information about scoring dates can be accessed on the NBCOT website.

When your score is released, you can view it in your MyNBCOT account. If you pass the exam, you will receive in the mail a packet containing a congratulatory letter with your overall score, an official NBCOT certificate, an identification card for your wallet, and information regarding your NBCOT benefits. Remember that by taking the exam, you have agreed not to share any information regarding the exam to others.

> 👍 **Remember**
>
> Candidates must obtain a scaled score of at least 450 points to pass the exam.

> 🔍 **Learn More**
>
> Review the Foundations of the NBCOT Certification Examinations at www.nbcot.org/foundations to learn more about psychometric principles used by NBCOT for certification exam development and scoring.

🔍 Learn More

Access the scoring calendar at www.nbcot.org/Students/get-certified#Schedule.

Score Transfer

Note that completion of the NBCOT Certification Exam Application is not the same as applying for state licensure. Sending a score transfer to a state regulatory board does not automatically initiate the process to obtain a license or permit to work in that state. Certification by NBCOT is independent and different from any state or jurisdiction's law/licensure. Almost all jurisdictions, including the District of Columbia and Puerto Rico, have some form of regulation for occupational therapists and occupational therapy assistants. Before a candidate begins practicing in any state or comparable jurisdiction, it is essential that all requirements for that jurisdiction are met. To practice without a license or permit is against the law.

Retaking the Exam

Not every candidate who takes the NBCOT OTR® Certification Exam will achieve a passing score.

Candidates who receive a failing score will be notified via email when their exam result has been posted in their MyNBCOT account. The downloadable PDF feedback report will include the overall score along with domain-level performance information and an explanation of the overall and domain-level performance. The feedback report also includes answers to frequently asked questions about the feedback report and preparation needed to retake the exam. While it is very disappointing to receive notification indicating failure to meet the passing requirement, it is essential to address the consequences of this occurrence. Not passing the OTR exam may impact your plans to begin an occupational therapy job. If you do not successfully pass the NBCOT certification exam and are negotiating with an employer about an OTR position, you must inform your potential employer of your need to retake the certification exam. Additionally, you should contact state regulatory entities for specific information regarding temporary licenses.

Preparing to Retake the Certification Exam

There are various reasons why a candidate might fail the OTR exam. Reflecting on potential reasons is an important first step in preparing to retake the exam. These reasons may include:

- Poor test-taking strategies
- Inadequate study habits
- Lack of preparation
- Test anxiety
- External stresses

Note

Refer to the "Retaking the Exam" section of the *NBCOT Certification Exam Handbook* for additional information about reapplying to take the exam.

Chapter 5

Certification Renewal

Your OTR credential and benefits of maintaining certification

🔍 Learn More

Review the *Certification Renewal Handbook* at www.nbcot.org/-/media/NBCOT/PDFs/Renewal_Handbook to learn more about certification renewal.

🔍 Learn More

You can access the Certification Renewal Activities Chart at www.nbcot.org/-/media/NBCOT/PDFs/Renewal_Activity_Chart.ashx?la=en to learn more about the required units for certification.

📄 Note

If you complete all the certification renewal requirements by your scheduled renewal date, you will be granted **Active in Good Standing** certification status for another 3-year period.

After earning your initial NBCOT certification, your OTR credential will be valid for a period of 3 years. The certification renewal season occurs annually between January and March, regardless of the month your initial certification was received.

Certification renewal is required to maintain active certification. Your initial certification as an OTR is highly valued by you, the public, and your employers. NBCOT is your lifelong partner as you continue to grow and develop as a certified professional.

The requirements for certification renewal are:

- Accrue 36 units in the 3 years between your initial certification date and the date you renew your certification

- Abide by the NBCOT Practice Standards/Code of Conduct

- Complete a Certification Renewal Application

- Submit the appropriate renewal application fee

Benefits of Certification Renewal

OTR CREDENTIAL

One of the benefits of certification is having the privilege to use the OTR certification mark. It is necessary to maintain an **Active in Good Standing** certification status to use the OTR certification mark.

Fulfilling the certification renewal requirements entitles you to continue using the OTR credential.

NBCOT Navigator® Competency Assessment Platform

If you have earned a passing score on the OTR exam and have maintained an Active in Good Standing certification status, you will continue to have access to the latest evidence-based research through the NBCOT Navigator® suite.

The NBCOT Navigator is a suite of online tools designed to help you assess your competency across all areas of occupational therapy. All tools were created based on current practice and evidence-based literature. You can complete the tools to earn Competency Assessment Units (CAU) toward renewal, develop your occupational therapy knowledge and skills, and stay current in your practice.

The tools are available, at no charge, to individuals currently certified as an Occupational Therapist Registered OTR® and can be accessed through your MyNBCOT account. Competency Assessment Units (CAU) are awarded for successful completion of tools. You can accrue up to a maximum of 14 CAU per renewal period by completing tools in the NBCOT Navigator suite to use toward your NBCOT certification renewal requirements.

Note

The NBCOT Navigator is only available to active OTR certificants.

NBCOT Navigator® Tools

There is a wide range of competency assessment tools available on the NBCOT Navigator for the OTR, including: PICO, Case Simulations, Mini Games, Mini Practice Quizzes, and the OT Knowledge Library.

PICO

PICO is a tool that contains a series of simulated games that introduce you to the process of evaluating appropriate, evidence-based research in order to make informed decisions about OT practice.

CASE SIMULATIONS

Case simulations bring OT practice to life with a focus on clinical reasoning. Each case simulation starts with an opening scene that provides background information about the scenario. This is followed by a series of modules that engage you in providing OT services to a virtual client. Modules may include: client interviews and chart reviews; selection of appropriate screening and assessment tools; completion of evaluations; interpretation of assessment results; interprofessional team discussions; intervention planning; provision of intervention services; and discharge planning.

MINI GAMES

Mini games assess specific practice knowledge. Each game is uniquely designed for its specific topic. Mini games included in the Navigator are as follows:

Management Challenge
Assess your skills managing the day-to-day operations of a busy outpatient rehabilitation facility. This tool reflects typical challenges facing the OT manager today.

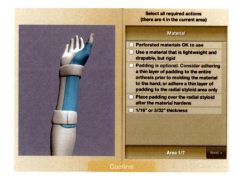

Orthotic Builder
Assess your competency to select the optimal orthosis and make best-practice fabrication decisions to support recovery from a range of hand injuries and conditions.

Physical Agent Modalities (PAMs)
Select and administer the most appropriate PAM as part of the client's intervention plan, based on the presenting condition, past medical history, and the physician's referral.

NBCOT® Study Guide for the OTR Certification Examination

MINI PRACTICE QUIZZES

Mini Practice Quizzes are short, multiple choice quizzes grounded in evidence-based literature that are designed to assess knowledge of contemporary OT practice. Topic quizzes cover the major practice areas identified in the *NBCOT Certification Renewal Practice Analysis Study*, which include: pediatrics, school system, administration/management, acute care, rehabilitation, education/research, work/industry, wellness, and home health.

OT KNOWLEDGE LIBRARY

The OT Knowledge Library is a stylized matching tool that covers a broad range of occupational therapy knowledge.

🔍 Learn More

For more information on the Navigator suite, visit www.nbcot.org/navigator.

Section 2
Preparing for the Exam

Chapter 6

NBCOT Illustrated Description to Entry-Level OTR® Practice

Critical thinking and self-reflection

> **☐ Note**
>
> The critical thinking skills that you use to make practice decisions can help when you are developing a personalized study plan.

Critical Thinking

Critical thinking is a core skill for all successful occupational therapy practitioners. It is through critical thinking that the occupational therapy practitioner effectively completes the occupational therapy process. You can use your critical thinking skills to frame how you study for the NBCOT OTR® Certification Exam.

Define what you want to learn

For example, you may be familiar with the anatomical implications of ulnar nerve palsy but want to know more about how it impacts thumb mobility and the challenges this condition poses to a homemaker caring for a young child. You can use critical thinking to help you understand the perspective of this homemaker. Define your learning using simple questions, such as:

- How does the impairment affect the homemaker's ability to button the baby's clothes?

- How might this impact the homemaker's ability to perform grooming tasks?

- Are adaptations needed to help the homemaker open packets of formula?

Consider what you already know about the subject

Critical thinking will help you identify strengths and gaps in your knowledge. Tapping into your previous experiences from fieldwork, labs, case studies, and readings will give you a foundation upon which to build your personalized study plan based on your learning needs.

Identify resources

Critical thinking is about recognizing and using all the resources available to you. Consider resources in the widest possible context; have an open mind.

Here are a few resources you may consider. Expand on these and design your own list.

- **People**—professors, fieldwork educators, mentors, peer group, community members
- **Materials**—textbooks, journal readings, reflective journals, class notes, lab exercises, exam prep tools
- **Environments**—fieldwork, community facilities, specialist clinics, adaptive workplaces, inpatient services

Challenge yourself and ask questions

Use your critical thinking skills to enhance your understanding and application of knowledge to various situations. For example:

- What interventions are beneficial and effective during the acute phase of a condition versus during the rehabilitation phase?
- Why would a client respond differently to the same intervention when it is applied in different practice settings?
- How would I measure outcomes for a student in the school setting versus an older adult in a home health setting?

 Tip

Use creative problem-solving strategies to identify topics you want to learn more about and to trigger new learning experiences.

Organize the information you have gathered

Your critical thinking skills can help you examine patterns and make connections across your learning. For example, you can further your understanding of ulnar nerve palsy by reviewing your class notes, talking to an occupational therapy practitioner who has provided services to people who have this condition, discussing with your peers about the variety of ways this condition may affect household occupations, and identifying possible short-term and long-term treatment goals from key textbooks. **Figure 6.1** below shows the areas of learning you may choose to consult to enhance your knowledge of ulnar nerve palsy.

Figure 6.1
Areas of learning to enhance your knowledge of ulnar nerve palsy

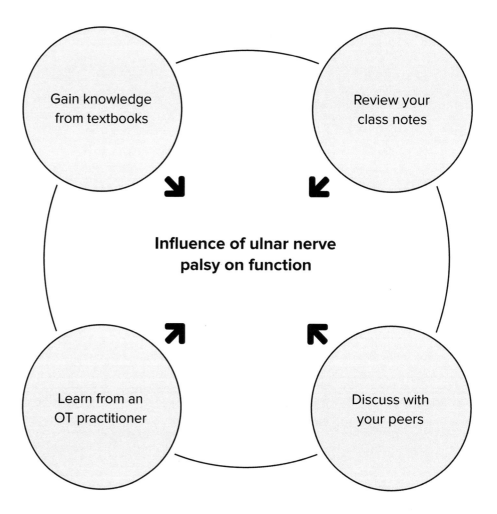

NBCOT's Illustrated Description of Entry-Level OTR® Practice

The *Illustrated Description of Entry-Level OTR® Practice* details the results of the *2017 NBCOT Practice Analysis Study*. It presents sample scenarios across a variety of practice settings that depict the tasks OTR practitioners complete in practice. Alongside each scenario is a description of how the knowledge required to competently perform a task is applied throughout the occupational therapy process. You can use the sample scenarios and associated application to practice to support your understanding of entry-level practice, as described in the practice analysis study, and to prepare for the OTR certification exam.

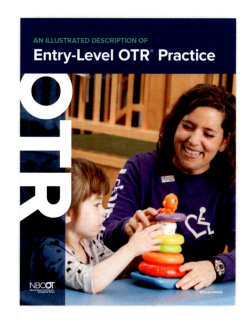

 See Appendix B to read the Illustrated Description of Entry-Level OTR® Practice.

The *Illustrated Description of Entry-Level OTR® Practice* is a useful tool to jump-start a self-reflective process about your level of experience and knowledge in various areas of occupational therapy practice. As you read each scenario and application to practice, think about a similar client you encountered during fieldwork or knowledge you have that relates to the scenario.

 Access the Illustrated Guide Worksheet in Appendix C to support your self-reflection process.

When using the worksheet, consider what additional information you want to learn, or brainstorm other scenarios that align with the class code of the exam. You can also bring the *Illustrated Description of Entry-Level OTR® Practice* to a study group to discuss the scenarios and the strengths and gaps in your associated knowledge.

>  **❶ Important**
>
> Determine what content YOU need to review and study when preparing for the NBCOT OTR® Certification Exam.

Chapter 7

NBCOT OTR® Entry-Level Self-Assessment

Identifying your strengths and learning needs

Note

The NBCOT OTR® Entry-Level Self-Assessment enables you to self-assess how prepared you are for the OTR certification exam.

NBCOT OTR® Entry-Level Self-Assessment

The NBCOT OTR® Entry-Level Self-Assessment is a free resource that can help you determine your overall perceived competency for entry-level practice. The self-assessment is built in relation to the validated domain, task, and knowledge statements of the NBCOT exam content outline, and it sorts practice skills by the overarching domains of entry-level practice. The feedback report provided at the end of the self-assessment is designed to help you develop or adjust your personalized study plan.

The self-assessment can be used more than once. Some students complete the self-assessment at certain points during their OT program, while others do so before and after fieldwork. See **Figure 7.1**, which shows options for when to complete the NBCOT OTR® Entry-Level Self-Assessment.

Learn More

Visit www.nbcot.org/en/Students/Study-Tools/Self-Assessments to access the NBCOT OTR® Entry-Level Self-Assessment.

 The NBCOT OTR® Entry-Level Self-Assessment is available in Appendix D.

NBCOT OTR® Illustrated Entry-Level Self-Assessment

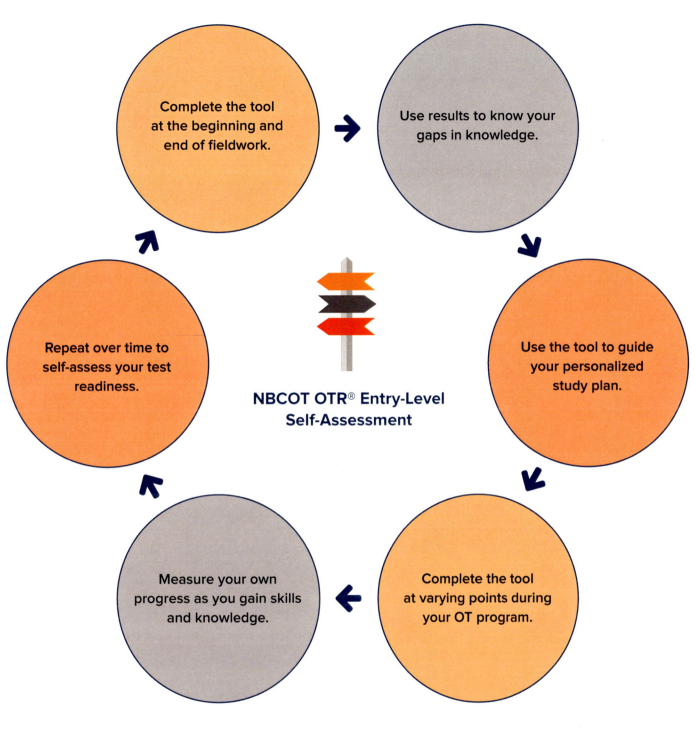

Figure 7.1
Options for using NBCOT OTR® Entry-Level Self-Assessment

29

NBCOT® Study Guide for the OTR Certification Examination

How to Complete the Self-Assessment

Step 1

To complete the self-assessment, consider your competence for each skill statement based on the following question:

What knowledge and experience do you have related to these entry-level OTR skills?	Ratings
Methods for defining a clinical question and performing a critical appraisal to support evidence-based practice	○0 ○1 ○2 ○3
Methods for applying continuous quality improvement processes and procedures to occupational therapy service delivery	○0 ○1 ○2 ○3
Methods for evaluating, monitoring, and documenting service competency and professional development needs of self and assigned personnel based on scope of practice and certification standards for occupational therapy	○0 ○1 ○2 ○3
Methods for developing, analyzing, and applying evidence that supports occupation-based programming to advance positive health outcomes for individuals, groups, and specific populations	○0 ○1 ○2 ○3

Step 2

Determine a rating for your knowledge and skills in the featured practice area by using the following rating scale:

0	**No knowledge or skills:** Unfamiliar with concept or practice of the skill
1	**General knowledge through observation and academic learning:** Familiar with general knowledge related to the skill through academic learning and observation but did not have an opportunity to apply this during fieldwork
2	**General clinical skills under supervision:** Familiar with general clinical application of the skill and occasionally applied this under direct supervision during Level II fieldwork
3	**Entry-level competence:** Implemented the skill across routine situations within guidelines of Level II fieldwork practice setting

30

Step 3

Review your results. If you complete the online version of the NBCOT OTR® Entry-Level Self-Assessment, you will receive a feedback report containing a visual key that allows you to view your results. You can develop or adjust your personalized study plan based on these results and assess your perceived knowledge and learning needs based on the validated domain, task, and knowledge statements.

🔴	**No knowledge or skills:** You are unfamiliar with concept or practice of the skill
➕	**General knowledge through observation and academic learning:** You are familiar with general knowledge related to the skill through academic learning and observation but have had limited opportunities to apply this during fieldwork. You should focus on strategies for gaining more knowledge about this skill and ways to demonstrate this knowledge in clinical situations.
🚩	**General clinical skills under supervision:** You are familiar with general clinical application of this skill and have occasionally applied the skill under direct supervision. You may want to collaborate with an experienced OTR clinician to plan independent practice-based learning activities requiring these skills.
⭐	**Entry-level competence:** You have implemented the skill across routine situations within guidelines of Level II fieldwork practice setting. Your responses indicate you have experience associated with entry-level competence.

> **ⓘ Tip**
>
> After completing the self-assessment, take some time to reflect on areas in which you feel competent and areas in which you need more knowledge.

Chapter 8

Personalized Study Plan

A method for developing a study plan that works for you

The sample planning tool on the following pages may be useful in helping you develop a personalized study plan to structure your studying. The tool allows you to pull various pieces of information together into one place.

NBCOT OTR® CERTIFICATION EXAM

Personalized STUDY PLAN

Tip

Use this STUDY PLAN worksheet to reflect on the details of a personalized study plan that will work for you.

S	Start by completing the self-assessment.
T	Target a date to sit for the NBCOT OTR® Certification Exam.
U	Understand your personal life circumstances.
D	Develop a realistic study schedule.
Y	You need to determine where you study best.
P	Pick a method to track your progress.
L	List available resources and study tools.
A	Ask yourself how you will stick to your plan.
N	Note additional actions you need to take to prepare for exam day.

Start by completing the self-assessment.

Write down your key learning needs based on the results of the self-assessment.

Target a date to sit for the NBCOT OTR® Certification Exam.

Think about the length of time you need to study.

Understand your personal life circumstances.

Think about the commitments in your life (e.g., family responsibilities, work, personal needs) that will influence your ability to commit to your study plan.

Develop a realistic study schedule.

Use a calendar to map out a study schedule that includes the number of hours per day you will dedicate to studying.

You need to determine where you study best.

Write down where you like to study and key features of that environment.

Pick a method to track your progress.

Brainstorm options, such as taking practice tests or measuring change with a self-assessment, and pick methods that work for you.

List available resources and study tools.

Think about the resources (e.g., textbooks, class notes, case studies) and study tools (e.g., practice tests, flashcards) you will need.

Ask yourself how you will stick to your plan.

Determine how to pace your study and think of methods for rewarding yourself for committing to your study schedule.

Note additional actions you need to take to prepare for exam day.

Keep an ongoing "to do" list, for example: review my Authorization to Test (ATT) letter, watch exam tutorials at www.nbcot.org, plan the route to the test center, research state licensure requirements, etc.

Exam Preparation Tools

In addition to this study guide, NBCOT offers a variety of test preparation resources. NBCOT's Aspire study tools are designed using the validated domain, task, and knowledge statements on which the OTR certification exams are based.

NBCOT Aspire is a suite of tools to help you prepare for the certification exam.

🔍 Learn More

To learn more about the NBCOT Aspire study tools, go to: www.nbcot.org/en/Students/Study-Tools.

The NBCOT Exam StudyPack

The NBCOT Exam StudyPack is a comprehensive exam prep platform to support you as you prepare for the exam. The StudyPack is filled with exam prep tools and easy-to-access resources to challenge your knowledge and assist you in meeting your goal for the certification exam! You can follow a guided study pathway or self-navigate from study tool to study tool in whichever way suits your studying style and needs.

> ❗ **Important**
>
> The NBCOT Exam StudyPack is a comprehensive exam prep platform with expanded content that is only available in the StudyPack.

Flashcards

Study for the certification exam anywhere, at any time. The online flashcards are easy to use and filled with practice-relevant content.

Knowledge Match Games

Test your OT knowledge in a fun and interactive online environment with the Knowledge Match Game. Use your speed and recall ability to match statements to corresponding categories.

Practice Tests

Test your readiness by simulating the computer-based format and flow of the real exam.

🔍 Learn More

Find more information on the NBCOT Aspire study tools at www.nbcot.org/aspire.

Chapter 9

Exam Day

Planning for exam day and test-taking tips

.

Take some time to think of strategies that can help you feel relaxed in the days leading up to your test day. Remind yourself of the progress you have made to date: you completed an occupational therapy program, you took many academic courses, you successfully completed assignments, and you passed several major tests. Think back to how much you knew about occupational therapy at the start of your program compared to how much you know now.

The night before the test:

- Remind yourself that you have been preparing for this day for a long time.

- Think about where the test center is located and how long it will take you to get there.

- Make sure you have all the documents you must take to the test site—refer to the latest copy of the *NBCOT Certification Exam Handbook* at www.nbcot.org for details about the documents you need to bring.

- Decide what clothes you plan to wear: comfortable, layered clothes are key considerations.

- Have a plan for what you want to do the night before—such as exercise or spend time with friends—to alleviate pretest nerves.

- Try to get a good night's sleep and remember to set your alarm.

⊕ Learn More

To prepare for your test day, you can access and watch the video *What to Expect on Test Day* at www.nbcot.org/Students/get-certified#testday.

> ❗ **Important**
>
> Review your Authorization to Test (ATT) letter and follow the instructions.

Test-Taking Tips

It's test day! This is the day you have been preparing for since the beginning of your journey to become an Occupational Therapist Registered. Your NBCOT OTR® Certification Exam will be administered at the Prometric test center you selected at the time you scheduled your exam.

> **ⓘ Tips**
> - Arrive at the test site early.
> - Follow the instructions in your ATT letter.
> - Use strategies to feel calm.

Remember that you have 4 hours to take the exam, but your scheduled appointment time at the test center is for 5 hours and 15 minutes to allow you to complete all administrative requirements.

Prometric employs biometric-enabled check-in services at all of its test sites. This procedure consists of a number of steps to verify your eligibility to test, including taking an electronic record of your ID, photo imaging, and a digital fingertip record. You are required to undergo fingertip analysis any time you leave and re-enter the testing room for validation purposes. There is video surveillance in all candidate-accessible areas of the testing center.

A common question asked is: "Can I eat/drink in the testing room?" The answer to this question is: No, however beverages and snacks can be stored in lockers located in the testing center waiting area. You may eat or drink in the waiting area only.

After you are assigned a workspace at the testing site, familiarize yourself with the computer and make certain you can see the clock on the screen. You may request headphones if you will be distracted by others working around you. You may also ask the proctor for a marker board to use during your test time. Advise the test proctor of any problems or concerns you have regarding the test environment prior to beginning the exam.

> **❗ Important**
>
> Plan to arrive at least 30 minutes before your scheduled appointment time.

⊕ Learn More

To learn more read the *Certification Exam Handbook* at www.nbcot.org/-/media/NBCOT/PDFs/Cert_Exam_Handbook.

Test-Taking Strategies

Manage Your Time

Make a plan for managing your test time. You have 4 hours to take the exam. There are two sections on the exam: section one contains three clinical simulation test problems and section two contains 170 multiple choice items.

Exam Tutorial

A tutorial precedes each section of the exam. One appears before the section containing the clinical simulation test (CST) problems and another appears before the section containing the single-response multiple choice items.

Organize Your Thinking

Use the marker board to help you organize and clarify your thinking.

Maintain Good Posture

Manage your posture and change your position regularly. Sit in an upright position. If you feel tension, stretch, drop your shoulders, open and close your fingers, or shift in your chair.

Read the Instructions

Be sure to read the instructions before answering each item type.

Stay Calm

If you feel anxious during the exam, take some deep, slow breaths. Don't worry if other people in the room finish before you do. You do not need to leave the room until you have used all your allotted time. If you experience a technical problem during the exam, inform the test center proctor.

> 👆 **Remember**
>
> Time spent using a tutorial is NOT deducted from the 4-hour testing time.

☝ **Remember**

When answering clinical simulation problems:

- You cannot change your mind and deselect an option after you have made an initial selection.

- Although you can scroll back to a previous section within a single simulation problem, you cannot add to or change the selections you made on those screens.

- Each clinical simulation problem is presented sequentially and is distinct from the other problems. When you have made your selections for the first problem, the next problem will begin, and you will not be able to access the previous problem(s).

When answering multiple choice items:

- Use the "Mark" button on the computer screen to review items later if time permits.

- Only change an answer you initially selected if you are sure it is an incorrect response. The answer that comes to mind first is often correct.

- Rely on your knowledge and do not watch for patterns. The test answers are randomized.

ⓘ **Tips**

After the exam:

- Resist the urge to discuss the test items and potential answers with your peer group. You have completed the exam and it is too late to change your answers.

- Resist the urge to open your study notes, texts, and review guides for the same reason given above.

- Remember, it is against the NBCOT Candidate/Certificant Code of Conduct to discuss test items with other candidates or to record test information from memory.

- Relax. You have completed the exam. Reward yourself for accomplishing this stage.

Section 3
Time to Practice

NBCOT® Study Guide for the OTR Certification Examination

Chapter 10

Sample CST Problem

Sample CST problem with answer key and references

⊕ Learn More

Visit MyNBCOT (www.nbcot.org) for more information about these CST practice tests and other practice tools available in the Aspire suite. You can also refer back to Chapter 3 of this study guide for additional detail about the CST problem format.

Sample Clinical Simulation Test Problems

The sample CST problem presented in this study guide closely mimics the format of the computer-delivered CST problems on the exam. However, this sample is not interactive.

Steps for Using the Sample:

This sample CST problem contains four sections. The opening scene for each section is the same.

- Read the opening scene and the "Section A" header.

- Read each response option and select "Yes" for the optimal responses and "No" for responses that are not optimal based on information from the opening scene, the section header, and feedback information provided in previously marked options and sections.

- Think about your rationale for why your response is "Yes" or "No."

- Mark your responses to "Section A," then turn the page. Transfer your responses from the previous page and read the information provided in the feedback box associated with your "Yes" responses. (Remember that the highlight and strike out features are available on the exam to aid your decision-making process.)

- Keep in mind the information from the "Opening Scene" and "Section A" as you proceed through the remaining three sections.

42

Sample CST Problem

Sample Clinical Simulation Test Problem

OPENING SCENE

An older adult is admitted to an acute care inpatient facility following a fall. The fall resulted in a right hip fracture. The patient has a pre-morbid diagnosis of moderate dementia. The patient's caregiver indicates the patient was dependent with lower body dressing and bathing prior to the fall. A day after undergoing an open reduction internal fixation of the affected hip, the patient is referred for occupational therapy.

SECTION A

Before meeting with the patient for the initial evaluation, what information from the patient's medical record is important for the OTR to gather?

Select "Yes" next to those options that are appropriate at this time. Select "No" if the option is not appropriate at this time. You must select either "Yes" or "No" for every option.

	Yes	No		
A.	☐	☐	Review all nursing entries for this patient's hospitalization.	
B.	☐	☐	Obtain the patient's prior functional level.	
C.	☐	☐	Note the patient's prior social and living history.	
D.	☐	☐	Note if the patient has a history of falls.	
E.	☐	☐	Note if the family has a history of osteoporosis disease.	
F.	☐	☐	Review the patient's weight-bearing status.	
G.	☐	☐	Review the patient's post-operative hematocrit level.	

Turn the page, and read **ONLY** the feedback boxes where you have selected a "Yes" response.

43

NBCOT® Study Guide for the OTR Certification Examination

Instructions

Place a checkmark beside your "Yes" responses from the previous page.
Read **ONLY** the feedback boxes where you have selected a "Yes" response.

SECTION A: FEEDBACK

Before meeting with the patient for the initial evaluation, what information from the patient's medical record is important for the OTR to gather?

Select "Yes" next to those options that are appropriate at this time. Select "No" if the option is not appropriate at this time. You must select either "Yes" or "No" for every option.

	Yes	No		
A.	☐	☐	Review all nursing entries for this patient's hospitalization.	The notes are complete.
B.	☐	☐	Obtain the patient's prior functional level.	The notes indicate that the patient required moderate assistance for most multi-step ADL tasks
C.	☐	☐	Note the patient's prior social and living history.	The notes indicate that the patient lives locally in a one-story home with an adult child who is the primary caregiver.
D.	☐	☐	Note if the patient has a history of falls.	The notes indicate no record of patient fall prior to this admission.
E.	☐	☐	Note if the family has a history of osteoporosis disease.	The notes do not include this information.
F.	☐	☐	Review the patient's weight-bearing status.	The notes indicate that the patient is restricted to partial weight-bearing status on the operated limb.
G.	☐	☐	Review the patient's post-operative hematocrit level.	The notes indicate the patient's lab values are within normal range.

Proceed to the next section of the CST problem.

Sample CST Problem

SECTION B

Following the review of the patient's medical record, the OTR begins the patient's evaluation. What actions should the OTR take as part of the patient's evaluation prior to establishing the patient's intervention plan?

Select "Yes" next to those options that are appropriate at this time. Select "No" if the option is not appropriate at this time. You must select either "Yes" or "No" for every option.

	Yes	No		
A.	☐	☐	Assess the patient's ability to complete lower extremity dressing when adhering to total hip precautions.	
B.	☐	☐	Determine the patient's ability to transfer from the wheelchair to a shower seat.	
C.	☐	☐	With the head of the bed elevated between 75° and 90°, provide the patient with set up to complete a grooming task.	
D.	☐	☐	With the patient sitting bedside, provide an ADL checklist for the patient to complete.	
E.	☐	☐	Identify the patient's pain level using a visual analogue scale.	
F.	☐	☐	Ask the patient to read a handout on movement precautions aloud.	
G.	☐	☐	Determine the amount of assistance the caregiver is able to provide the patient after discharge.	

NBCOT® Study Guide for the OTR Certification Examination

Instructions

Place a checkmark beside your "Yes" responses from the previous page.
Read **ONLY** the feedback boxes where you have selected a "Yes" response.

	SECTION B: FEEDBACK	

Following the review of the patient's medical record, the OTR begins the patient's evaluation. What actions should the OTR take as part of the patient's evaluation prior to establishing the patient's intervention plan?

Select "Yes" next to those options that are appropriate at this time. Select "No" if the option is not appropriate at this time. You must select either "Yes" or "No" for every option.

	Yes	No		
A.	☐	☐	Assess the patient's ability to complete lower extremity dressing when adhering to total hip precautions.	The patient cannot follow the hip precautions and the assessment is terminated.
B.	☐	☐	Determine the patient's ability to transfer from the wheelchair to a shower seat.	The patient indicates understanding of the procedures.
C.	☐	☐	With the head of the bed elevated between 75° and 90°, provide the patient with set up to complete a grooming task.	The patient requires verbal prompting to initiate and complete the grooming task.
D.	☐	☐	With the patient sitting bedside, provide an ADL checklist for the patient to complete.	After verbal prompting, the patient indicates ability to complete all ADL tasks independently.
E.	☐	☐	Identify the patient's pain level using a visual analogue scale.	The patient indicates pain is a 3 out of 10.
F.	☐	☐	Ask the patient to read a handout on movement precautions aloud.	The patient skips lines when reading but likes the pictures.
G.	☐	☐	Determine the amount of assistance the caregiver is able to provide the patient after discharge.	The caregiver is making arrangements to have family available at all times to assist the patient.

Proceed to the next section of the CST problem.

46

SECTION C

The family's discharge preference for the patient is direct discharge home from the acute care inpatient facility in 3 days. The patient's primary caregiver will provide 24-hour caregiver assistance to the patient. In preparation for discharge, the caregiver agrees to participate in the patient's intervention sessions. What ADL tasks should the OTR select for the patient's intervention sessions prior to discharge?

Select "Yes" next to those options that are appropriate at this time. Select "No" if the option is not appropriate at this time. You must select either "Yes" or "No" for every option.

	Yes	No		
A.	☐	☐	Demonstrate a transfer from the bed to a bedside commode using verbal and visual cues.	
B.	☐	☐	Demonstrate a transfer in and out of a vehicle.	
C.	☐	☐	Observe while the caregiver assists the patient in completing a transfer from the bed to a bedside commode.	
D.	☐	☐	Instruct the patient on the completion of grooming and hygiene activities while standing at the sink.	
E.	☐	☐	Instruct the patient and the caregiver on minimizing environmental hazards in the home.	
F.	☐	☐	Instruct the patient on lower extremity dressing in compliance with postsurgical hip precaution guidelines.	

NBCOT® Study Guide for the OTR Certification Examination

Instructions

Place a checkmark beside your "Yes" responses from the previous page.
Read **ONLY** the feedback boxes where you have selected a "Yes" response.

SECTION C: FEEDBACK

The family's discharge preference for the patient is direct discharge home from the acute care inpatient facility in 3 days. The patient's primary caregiver will provide 24-hour caregiver assistance to the patient. In preparation for discharge, the caregiver agrees to participate in the patient's intervention sessions. What ADL tasks should the OTR select for the patient's intervention sessions prior to discharge?

Select "Yes" next to those options that are appropriate at this time. Select "No" if the option is not appropriate at this time. You must select either "Yes" or "No" for every option.

	Yes	No		
A.	☐	☐	Demonstrate a transfer from the bed to a bedside commode using verbal and visual cues.	The caregiver demonstrates understanding and agrees to follow the guidelines.
B.	☐	☐	Demonstrate a transfer in and out of a vehicle.	The caregiver demonstrates understanding and agrees to follow the guidelines.
C.	☐	☐	Observe while the caregiver assists the patient in completing a transfer from the bed to a bedside commode.	The caregiver safely assists the patient in completing this transfer by following the guidelines.
D.	☐	☐	Instruct the patient on the completion of grooming and hygiene activities while standing at the sink.	The patient refuses to complete this activity due to pain but accepts written informational handouts on the activity.
E.	☐	☐	Instruct the patient and the caregiver on minimizing environmental hazards in the home.	The patient and caregiver accept written informational handouts on minimizing hazards.
F.	☐	☐	Instruct the patient on lower extremity dressing in compliance with postsurgical hip precaution guidelines.	The patient accepts written informational handouts on the precautions.

Proceed to the next section of the CST problem.

48

Sample CST Problem

SECTION D

To prepare for the patient's upcoming discharge, which pieces of durable medical equipment or assistive devices should the OTR recommend that the caregiver have available at the patient's home?

Select "Yes" next to those options that are appropriate at this time. Select "No" if the option is not appropriate at this time. You must select either "Yes" or "No" for every option.

	Yes	No	
A.	☐	☐	Dressing stick
B.	☐	☐	Hand-held shower attachment
C.	☐	☐	Overhead trapeze
D.	☐	☐	Quad cane
E.	☐	☐	Three-in-one commode
F.	☐	☐	Transfer tub bench
G.	☐	☐	Bathroom grab bars
H.	☐	☐	Flexible sock aid

NBCOT® Study Guide for the OTR Certification Examination

Instructions

Place a checkmark beside your "Yes" responses from the previous page.
Read **ONLY** the feedback boxes where you have selected a "Yes" response.

SECTION D: FEEDBACK

To prepare for the patient's upcoming discharge, which pieces of durable medical equipment or assistive devices should the OTR recommend that the caregiver have available at the patient's home?

Select "Yes" next to those options that are appropriate at this time. Select "No" if the option is not appropriate at this time. You must select either "Yes" or "No" for every option.

	Yes	No		
A.	☐	☐	Dressing stick	The caregiver would like more instruction about how to use this equipment.
B.	☐	☐	Hand-held shower attachment	The caregiver states the home shower will accommodate this attachment.
C.	☐	☐	Overhead trapeze	The caregiver will contact the durable medical equipment company to inquire about this device.
D.	☐	☐	Quad cane	The caregiver will talk with Physical Therapy about walking aids.
E.	☐	☐	Three-in-one commode	The caregiver asks for clarification on the best location in the home to place this device.
F.	☐	☐	Transfer tub bench	The caregiver has arranged to purchase a tub bench.
G.	☐	☐	Bathroom grab bars	The caregiver has arranged for the installation of grab bars.
H.	☐	☐	Flexible sock aid	The caregiver would like more instruction about how to use this equipment.

Answer key and references for clinical simulation test sample problem

Answer Key:

	YES	NO
Section A	B, C, D, F, G	A, E
Section B	B, C, E, G	A, D, F
Section C	A, B, C, E	D, F
Section D	B, E, F, G	A, C, D, H

References:
Pendleton, H. M., & Schultz-Krohn, W. (Eds.). (2018). *Pedretti's occupational therapy: Practice skills for the physical dysfunction* (8th ed.). St. Louis, MO: Mosby Elsevier.

Smith-Gabai, H., & Holm, S. (Eds.). (2017). *Occupational therapy in acute care* (2nd ed.). Bethesda, MD: AOTA Press.

 Note

The NBCOT Aspire suite of exam practice tools include clinical simulation practice tests designed to mirror the format and flow of the computer-delivered clinical simulation problems.

Chapter 11

Domain 1: Multiple Choice Sample Questions

Practice questions with answer key and references

The following multiple choice items are samples related to Domain 1.

Evaluation and Assessment

Acquire information regarding factors that influence occupational performance on an ongoing basis throughout the occupational therapy process.

NOTES

1. Which dressing task requires the **MOST** challenging integration of performance skills and patterns for a typically developing 3-year-old child?

   A. Finding armholes in a pull-over shirt

   B. Unfastening the zipper of a front-opening jacket

   C. Pulling down a pair of elastic waist pants

   D. Taking off a pair of ankle-high socks

2. A 2-year-old toddler, who has a developmental delay, recently learned to release a 2-inch (5.08 cm) ball into a large toy box. What fine motor skill should the OTR work on **NEXT**?

   A. Color within the lines on a page.

   B. Transfer toys from hand to hand.

   C. Complete a 3- to 4-piece puzzle.

Domain 1: Multiple Choice Sample Questions

3. For a typically developing child, which postural reflex becomes evident between 6-9 months of age and continues throughout life?

   A. Asymmetrical tonic neck

   B. Forward protective extension

   C. Head righting

   D. Tonic labyrinthine

4. An OTR is assessing the reflexes of a 4-month-old infant. The OTR places the infant in a sitting position and encourages the infant to actively flex the neck forward to look at an object held near the infant's chest. Which of the following responses to this movement indicates the presence of the symmetrical tonic neck reflex?

   A. Flexion of the upper extremities and extension of the lower extremities

   B. Flexion in both the upper and lower extremities

   C. Flexion of the lower extremities and extension of the upper extremities

5. A 2-year-old child has developmental delay due to mild spastic cerebral palsy. The child has mastered four-point positioning. Which movement component should the OTR plan to facilitate **NEXT**?

   A. Scooting on the belly

   B. Unsupported upright sitting

   C. Rocking on hands and knees

   D. Creeping on hands and knees

NBCOT® Study Guide for the OTR Certification Examination

NOTES

6. Which of the following symptoms **TYPICALLY** indicates that a client who has been on prolonged bed rest is experiencing orthostatic hypotension?

   A. Diaphoresis when turning over from supine to side-lying position

   B. Lightheadedness upon moving from a supine to seated position

   C. Shortness of breath when sitting up from a supine position

   D. Pounding headache upon moving into a semi-reclined position

7. A client has constructional disorder secondary to an excision of a brain tumor. One of the client's goals is to resume work in a garden center. During which of the following gardening activities would this deficit be **MOST** evident?

   A. Distinguishing between weeds and flowers in a garden bed

   B. Determining how much water to use when watering plants

   C. Duplicating garden designs based on a magazine picture

   D. Placing seeds in small containers filled with potting soil

8. What critical functional advantage is **TYPICALLY** observed in a client who has a complete C_6 spinal cord injury compared to a client who has a complete C_5 spinal cord injury?

   A. Improved gross grasp from innervation of the extrinsic flexors

   B. Ability to use triceps strength during transfers

   C. Improved trunk control to bend side to side without falling

   D. Ability to use the radial wrist extensors to supplement grasp

Domain 1: Multiple Choice Sample Questions

9. A client has a peripheral neuropathy of the dominant hand. A screening indicates thenar muscle atrophy with loss of thumb opposition and palmar abduction, inability to pick up a key or coin from a table top, and decreased grip and pinch strength compared to the non-affected hand. Based on these findings, where on the client's hand would an OTR expect to find sensory disturbances during a Semmes-Weinstein monofilament assessment?

   A. Volar surface of the thumb, index, long, and radial half of the ring fingers

   B. Entire palm and tips of the index, long, ring, and small fingers

   C. Volar and dorsal surfaces of the small finger and radial half of the ring finger

10. A student who is 8 years old has severe diplegia and is non-ambulatory. The student is referred to OT after the family relocates to a new school district. Which area of occupation should be a priority for the school-based OTR to assess during the **INITIAL** evaluation?

   A. Prehensile skills for manipulating eating utensils during lunchtime

   B. Perceptual abilities for copying from the classroom lesson board

   C. Motor skills for managing clothing during toilet transfers

11. An OTR is evaluating an inpatient who recently had a severe TBI and is emerging from coma. The patient is functioning at a Level III (Localized response) on the Rancho Los Amigos scale. Which is the **FIRST** cognitive function the OTR should assess?

   A. Ability to learn new information

   B. Orientation to place and time

   C. Level of arousal

55

NBCOT® Study Guide for the OTR Certification Examination

NOTES

12. Which of the following options represent a condition that requires close monitoring of a client's wound due to having the **GREATEST** risk for infection?

   A. Vascular ulcer left uncovered during healing

   B. Traumatic laceration immediately closed with clips for healing

   C. Abdominal surgical wound left open to heal

13. An inpatient had a myocardial infarction 2 days ago and is beginning phase I cardiac rehabilitation. Which activity is an **ESSENTIAL** component of the initial assessment with this patient?

   A. Monitoring the patient's orthostatic tolerance during movement

   B. Measuring the patient's upper extremity grip and pinch strength

   C. Determining the patient's typical daily energy expenditure

14. An OTR is evaluating an inpatient diagnosed with a glioblastoma multiform in the right frontal lobe. The patient has an extensive fund of knowledge and intact long-term memory, but does not understand the meaning of a joke when engaged in social conversation with family members. Which option **BEST** describes this behavior?

   A. Flight of ideas

   B. Concrete thinking

   C. Confabulation

56

Domain 1: Multiple Choice Sample Questions

15. An OTR is working with a 5-year-old child who has severe spastic diplegic cerebral palsy and will soon be attending kindergarten. The child has been approved for a power wheelchair. Before beginning training in the use of the chair in a school setting, which client factor is **MOST IMPORTANT** for the OTR to re-evaluate?

    A. Upper extremity range of motion

    B. Object permanence

    C. Visual perceptual skills

16. A client in an outpatient setting sustained a frontal lobe TBI 2 months ago. The client has good motor control, but has residual problems with executive functioning. One of the client's goals is to be independent with homemaking tasks. During a meal preparation session, the client cooks a meal, but makes no attempt to clean the cooking utensils and dishes or put the food items away after completing the cooking task. Which area of executive function appears to be **MOST** affected by the TBI as evidenced by this behavior?

    A. Emergent awareness

    B. Selective attention

    C. Episodic memory

    D. Environmental gnosia

17. A client in an outpatient setting has early relapsing-remitting multiple sclerosis. The client lives at home with a spouse and two adolescent children. The client wants to remain independent with homemaking tasks, but finds these daily routines are physically exhausting. What **INITIAL** action should the OTR take to acquire more information related to the client's priorities?

    A. Administer standardized assessments of client factors.

    B. Collaborate with the family regarding typical occupational roles.

    C. Complete a client-centered occupational profile.

57

NBCOT® Study Guide for the OTR Certification Examination

NOTES

18. An OTR has completed an initial neuromotor assessment of a 4-year-old child who has moderate athetoid cerebral palsy. Results indicate persistent primitive reflexes and decreased oral motor control interfere with feeding and functional communication. The parents want the child to be able to self-feed, eat family meals and communicate with others. What additional information is **MOST IMPORTANT** for the OTR to collect prior to developing the intervention plan?

   A. Contextual features that support the child's typical participation in occupation

   B. Early intervention programs available for supporting the child's academic readiness

   C. Medical reports that include the child's past medical history and developmental prognosis

19. An OTR working in an outpatient setting is completing an initial interview with an older adult client who has recently been diagnosed with a progressive neurological disease. What method should the OTR use during the course of the interview to communicate effective listening and client-centered understanding?

   A. Use head gestures to indicate empathy and understanding.

   B. Offer suggestions as the client discloses concerns and problems.

   C. Provide examples of how other clients have overcome similar adversity.

   D. Share examples of adaptations that help to overcome adversity.

20. A 5-year-old child has mild developmental delay. Motor and praxis skills are intact. Which action would be **BEST** to observe when screening emotional regulation skills?

   A. Sharing toys during unstructured play

   B. Responding to the feelings of others

   C. Taking turns while playing a board game

Domain 1: Multiple Choice Sample Questions

21. An inpatient in a rehabilitation setting sustained a C_7 spinal cord injury 2 months ago. One of the patient's goals is to be able to prepare family meals when discharged home. What **INITIAL** action should the OTR complete to support the patient's success with this goal?

    A. Observe current physical skills and abilities during a typical kitchen task.

    B. Identify the patient's typical mealtime routines and habits.

    C. Provide the patient with assistive devices to use in the kitchen.

22. A high-school student with autism spectrum disorder excels academically but has difficulty organizing assignments and homework. The OTR plans to evaluate the student's relative strengths and weaknesses to guide intervention planning. One of the student's goals is to learn an organization system. Which of the following is the **BEST** assessment for this purpose?

    A. Canadian Occupational Performance Measure (COPM)

    B. Executive Function Performance Test (EFPT)

    C. Behavior Rating Inventory of Executive Function (BRIEF)

23. An OTR, who works in the home health setting, is evaluating a client with pneumonia who was recently discharged home from the hospital. The OTR plans to interview the client and administer a standardized assessment to gather information about the client and the home environment. Which additional evaluation method is **MOST BENEFICIAL** for the OTR to include in the information-gathering process to understand the client's priorities?

    A. Measure spaces and features in the natural environment.

    B. Conduct skilled observations while in the client's home.

    C. Complete a comprehensive social participation inventory.

24. Which option represents the **MOST EFFECTIVE** method to screen an 8-month-old infant for neck-on-body automatic righting reaction?

A. Place the child in a sitting position and observe for arm extension while gently pushing the child off balance to the front, back, and each side.

B. Place the child in a supine position and observe body movements while rotating the child's head to one side and then to the other.

C. Hold the child in vertical suspension and observe head position while gently tilting the child from side to side then from front to back.

25. An OTR who works in a community mental health program is preparing to evaluate a 15-year-old client who has bulimia nervosa and frequently engages in self-injurious behaviors by superficially cutting the skin. Which standardized assessments would be **MOST EFFECTIVE** for the OTR to include as part of the evaluation process?

A. Numeric Pain Rating Scale and Sensory Integration and Praxis Test

B. Piers Harris Children's Self Concept Scale and Adolescent Role Assessment

C. Sensory Profile and Ranchos Los Amigos Levels of Cognitive Function-Revised™

26. During the administration of a standardized assessment, a client demonstrates difficulty initiating a motor task. What action **MUST** the OTR take to obtain accurate results from this assessment tool?

A. Provide prompts and tactile cues, as needed

B. Follow the test protocol for giving additional directions

C. Modify the instructions to enhance clarity

Domain 1: Multiple Choice Sample Questions

27. An OTR is a contributing investigator for a unit-wide research project. The focus of the project is to determine if participation in rehabilitation is beneficial to a client's health, well-being, and general quality of life. Which standardized assessment should the OTR use for gathering the **MOST RELIABLE** evidence for this study?

   A. Short Form-36 Health Survey (SF-36)

   B. Kohlman Evaluation of Living Skills (KELS)

   C. Barthel Index of ADL (BI)

28. An OTR is evaluating the visual function of a patient who is emerging from com**a.** The patient opens eyes spontaneously and in response to auditory stimulation. What visual function is **MOST IMPORTANT** for the OTR to observe in a patient at this level of function?

   A. Oculomotor control

   B. Scanning

   C. Pattern recognition

29. An OTR who works in an elementary school is preparing to evaluate a student in fifth grade who has a learning disability and ADHD. Which standardized assessments would be **MOST EFFECTIVE** for the OTR to include as part of the evaluation process?

   A. Hawaii Early Learning Profile (HELP) and Barthel Index of ADL

   B. Bruininks-Oseretsky Test of Motor Proficiency (BOT) and Evaluation Tool of Children's Handwriting (ETCH)

   C. Wee-FIM™ and Ranchos Los Amigos Levels of Cognitive Function-Revised™

NBCOT® Study Guide for the OTR Certification Examination

NOTES

30. A young adult client sustained transfemoral amputations to both legs after a recent accident. The OTR is gathering information to identify the client's priorities and personal goals regarding engagement in daily activities. Which standardized assessment tool would be **MOST BENEFICIAL** to use for obtaining this information?

   A. Kohlman Evaluation of Living Skills (KELS)

   B. Functional Independence Measure (FIM™)

   C. Canadian Occupational Performance Measure (COPM)

31. A client has persistent pitting edema of the hand secondary to mild hemiplegia. Which method would be **MOST RELIABLE** for monitoring the client's edema over time?

   A. Measure the hand circumference at the MCP joint level.

   B. Trace an outline of the hand and fingers placed flat on a tabletop.

   C. Use a volumeter to measure water displacement.

32. A patient in a skilled nursing facility had a CVA one week ago. An initial screening indicates the patient has hemiplegia, ambulates using a quad cane and has good memory. Nursing staff report the patient consistently has difficulty finding the way from the dayroom to the dining room. What type of assessment should be included as part of the initial evaluation to determine the underlying neurobehavioral problem associated with this difficulty?

   A. Functional assessment of topographical orientation and visual perception

   B. Attention and depth perception subtests from a standardized cognitive assessment

   C. Cognitive-behavioral assessment of executive function during a familiar ADL task

62

Domain 1: Multiple Choice Sample Questions

33. A client sustained a closed fracture of the humeral shaft 6 weeks ago. The physician refers the client to OT with a consult that reads: "Begin elbow and shoulder ROM." An initial screening of the affected upper extremity indicates the client has elbow and shoulder stiffness and mild swelling of the hand. The client has full active flexion and full passive extension and flexion of the wrist and digits. Active extension of the wrist and digits is absent. What **INITIAL** action should the OTR take based on these findings?

   A. Confirm whether the client has a secondary radial nerve injury.

   B. Fabricate a dynamic splint to compensate for loss of finger extension.

   C. Complete a comprehensive manual muscle test of the affected upper extremity.

34. An OTR is administering the Functional Independence Measure (FIM™) as part of the initial evaluation of an inpatient who had a left CVA with aphasia 5 days ago. The patient has right hemiparesis and requires moderate assistance to maintain balance while standing. What action should the OTR take when completing this assessment?

   A. Introduce a reacher and other adaptive equipment to maximize patient's level of performance.

   B. Observe as the patient performs ADL routines with the typical methods used prior to admission.

   C. Provide the patient with visual and tactile cues to sequence each step of the task.

35. A student in the second grade has autism spectrum disorder and is scheduled to begin school-based OT. The teacher reports the student has difficulty attending to academic tasks and typically has outbursts when in close proximity to other people. In which environment should the majority of the student's intervention sessions take place?

   A. Self-contained occupational therapy treatment room

   B. Playground in an area apart from other students

   C. Classroom during routine curriculum-based activities

NBCOT® Study Guide for the OTR Certification Examination

NOTES

36. An OTR is developing an intervention plan for an inpatient who has severe post-traumatic stress disorder (PTSD). Symptoms of PTSD started several weeks after the patient was robbed in a convenience store where the patient was working. The patient's goal is to resume work at the store, but extreme fear and distrust interfere with the ability to interact with customers. Which environment is **MOST** conducive for promoting initial progress toward a return-to-work goal with this patient?

   A. One-on-one in the patient's hospital room

   B. During a role-play session in the therapy room

   C. Discussion group with several other patients

37. An OTR working in an inpatient rehabilitation facility is scheduled to complete an initial grooming and hygiene assessment with a patient. The patient has mild hemiplegia and neurobehavioral deficits secondary to a CVA one week ago. Which area of the facility should the assessment take place in order to obtain the **MOST BENEFICIAL** information about the impact of these symptoms on the patient's occupational performance?

   A. Bedside in the patient's hospital room

   B. Bathroom in the patient's hospital room

   C. Simulated environment in the OT clinic

38. An inpatient in a rehabilitation facility has hemiplegia secondary to a CVA. The patient is independent with BADL. The OTR, who uses the ecology of human performance model, is preparing the patient's discharge summary. What information reflects this approach and should be included as part of this report?

   A. Recommendations for home modifications to maximize accessibility and task performance

   B. Exercise protocols for maintaining physical strength and cardiovascular endurance

   C. Current functional status and anticipated occupational performance upon return home

   D. Support groups for promoting the patient's acceptance of the physical impairments

64

Domain 1: Multiple Choice Sample Questions

39. An OTR and a vocational rehabilitation team are using the Individual Placement and Support (IPS) model to support a client, who has schizophrenia and anxiety, in gaining employment. One of the intervention goals is for the client to achieve competitive employment. When using the IPS model, which approach should be included in the vocational intervention to support this goal?

    A. Provide education in general work behaviors, then conduct an extensive job search.

    B. Secure a job placement site, then teach the client the specific job skills for that workplace.

    C. Complete a detailed resume of job skills, then teach the client effective work behaviors.

40. An OTR is developing an intervention plan using a bottom-up approach for clients who have hemiplegia and hemi-neglect secondary to having a CVA more than one year ago. Which of the following intervention techniques has evidence supporting its efficacy for reducing the effects of "learned non-use" through cortical reorganization?

    A. Proprioceptive neuromuscular facilitation (PNF)

    B. Occupational adaptation (OA)

    C. Constraint-induced movement therapy (CIMT)

41. An OTR is providing consultative services at an assisted living facility. Facility administrators are concerned that some residents may be at risk for falls. Using a primary prevention model, what **INITIAL** recommendation should the OTR make to the management of the facility?

    A. Analysis of resident injuries that have occurred at the facility over the past 5 years

    B. Ongoing monitoring and observation of the residents to decrease liability

    C. Screening of all residents prior to determining needs of the facility

65

42. A client in an outpatient setting sustained an acquired brain injury 2 months ago. Evaluation results indicate the client has functional ROM and strength, but continues to require assistance with ADL due to moderate visual and vestibular processing deficits. Which intervention represents an adaptive approach for improving the client's performance in areas of occupation?

A. Providing the client with an exercise program for improving gaze stabilization

B. Teaching the client to use proprioceptive cues during functional activities

C. Incorporating progressively more challenging tasks into a functional activity

D. Engaging the client in valued activities that promote postural stability and balance

43. An OTR is using a top-down approach to select interventions for a client who has unilateral neglect secondary to a CVA. Which intervention would be **MOST BENEFICIAL** to include as part of the client's intervention when using this approach?

A. Determine compensatory options the client can use in the home environment.

B. Teach drills for practicing head turning to find an object placed near the affected side.

C. Place commonly used toiletry items to the client's affected side during self-care tasks.

D. Use tactile-kinesthetic guiding to the client's involved extremity during a dressing task.

Domain 1: Multiple Choice Sample Questions

44. An OTR working in an inpatient mental health setting is using a cognitive behavioral approach to select an intervention activity for a young adult undergoing treatment for symptoms associated with body dysmorphic disorder. The patient is employed in a successful career and enjoys outdoor activities such as jogging and hiking, but has difficulty forming and maintaining interpersonal relationships. One of the patient's goals is to improve self-image and the ability to express feelings. Which activity would be **MOST BENEFICIAL** to include as part of the intervention for supporting this goal when using this approach?

A. Engaging the patient in an art project using a variety of media during which the patient is encouraged to release emotions

B. Teaching the patient to use a dysfunctional thought record for describing distressing situations and emotional responses

C. Guiding the patient through avocational exploration of activities that provide opportunities for social interaction

45. An inpatient in a rehabilitation facility has a C_6 tetraplegia with a rating of "A" on the ASIA impairment scale. The patient has achieved BADL goals and now wants to be as independent as possible with homemaking tasks. Which intervention approach would be effective to use as the **PRIMARY** strategy for promoting progress toward the patient's goal?

A. Behavioral

B. Remedial

C. Biomechanical

D. Compensatory

NBCOT® Study Guide for the OTR Certification Examination

NOTES

46. An OTR completed an initial assessment of a student in the second grade. Results indicate the student has age-appropriate comprehension, visual object gnosia, and visual acuity, but standardized test scores on figure-ground subtests are well below the norm. Which of the following school art class activities would present the **MOST** challenge to this student based on the outcomes of this evaluation?

   A. Painting a free form design on a clay pot using a variety of paint colors

   B. Selecting a round bead from a bag of multi-shaped beads to complete a necklace

   C. Using plastic templates to trace basic geometric shapes on colored paper

   D. Placing tiles of the same color and shape in a straight line when making a trivet

47. A client who has schizophrenia is participating in OT to improve functional living skills. The client's goal is to be able to independently prepare family meals. The client has successfully used a checklist strategy to gather and keep track of items while preparing a simple cold snack. Which of the following tasks would present a "just right" challenge when using the checklist strategy to progress towards the client's goal?

   A. Setting the dining table for a group meal

   B. Cooking a three-course meal for the family

   C. Purchasing groceries for a pre-set weekly menu

48. Which activity involves the use of a closed kinetic chain movement of the upper extremity?

   A. Lifting a suitcase off the floor to carry by the handle

   B. Pulling up on an overhead trapeze during bed mobility

   C. Hand-to-mouth patterns used for self-feeding

Domain 1: Multiple Choice Sample Questions

49. An OTR is evaluating a client who has an ulnar nerve injury at the wrist level of the right dominant extremity. During which task would this injury be **MOST** evident?

   A. Carrying a briefcase

   B. Turning a key in the car ignition

   C. Operating a desktop calculator

   D. Holding coins in the palm of the hand

50. An older adult in an inpatient setting has moderate-severe debilitation from prolonged bed rest secondary to general medical-surgical post-operative complications. The patient's primary goal is to be as independent as possible with BADL prior to discharge home. The patient has full passive ROM and Fair minus (3-/5) functional muscle strength of the upper extremities. The patient can ambulate for several feet using a walker and contact guard assistance, but uses a wheelchair in the hospital room and depends on caregivers for wheelchair transport to various areas of the hospital. Based on the patient's current status, which dressing activity would be **MOST** difficult for this patient to complete while seated in the wheelchair?

   A. Crossing one leg over the other and putting on loose-fitting slip-on shoes

   B. Putting on a front-opening shirt after reaching for the shirt off a bedside stand

   C. Getting a pair of pants hanging in the closet and putting them on

   D. Washing hands at a sink and drying the hands using a towel placed next to the sink

69

NBCOT® Study Guide for the OTR Certification Examination

Answer Key

Domain 1 Sample Items

Item Number	Key
1.	B
2.	C
3.	B
4.	A
5.	C
6.	B
7.	C
8.	D
9.	A
10.	C
11.	C
12.	C
13.	A
14.	B
15.	C
16.	A
17.	C
18.	A
19.	D
20.	B
21.	B
22.	C
23.	B
24.	B
25.	B

Item Number	Key
26.	B
27.	A
28.	A
29.	B
30.	C
31.	C
32.	A
33.	A
34.	B
35.	C
36.	A
37.	B
38.	A
39.	B
40.	C
41.	C
42.	B
43.	A
44.	B
45.	D
46.	B
47.	A
48.	B
49.	B
50.	C

NBCOT® Study Guide for the OTR Certification Examination

DOMAIN 01: Multiple Choice Answers, Rationales, and References

NOTES

1. Which dressing task requires the **MOST** challenging integration of performance skills and patterns for a typically developing 3-year-old child?

    A. Finding armholes in a pull-over shirt

    B. Unfastening the zipper of a front-opening jacket

    C. Pulling down a pair of elastic waist pants

    D. Taking off a pair of ankle-high socks

Correct Answer: B

RATIONALE:
This skill requires a complex integration of visual and somatosensory systems that typically develops by the third year of age.

Reference:
Case-Smith, J., & O'Brien, J. C. (2015). *Occupational therapy for children and adolescents* (7th ed., p. 439). St. Louis, MO: Mosby Elsevier.

2. A 2-year-old toddler, who has a developmental delay, recently learned to release a 2-inch (5.08 cm) ball into a large toy box. What fine motor skill should the OTR work on **NEXT**?

    A. Color within the lines on a page.

    B. Transfer toys from hand to hand.

    C. Complete a 3- to 4-piece puzzle.

Correct Answer: C

RATIONALE:
In the development of play occupations, a child who is able to release an object into a toy box would **NEXT** be expected to be able to put together a 3- to 4-piece puzzle.

Reference:
Case-Smith, J., & O'Brien, J. C. (2015). *Occupational therapy for children and adolescents* (7th ed., pp. 80-81, 88). St. Louis, MO: Mosby Elsevier.

NBCOT® Study Guide for the OTR Certification Examination

NOTES

3. For a typically developing child, which postural reflex becomes evident between 6-9 months of age and continues throughout life?

   A. Asymmetrical tonic neck

   B. Forward protective extension

   C. Head righting

   D. Tonic labyrinthine

Correct Answer: B

RATIONALE:
Forward protective extension is a postural reflex that typically becomes evident between 6-9 months of age and continues throughout life.

Reference:
Case-Smith, J., & O'Brien, J. C. (2015). *Occupational therapy for children and adolescents* (7th ed., p. 198). St. Louis, MO: Mosby Elsevier.

4. An OTR is assessing the reflexes of a 4-month-old infant. The OTR places the infant in a sitting position and encourages the infant to actively flex the neck forward to look at an object held near the infant's chest. Which of the following responses to this movement indicates the presence of the symmetrical tonic neck reflex?

   A. Flexion of the upper extremities and extension of the lower extremities

   B. Flexion in both the upper and lower extremities

   C. Flexion of the lower extremities and extension of the upper extremities

Correct Answer: A

RATIONALE:
This movement pattern indicates the presence of the symmetrical tonic neck reflex (STNR).

Reference:
Pendleton, H. M., & Schultz-Krohn, W. (Eds.). (2018). *Pedretti's occupational therapy: Practice skills for the physical dysfunction* (8th ed., p. 456). St. Louis, MO: Mosby Elsevier.

74

Domain 1: Multiple Choice Answers, Rationales, and References

5. A 2-year-old child has developmental delay due to mild spastic cerebral palsy. The child has mastered four-point positioning. Which movement component should the OTR plan to facilitate **NEXT**?

    A. Scooting on the belly

    B. Unsupported upright sitting

    C. Rocking on hands and knees

    D. Creeping on hands and knees

Correct Answer: C

RATIONALE:
In the developmental sequence of gross motor development and mobility skills, a child who has mastered four-point positioning would be expected to progress to rocking on hands and knees **NEXT**.

Reference:
Case-Smith, J., & O'Brien, J. C. (2015). *Occupational therapy for children and adolescents* (7th ed., p. 83). St. Louis, MO: Mosby Elsevier.

6. Which of the following symptoms **TYPICALLY** indicates that a client who has been on prolonged bed rest is experiencing orthostatic hypotension?

    A. Diaphoresis when turning over from supine to side-lying position

    B. Lightheadedness upon moving from a supine to seated position

    C. Shortness of breath when sitting up from a supine position

    D. Pounding headache upon moving into a semi-reclined position

Correct Answer: B

RATIONALE:
Orthostatic hypotension is a decrease in blood pressure that reduces blood flow to the brain and results in lightheadedness.

Reference:
Pendleton, H. M., & Schultz-Krohn, W. (Eds.). (2018). *Pedretti's occupational therapy: Practice skills for the physical dysfunction* (8th ed., p. 909). St. Louis, MO: Mosby Elsevier.

NBCOT® Study Guide for the OTR Certification Examination

NOTES

7. A client has constructional disorder secondary to an excision of a brain tumor. One of the client's goals is to resume work in a garden center. During which of the following gardening activities would this deficit be **MOST** evident?

   A. Distinguishing between weeds and flowers in a garden bed

   B. Determining how much water to use when watering plants

   C. Duplicating garden designs based on a magazine picture

   D. Placing seeds in small containers filled with potting soil

Correct Answer: C

RATIONALE:
Constructional disorder is characterized by difficulty or inability to assemble separate parts to build an end-product.

Reference:
Pendleton, H. M., & Schultz-Krohn, W. (Eds.). (2018). *Pedretti's occupational therapy: Practice skills for the physical dysfunction* (8th ed., p. 640). St. Louis, MO: Mosby Elsevier.

8. What critical functional advantage is **TYPICALLY** observed in a client who has a complete C_6 spinal cord injury compared to a client who has a complete C_5 spinal cord injury?

   A. Improved gross grasp from innervation of the extrinsic flexors

   B. Ability to use triceps strength during transfers

   C. Improved trunk control to bend side to side without falling

   D. Ability to use the radial wrist extensors to supplement grasp

Correct Answer: D

RATIONALE:
Clients who have a complete C_6 spinal cord injury **TYPICALLY** have innervation of the radial wrist extensors. This allows the use of a tenodesis grasp to attain a higher level of functional independence.

Reference:
Pendleton, H. M., & Schultz-Krohn, W. (Eds.). (2018). *Pedretti's occupational therapy: Practice skills for the physical dysfunction* (8th ed., pp. 915-920). St. Louis, MO: Mosby Elsevier.

Domain 1: Multiple Choice Answers, Rationales, and References

9. A client has a peripheral neuropathy of the dominant hand. A screening indicates thenar muscle atrophy with loss of thumb opposition and palmar abduction, inability to pick up a key or coin from a table top, and decreased grip and pinch strength compared to the non-affected hand. Based on these findings, where on the client's hand would an OTR expect to find sensory disturbances during a Semmes-Weinstein monofilament assessment?

A. Volar surface of the thumb, index, long, and radial half of the ring fingers

B. Entire palm and tips of the index, long, ring, and small fingers

C. Volar and dorsal surfaces of the small finger and radial half of the ring finger

Correct Answer: A

RATIONALE:
The client's clinical symptoms are indicative of a median nerve injury. Sensory distribution for the median nerve is to the volar surface of the thumb, index, long, and radial half of the ring fingers.

Reference:
Pendleton, H. M., & Schultz-Krohn, W. (Eds). (2018). *Pedretti's occupational therapy: Practice skills for the physical dysfunction* (8th ed., pp. 978, 982-983). St. Louis, MO: Mosby Elsevier.

10. A student who is 8-years-old has severe diplegia and is non-ambulatory. The student is referred to OT after the family relocates to a new school district. Which area of occupation should be a priority for the school-based OTR to assess during the **INITIAL** evaluation?

   A. Prehensile skills for manipulating eating utensils during lunchtime

   B. Perceptual abilities for copying from the classroom lesson board

   C. **Motor skills for managing clothing during toilet transfers**

Correct Answer: C

RATIONALE:
A student with spastic diplegia typically has motor involvement of the lower extremity that may influence ability to manage clothing during toilet transfers.

Reference:
Case-Smith, J., & O'Brien, J. C. (2015). *Occupational therapy for children and adolescents* (7th ed., pp. 673, 796). St. Louis, MO: Mosby Elsevier.

Domain 1: Multiple Choice Answers, Rationales, and References

11. An OTR is evaluating an inpatient who recently had a severe TBI and is emerging from coma. The patient is functioning at a Level III (Localized response) on the Rancho Los Amigos scale. Which is the **FIRST** cognitive function the OTR should assess?

   A. Ability to learn new information

   B. Orientation to place and time

   C. Level of arousal

Correct Answer: C

RATIONALE:
A component of the evaluation for a patient who is functioning at a Level III (Localized Response) on the Rancho Los Amigos scale is to screen the patient's level of arousal and alertness.

References:
Gutman, S. A., & Schonfeld, A. B. (2009). *Screening adult neurologic populations: A step-by-step instruction manual* (2nd ed., pp. 8-9). Bethesda, MD: AOTA Press.

Smith-Gabai, H., & Holm, S. (Eds.). (2017). *Occupational therapy in acute care* (2nd ed., pp. 382-383). Bethesda, MD: AOTA Press

12. Which of the following options represent a condition that requires close monitoring of a client's wound due to having the **GREATEST** risk for infection?

   A. Vascular ulcer left uncovered during healing

   B. Traumatic laceration immediately closed with clips for healing

   C. Abdominal surgical wound left open to heal

Correct Answer: C

RATIONALE:
The surgeon may leave a deep wound open to heal through the granulation process. This type of wound requires skilled wound care and close monitoring due to the risk of infection.

Reference:
Cooper, C. (2014). *Fundamentals of hand therapy: Clinical reasoning and treatment guidelines for common diagnoses of the upper extremity* (2nd ed., p. 212). St. Louis, MO: Mosby Elsevier.

NBCOT® Study Guide for the OTR Certification Examination

NOTES

13. An inpatient had a myocardial infarction 2 days ago and is beginning phase I cardiac rehabilitation. Which activity is an **ESSENTIAL** component of the initial assessment with this patient?

    A. **Monitoring the patient's orthostatic tolerance during movement**

    B. Measuring the patient's upper extremity grip and pinch strength

    C. Determining the patient's typical daily energy expenditure

Correct Answer: A

RATIONALE:
For the safety of the patient, the patient's physiologic response to activity must be monitored during this early phase of cardiac rehabilitation.

Reference:
Pendleton, H. M., & Schultz-Krohn, W. (Eds.). (2018). *Pedretti's occupational therapy: Practice skills for the physical dysfunction* (8th ed., pp. 1124-1125). St. Louis, MO: Mosby Elsevier.

14. An OTR is evaluating an inpatient diagnosed with a glioblastoma multiform in the right frontal lobe. The patient has an extensive fund of knowledge and intact long-term memory, but does not understand the meaning of a joke when engaged in social conversation with family members. Which option **BEST** describes this behavior?

    A. Flight of ideas

    B. **Concrete thinking**

    C. Confabulation

Correct Answer: B

RATIONALE:
A client who exhibits concrete thinking interprets events and communication in a literal fashion, making it difficult to understand the underpinnings of a joke.

Reference:
Gutman, S. A., & Schonfeld, A. B. (2009). *Screening adult neurologic populations: A step-by-step instruction manual* (2nd ed., pp. 19, 23). Bethesda, MD: AOTA Press.

80

Domain 1: Multiple Choice Answers, Rationales, and References

15. An OTR is working with a 5-year-old child who has severe spastic diplegic cerebral palsy and will soon be attending kindergarten. The child has been approved for a power wheelchair. Before beginning training in the use of the chair in a school setting, which client factor is **MOST IMPORTANT** for the OTR to re-evaluate?

    A. Upper extremity range of motion

    B. Object permanence

    C. Visual perceptual skills

Correct Answer: C

RATIONALE:
Cerebral palsy is associated with visual impairments that need to be screened prior to initiating power mobility training.

Reference:
Case-Smith, J., & O'Brien, J. C. (2015). *Occupational therapy for children and adolescents* (7th ed., pp. 582, 798). St. Louis, MO: Mosby Elsevier.

NBCOT® Study Guide for the OTR Certification Examination

NOTES

16. A client in an outpatient setting sustained a frontal lobe TBI 2 months ago. The client has good motor control, but has residual problems with executive functioning. One of the client's goals is to be independent with homemaking tasks. During a meal preparation session, the client cooks a meal, but makes no attempt to clean the cooking utensils and dishes or put the food items away after completing the cooking task. Which area of executive function appears to be **MOST** affected by the TBI as evidenced by this behavior?

A. **Emergent awareness**

B. Selective attention

C. Episodic memory

D. Environmental gnosia

Correct Answer: A

RATIONALE:
Deficits in emergent awareness are characterized by difficulty or inability to recognize and correct errors in performance.

References:
Gillen, G. (2016). *Stroke rehabilitation: A function-based approach* (4th ed., p. 582). St. Louis, MO: Elsevier.

Zoltan, B. (2007). *Vision, perception, and cognition: A manual for the evaluation and treatment of the adult with acquired brain injury* (4th ed., pp. 236-238, 244-245). Thorofare, NJ: SLACK, Inc.

Domain 1: Multiple Choice Answers, Rationales, and References

17. A client in an outpatient setting has early relapsing-remitting multiple sclerosis. The client lives at home with a spouse and two adolescent children. The client wants to remain independent with homemaking tasks, but finds these daily routines are physically exhausting. What **INITIAL** action should the OTR take to acquire more information related to the client's priorities?

    A. Administer standardized assessments of client factors.

    B. Collaborate with the family regarding typical occupational roles.

    C. Complete a client-centered occupational profile.

Correct Answer: C

RATIONALE:
Completing an occupational profile as part of the **INITIAL** action provides the OTR information about the client's priorities. This leads to a more individualized approach to evaluation and intervention planning.

Reference:
Pendleton, H. M., & Schultz-Krohn, W. (Eds.). (2018). *Pedretti's occupational therapy: Practice skills for the physical dysfunction* (8th ed., pp. 891-892). St. Louis, MO: Mosby Elsevier.

NOTES

18. An OTR has completed an initial neuromotor assessment of a 4-year-old child who has moderate athetoid cerebral palsy. Results indicate persistent primitive reflexes and decreased oral motor control interfere with feeding and functional communication. The parents want the child to be able to self-feed, eat family meals and communicate with others. What additional information is **MOST IMPORTANT** for the OTR to collect prior to developing the intervention plan?

   A. Contextual features that support the child's typical participation in occupation

   B. Early intervention programs available for supporting the child's academic readiness

   C. Medical reports that include the child's past medical history and developmental prognosis

Correct Answer: A

RATIONALE:
An understanding of the contexts that impact a child's performance is critical to effective intervention planning.

Reference:
Case-Smith, J., & O'Brien, J. C. (2015). *Occupational therapy for children and adolescents* (7th ed. pp. 9-12, 396-397). St. Louis, MO: Mosby Elsevier.

19. An OTR working in an outpatient setting is completing an initial interview with an older adult client who has recently been diagnosed with a progressive neurological disease. What method should the OTR use during the course of the interview to communicate effective listening and client-centered understanding?

A. Use head gestures to indicate empathy and understanding.

B. Offer suggestions as the client discloses concerns and problems.

C. Provide examples of how other clients have overcome similar adversity.

D. Share examples of adaptations that help to overcome adversity.

Correct Answer: D

RATIONALE:
The OTR is demonstrating client-centered practice by using active listening skills and encouraging the client to continue to participate in the discussion.

Reference:
Schell, B. A. B., Gillen, G., & Scaffa, M. E. (2014). *Willard & Spackman's occupational therapy* (12th ed., pp. 432-433). Philadelphia, PA: Lippincott Williams & Wilkins.

NBCOT® Study Guide for the OTR Certification Examination

NOTES

20. A 5-year-old child has mild developmental delay. Motor and praxis skills are intact. Which action would be **BEST** to observe when screening emotional regulation skills?

   A. Sharing toys during unstructured play

   B. Responding to the feelings of others

   C. Taking turns while playing a board game

Correct Answer: B

RATIONALE:
Emotional self-regulation is **BEST** observed during a situation where the child is responding to the feelings of others.

References:
Case-Smith, J., & O'Brien, J. C. (2015). *Occupational therapy for children and adolescents* (7th ed., p. 73). St. Louis, MO: Mosby Elsevier.

Mulligan, S. (2014). *Occupational therapy evaluation for children: A pocket guide* (2nd ed., p. 65). Philadelphia, PA: Lippincott Williams & Wilkins.

21. An inpatient in a rehabilitation setting sustained a C_7 spinal cord injury 2 months ago. One of the patient's goals is to be able to prepare family meals when discharged home. What **INITIAL** action should the OTR complete to support the patient's success with this goal?

   A. Observe current physical skills and abilities during a typical kitchen task.

   B. Identify the patient's typical mealtime routines and habits.

   C. Provide the patient with assistive devices to use in the kitchen.

Correct Answer: B

RATIONALE:
An integral part of developing a client-centered intervention plan is to learn about the client's typical mealtime routines and habits.

Reference:
Pendleton, H. M., & Schultz-Krohn, W. (Eds.). (2018). *Pedretti's occupational therapy: Practice skills for the physical dysfunction* (8th ed., pp. 7, 160). St. Louis, MO: Mosby Elsevier.

22. A high-school student with autism spectrum disorder excels academically but has difficulty organizing assignments and homework. The OTR plans to evaluate the student's relative strengths and weaknesses to guide intervention planning. One of the student's goals is to learn an organization system. Which of the following is the **BEST** assessment for this purpose?

   A. Canadian Occupational Performance Measure (COPM)

   B. Executive Function Performance Test (EFPT)

   C. Behavior Rating Inventory of Executive Function (BRIEF)

Correct Answer: C

RATIONALE:
The objective of the Behavior Rating Inventory of Executive Function (BRIEF) is to evaluate self-regulation and executive function in adolescents who have neurological or developmental conditions.

References:
Asher, I. E. (Ed.). (2014). *Asher's occupational therapy assessment tools: An annotated index* (4th ed., p. 31, 564, 594). Bethesda, MD: AOTA Press.

Kuhaneck, H. M., & Watling, R. (2010). *Autism: A comprehensive occupational therapy approach* (3rd ed. p. 686). Bethesda: AOTA Press.

NBCOT® Study Guide for the OTR Certification Examination

NOTES

23. An OTR, who works in the home health setting, is evaluating a client with pneumonia who was recently discharged home from the hospital. The OTR plans to interview the client and administer a standardized assessment to gather information about the client and the home environment. Which additional evaluation method is **MOST BENEFICIAL** for the OTR to include in the information-gathering process to understand the client's priorities?

A. Measure spaces and features in the natural environment.

B. **Conduct skilled observations while in the client's home.**

C. Complete a comprehensive social participation inventory.

Correct Answer: B

RATIONALE:

Observing while the client engages in functional tasks in the natural context of the home will provide the **MOST BENEFICIAL** information related to the client's priorities in this environment.

References:

Ainsworth, E., & de Jonge, D. (2011). *An occupational therapist's guide to home modification practice* (pp. 96, 113). Thorofare, NJ: SLACK, Inc.

Pendleton, H. M., & Schultz-Krohn, W. (Eds.). (2018). *Pedretti's occupational therapy: Practice skills for the physical dysfunction* (8th ed., p. 160). St. Louis, MO: Mosby Elsevier.

Domain 1: Multiple Choice Answers, Rationales, and References

24. Which option represents the **MOST EFFECTIVE** method to screen an 8-month-old infant for neck-on-body automatic righting reaction?

A. Place the child in a sitting position and observe for arm extension while gently pushing the child off balance to the front, back, and each side.

B. Place the child in a supine position and observe body movements while rotating the child's head to one side and then to the other.

C. Hold the child in vertical suspension and observe head position while gently tilting the child from side to side then from front to back.

Correct Answer: B

RATIONALE:
This method describes the stimulus, response, and reaction associated with testing for neck-on-body automatic righting reaction.

Reference:
Mulligan, S. (2014). *Occupational therapy evaluation for children: A pocket guide* (2nd ed., p. 151). Philadelphia, PA: Lippincott Williams & Wilkins.

NBCOT® Study Guide for the OTR Certification Examination

NOTES

25. An OTR who works in a community mental health program is preparing to evaluate a 15-year-old client who has bulimia nervosa and frequently engages in self-injurious behaviors by superficially cutting the skin. Which standardized assessments would be **MOST EFFECTIVE** for the OTR to include as part of the evaluation process?

    A. Numeric Pain Rating Scale and Sensory Integration and Praxis Test

    B. Piers Harris Children's Self Concept Scale and Adolescent Role Assessment

    C. Sensory Profile and Ranchos Los Amigos Levels of Cognitive Function-Revised™

Correct Answer: B

RATIONALE:
The Piers Harris Children's Self Concept Scale and the Adolescent Role Assessment are the most effective assessment tools to use to evaluate self-concept and role development in this adolescent client who has psychosocial dysfunction.

References:
Asher, I. E. (Ed.). (2014). *Asher's occupational therapy assessment tools: An annotated index* (4th ed., p. 535). Bethesda, MD: AOTA Press.

Mulligan, S. (2014). *Occupational therapy evaluation for children: A pocket guide* (2nd ed., pp. 50-52). Philadelphia, PA: Lippincott Williams & Wilkins.

Domain 1: Multiple Choice Answers, Rationales, and References

26. During the administration of a standardized assessment, a client demonstrates difficulty initiating a motor task. What action **MUST** the OTR take to obtain accurate results from this assessment tool?

    A. Provide prompts and tactile cues, as needed

    B. Follow the test protocol for giving additional directions

    C. Modify the instructions to enhance clarity

Correct Answer: B

RATIONALE:
When administering a standardized assessment, the OTR must follow the uniform administration procedures outlined in the test manual to obtain valid and reliable results.

References:
Asher, I. E. (Ed.). (2014). *Asher's occupational therapy assessment tools: An annotated index* (4th ed., p. 12). Bethesda, MD: AOTA Press.

Case-Smith, J., & O'Brien, J. C. (2015). *Occupational therapy for children and adolescents* (7th ed., p. 163). St. Louis, MO: Mosby Elsevier.

27. An OTR is a contributing investigator for a unit-wide research project. The focus of the project is to determine if participation in rehabilitation is beneficial to a client's health, well-being, and general quality of life. Which standardized assessment should the OTR use for gathering the **MOST RELIABLE** evidence for this study?

    A. Short Form-36 Health Survey (SF-36)

    B. Kohlman Evaluation of Living Skills (KELS)

    C. Barthel Index of ADL (BI)

Correct Answer: A

RATIONALE:
This is a survey used as a measure of general health and well-being. It has been used in medical outcomes studies and is sensitive to change in health status.

Reference:
Asher, I. E. (Ed.). (2014). *Asher's occupational therapy assessment tools: An annotated index* (4th ed., pp. 163, 210-211, 92-93). Bethesda, MD: AOTA Press.

NBCOT® Study Guide for the OTR Certification Examination

NOTES

28. An OTR is evaluating the visual function of a patient who is emerging from coma. The patient opens eyes spontaneously and in response to auditory stimulation. What visual function is **MOST IMPORTANT** for the OTR to observe in a patient at this level of function?

    A. **Oculomotor control**

    B. Scanning

    C. Pattern recognition

Correct Answer: A

RATIONALE:
It is beneficial to assess basic visual skills such as oculomotor control when a patient is emerging from coma.

References:
Gutman, S. A., & Schonfeld, A. B. (2009). *Screening adult neurologic populations: A step-by-step instruction manual* (2nd ed., p. 36). Bethesda, MD: AOTA Press.

Pendleton, H. M., & Schultz-Krohn, W. (Eds.). (2018). *Pedretti's occupational therapy: Practice skills for the physical dysfunction* (8th ed., p. 598). St. Louis, MO: Mosby Elsevier.

Domain 1: Multiple Choice Answers, Rationales, and References

29. An OTR who works in an elementary school is preparing to evaluate a student in fifth grade who has a learning disability and ADHD. Which standardized assessments would be **MOST EFFECTIVE** for the OTR to include as part of the evaluation process?

A. Hawaii Early Learning Profile (HELP) and Barthel Index of ADL

B. Bruininks-Oseretsky Test of Motor Proficiency (BOT) and Evaluation Tool of Children's Handwriting (ETCH)

C. Wee-FIM™ and Ranchos Los Amigos Levels of Cognitive Function-Revised™

Correct Answer: B

RATIONALE:
These assessment tools are used to measure skills and abilities that are associated with school-related occupation performance.

References:
Asher, I. E. (Ed.). (2014). *Asher's occupational therapy assessment tools: An annotated index* (4th ed., pp. 452-453, 268-269). Bethesda, MD: AOTA Press.

Case-Smith, J., & O'Brien, J. C. (2015). *Occupational therapy for children and adolescents* (7th ed., p. 673). St. Louis, MO: Mosby Elsevier.

Mulligan, S. (2014). *Occupational therapy evaluation for children: A pocket guide* (2nd ed., pp. 55-52). Philadelphia, PA: Lippincott Williams & Wilkins.

NBCOT® Study Guide for the OTR Certification Examination

NOTES

30. A young adult client sustained transfemoral amputations to both legs after a recent accident. The OTR is gathering information to identify the client's priorities and personal goals regarding engagement in daily activities. Which standardized assessment tool would be **MOST BENEFICIAL** to use for obtaining this information?

    A. Kohlman Evaluation of Living Skills (KELS)

    B. Functional Independence Measure (FIM™)

    C. Canadian Occupational Performance Measure (COPM)

Correct Answer: C

RATIONALE:
This assessment tool fosters collaboration between the client and the OTR and enables the development of a meaningful client-centered intervention plan. The tool can be used to measure change in a client's self-perception of occupational performance over time.

Reference:
Asher, I. E. (Ed.). (2014). *Asher's occupational therapy assessment tools: An annotated index* (4th ed., pp. 31-32, 124-125, 210-211). Bethesda, MD: AOTA Press.

31. A client has persistent pitting edema of the hand secondary to mild hemiplegia. Which method would be **MOST RELIABLE** for monitoring the client's edema over time?

    A. Measure the hand circumference at the MCP joint level.

    B. Trace an outline of the hand and fingers placed flat on a tabletop.

    C. Use a volumeter to measure water displacement.

Correct Answer: C

RATIONALE:
Volumetric measurement procedures are standardized and would produce the **MOST RELIABLE** results when measuring hand edema in clients with this diagnosis.

References:
Gillen, G. (2016). *Stroke rehabilitation: A function-based approach* (4th ed., pp. 514-515). St. Louis, MO: Elsevier.

Pendleton, H. M., & Schultz-Krohn, W. (Eds.). (2018). *Pedretti's occupational therapy: Practice skills for the physical dysfunction* (8th ed., pp. 979-980). St. Louis, MO: Mosby Elsevier.

NBCOT® Study Guide for the OTR Certification Examination

NOTES

32. A patient in a skilled nursing facility had a CVA one week ago. An initial screening indicates the patient has hemiplegia, ambulates using a quad cane and has good memory. Nursing staff report the patient consistently has difficulty finding the way from the dayroom to the dining room. What type of assessment should be included as part of the initial evaluation to determine the underlying neurobehavioral problem associated with this difficulty?

A. Functional assessment of topographical orientation and visual perception

B. Attention and depth perception subtests from a standardized cognitive assessment

C. Cognitive-behavioral assessment of executive function during a familiar ADL task

Correct Answer: A

RATIONALE:
Since the patient has intact memory, the behavior suggests topographical disorientation. The test for this is typically a functional test. Contributing visual perceptual deficits should also be considered.

References:
Gillen, G. (2016). *Stroke rehabilitation: A function-based approach* (4th ed., pp. 595-596, 587-590, 634). St. Louis, MO: Elsevier.

Pendleton, H. M., & Schultz-Krohn, W. (Eds.). (2018). *Pedretti's occupational therapy: Practice skills for the physical dysfunction* (8th ed., pp. 828-829). St. Louis, MO: Mosby Elsevier.

Domain 1: Multiple Choice Answers, Rationales, and References

33. A client sustained a closed fracture of the humeral shaft 6 weeks ago. The physician refers the client to OT with a consult that reads: "Begin elbow and shoulder ROM." An initial screening of the affected upper extremity indicates the client has elbow and shoulder stiffness and mild swelling of the hand. The client has full active flexion and full passive extension and flexion of the wrist and digits. Active extension of the wrist and digits is absent. What **INITIAL** action should the OTR take based on these findings?

    A. Confirm whether the client has a secondary radial nerve injury.

    B. Fabricate a dynamic splint to compensate for loss of finger extension.

    C. Complete a comprehensive manual muscle test of the affected upper extremity.

Correct Answer: A

RATIONALE:
The radial nerve is commonly injured with a fracture of the humerus. This results in weak or absent wrist and finger extensors. The OTR should contact the physician to confirm this diagnosis and to clarify the consult before proceeding with rehabilitation for the hand.

Reference:
Radomski, M. V., & Trombly Latham, C. A. (Eds.). (2014). *Occupational therapy for physical dysfunction* (7th ed., pp. 454-455). Philadelphia, PA: Lippincott Williams & Wilkins.

NBCOT® Study Guide for the OTR Certification Examination

NOTES

34. An OTR is administering the Functional Independence Measure (FIM™) as part of the initial evaluation of an inpatient who had a left CVA with aphasia 5 days ago. The patient has right hemiparesis and requires moderate assistance to maintain balance while standing. What action should the OTR take when completing this assessment?

A. Introduce a reacher and other adaptive equipment to maximize patient's level of performance.

B. Observe as the patient performs ADL routines with the typical methods used prior to admission.

C. Provide the patient with visual and tactile cues to sequence each step of the task.

Correct Answer: B

RATIONALE:
Administration of the Functional Independence Measure (FIM™) includes assessing the patient's complete ADL routines with the typical methods used prior to admission.

References:
Asher, I. E. (Ed.). (2014). *Asher's occupational therapy assessment tools: An annotated index* (4th ed., p. 124). Bethesda, MD: AOTA Press.

Pendleton, H. M., & Schultz-Krohn, W. (Eds.). (2018). *Pedretti's occupational therapy: Practice skills for the physical dysfunction* (8th ed., p. 820). St. Louis, MO: Mosby Elsevier.

98

Domain 1: Multiple Choice Answers, Rationales, and References

35. A student in the second grade has autism spectrum disorder and is scheduled to begin school-based OT. The teacher reports the student has difficulty attending to academic tasks and typically has outbursts when in close proximity to other people. In which environment should the majority of the student's intervention sessions take place?

    A. Self-contained occupational therapy treatment room

    B. Playground in an area apart from other students

    C. Classroom during routine curriculum-based activities

Correct Answer: C

RATIONALE:
OT goals and objectives in school-based settings support students' academic and functional abilities. Providing services in the natural classroom environment during typical routines would increase the likelihood for carry-over and consistency.

Reference:
Case-Smith, J., & O'Brien, J. C. (2015). *Occupational therapy for children and adolescents* (7th ed., pp. 685-687). St. Louis, MO: Mosby Elsevier.

NOTES

36. An OTR is developing an intervention plan for an inpatient who has severe post-traumatic stress disorder (PTSD). Symptoms of PTSD started several weeks after the patient was robbed in a convenience store where the patient was working. The patient's goal is to resume work at the store, but extreme fear and distrust interfere with the ability to interact with customers. Which environment is **MOST** conducive for promoting initial progress toward a return-to-work goal with this patient?

    A. **One-on-one in the patient's hospital room**

    B. During a role-play session in the therapy room

    C. Discussion group with several other patients

Correct Answer: A

RATIONALE:
One-on-one intervention sessions in the patient's room would be most conducive for promoting initial progress toward the goals. As progress is made, session contexts should be graded to reflect real-life situations.

Reference:
Cara, E., & MacRae, A. (2013). *Psychosocial occupational therapy: An evolving practice* (3rd ed., pp. 268, 277-278). Clifton Park, NY: Delmar Cengage Learning.

Domain 1: Multiple Choice Answers, Rationales, and References

37. An OTR working in an inpatient rehabilitation facility is scheduled to complete an initial grooming and hygiene assessment with a patient. The patient has mild hemiplegia and neurobehavioral deficits secondary to a CVA one week ago. Which area of the facility should the assessment take place in order to obtain the **MOST BENEFICIAL** information about the impact of these symptoms on the patient's occupational performance?

    A. Bedside in the patient's hospital room

    B. Bathroom in the patient's hospital room

    C. Simulated environment in the OT clinic

Correct Answer: B

RATIONALE:
The assessment should take place in the environment where the patient will typically complete this task. While an inpatient, this task would take place in the bathroom of the patient's room.

References:
Pendleton, H. M., & Schultz-Krohn, W. (Eds.). (2018). *Pedretti's occupational therapy: Practice skills for the physical dysfunction* (8th ed., pp. 160-161). St. Louis, MO: Mosby Elsevier.

Radomski, M. V., & Trombly Latham, C. A. (Eds.). (2014). *Occupational therapy for physical dysfunction* (7th ed., p. 93). Philadelphia, PA: Lippincott Williams & Wilkins.

NBCOT® Study Guide for the OTR Certification Examination

NOTES

38. An inpatient in a rehabilitation facility has hemiplegia secondary to a CVA. The patient is independent with BADL. The OTR, who uses the ecology of human performance model, is preparing the patient's discharge summary. What information reflects this approach and should be included as part of this report?

A. **Recommendations for home modifications to maximize accessibility and task performance**

B. Exercise protocols for maintaining physical strength and cardiovascular endurance

C. Current functional status and anticipated occupational performance upon return home

D. Support groups for promoting the patient's acceptance of the physical impairments

Correct Answer: A

RATIONALE:

The ecology of human performance approach considers the interaction between the context or the environment and the person.

Reference:
Pendleton, H. M., & Schultz-Krohn, W. (Eds.). (2018). *Pedretti's occupational therapy: Practice skills for the physical dysfunction* (8th ed., p. 33). St. Louis, MO: Mosby Elsevier.

Domain 1: Multiple Choice Answers, Rationales, and References

39. An OTR and a vocational rehabilitation team are using the Individual Placement and Support (IPS) model to support a client, who has schizophrenia and anxiety, in gaining employment. One of the intervention goals is for the client to achieve competitive employment. When using the IPS model, which approach should be included in the vocational intervention to support this goal?

    A. Provide education in general work behaviors, then conduct an extensive job search.

    B. Secure a job placement site, then teach the client the specific job skills for that workplace.

    C. Complete a detailed resume of job skills, then teach the client effective work behaviors.

Correct Answer: B

RATIONALE:
The Individual Placement and Support (IPS) model is a supportive employment approach that involves securing a job placement site, then teaching the client the specific job skills for that workplace.

Reference:
Brown, C., & Stoffel V. C. (2011). *Occupational therapy in mental health: A vision for participation* (p. 64). Philadelphia, PA: F.A. Davis Company.

NBCOT® Study Guide for the OTR Certification Examination

NOTES

40. An OTR is developing an intervention plan using a bottom-up approach for clients who have hemiplegia and hemi-neglect secondary to having a CVA more than one year ago. Which of the following intervention techniques has evidence supporting its efficacy for reducing the effects of "learned non-use" through cortical reorganization?

  A. Proprioceptive neuromuscular facilitation (PNF)

  B. Occupational adaptation (OA)

  C. **Constraint-induced movement therapy (CIMT)**

Correct Answer: C

RATIONALE:
This is an evidence-based functional approach for promoting use of a hemiparetic upper extremity.

Reference:
Pendleton, H. M., & Schultz-Krohn, W. (Eds.). (2018). *Pedretti's occupational therapy: Practice skills for the physical dysfunction* (8th ed., pp. 800-805). St. Louis, MO: Mosby Elsevier.

41. An OTR is providing consultative services at an assisted living facility. Facility administrators are concerned that some residents may be at risk for falls. Using a primary prevention model, what **INITIAL** recommendation should the OTR make to the management of the facility?

    A. Analysis of resident injuries that have occurred at the facility over the past 5 years

    B. Ongoing monitoring and observation of the residents to decrease liability

    C. Screening of all residents prior to determining needs of the facility

Correct Answer: C

RATIONALE:
The primary prevention model focuses on anticipating potential circumstances or conditions that threaten the function or well-being of healthy individuals and developing an associated prevention plan.

Reference:
Pendleton, H. M., & Schultz-Krohn, W. (Eds.). (2018). *Pedretti's occupational therapy: Practice skills for the physical dysfunction* (8th ed., pp. 62-63). St. Louis, MO: Mosby Elsevier.

NBCOT® Study Guide for the OTR Certification Examination

NOTES

42. A client in an outpatient setting sustained an acquired brain injury 2 months ago. Evaluation results indicate the client has functional ROM and strength, but continues to require assistance with ADL due to moderate visual and vestibular processing deficits. Which intervention represents an adaptive approach for improving the client's performance in areas of occupation?

    A. Providing the client with an exercise program for improving gaze stabilization

    B. Teaching the client to use proprioceptive cues during functional activities

    C. Incorporating progressively more challenging tasks into a functional activity

    D. Engaging the client in valued activities that promote postural stability and balance

Correct Answer: B

RATIONALE:
The adaptive approach places emphasis on the client's abilities. This top-down approach aims to facilitate functional performance through compensatory techniques.

References:
Pendleton, H. M., & Schultz-Krohn, W. (Eds.). (2018). *Pedretti's occupational therapy: Practice skills for the physical dysfunction* (8th ed., p. 127). St. Louis, MO: Mosby Elsevier.

Zoltan, B. (2007). *Vision, perception, and cognition: A manual for the evaluation and treatment of the adult with acquired brain injury* (4th ed., pp. 4-5, 100-103). Thorofare, NJ: SLACK, Inc.

Domain 1: Multiple Choice Answers, Rationales, and References

43. An OTR is using a top-down approach to select interventions for a client who has unilateral neglect secondary to a CVA. Which intervention would be **MOST BENEFICIAL** to include as part of the client's intervention when using this approach?

    A. Determine compensatory options the client can use in the home environment.

    B. Teach drills for practicing head turning to find an object placed near the affected side.

    C. Place commonly used toiletry items to the client's affected side during self-care tasks.

    D. Use tactile-kinesthetic guiding to the client's involved extremity during a dressing task.

Correct Answer: A

RATIONALE:
This represents a top-down approach because it focuses on a strategy the client can use in everyday life.

References:
Gillen, G. (2016). *Stroke rehabilitation: A function-based approach* (4th ed., pp. 600-601). St. Louis, MO: Elsevier.

Pendleton, H. M., & Schultz-Krohn, W. (Eds.). (2018). *Pedretti's occupational therapy: Practice skills for the physical dysfunction* (8th ed., pp. 816-817). St. Louis, MO: Mosby Elsevier.

NBCOT® Study Guide for the OTR Certification Examination

NOTES

44. An OTR working in an inpatient mental health setting is using a cognitive behavioral approach to select an intervention activity for a young adult undergoing treatment for symptoms associated with body dysmorphic disorder. The patient is employed in a successful career and enjoys outdoor activities such as jogging and hiking, but has difficulty forming and maintaining interpersonal relationships. One of the patient's goals is to improve self-image and the ability to express feelings. Which activity would be **MOST BENEFICIAL** to include as part of the intervention for supporting this goal when using this approach?

    A. Engaging the patient in an art project using a variety of media during which the patient is encouraged to release emotions

    B. Teaching the patient to use a dysfunctional thought record for describing distressing situations and emotional responses

    C. Guiding the patient through avocational exploration of activities that provide opportunities for social interaction

Correct Answer: B

RATIONALE:
Having the client maintain a journal of distressing events and associated feelings or thought processes is integral to a cognitive behavioral approach.

Reference:
Brown, C., & Stoffel V. C. (2011). *Occupational therapy in mental health: A vision for participation* (p. 272). Philadelphia, PA: F.A. Davis Company.

108

45. An inpatient in a rehabilitation facility has a C_6 tetraplegia with a rating of "A" on the ASIA impairment scale. The patient has achieved BADL goals and now wants to be as independent as possible with homemaking tasks. Which intervention approach would be effective to use as the **PRIMARY** strategy for promoting progress toward the patient's goal?

    A. Behavioral

    B. Remedial

    C. Biomechanical

    D. Compensatory

Correct Answer: D

RATIONALE:
Using this approach allows the patient to learn adaptive strategies, reestablish routines, and learn to function in a variety of contexts.

References:
Pendleton, H. M., & Schultz-Krohn, W. (Eds.). (2018). *Pedretti's occupational therapy: Practice skills for the physical dysfunction* (8th ed., pp. 917-919, 983). St. Louis, MO: Mosby Elsevier.

Radomski, M. V., & Trombly Latham, C. A. (Eds.). (2014). *Occupational therapy for physical dysfunction* (7th ed., pp. 38-39, 1173, 1196). Philadelphia, PA: Lippincott Williams & Wilkins.

NBCOT® Study Guide for the OTR Certification Examination

NOTES

46. An OTR completed an initial assessment of a student in the second grade. Results indicate the student has age-appropriate comprehension, visual object gnosia, and visual acuity, but standardized test scores on figure-ground subtests are well below the norm. Which of the following school art class activities would present the **MOST** challenge to this student based on the outcomes of this evaluation?

A. Painting a free form design on a clay pot using a variety of paint colors

B. **Selecting a round bead from a bag of multi-shaped beads to complete a necklace**

C. Using plastic templates to trace basic geometric shapes on colored paper

D. Placing tiles of the same color and shape in a straight line when making a trivet

Correct Answer: B

RATIONALE:
Figure-ground perception is the ability to distinguish foreground from background. A student who has figure-ground deficits would have difficulty finding a bead of a specific size or shape in a bag of beads.

References:
Case-Smith, J., & O'Brien, J. C. (2015). *Occupational therapy for children and adolescents* (7th ed., p. 271). St. Louis, MO: Mosby Elsevier.

Zoltan, B. (2007). *Vision, perception, and cognition: A manual for the evaluation and treatment of the adult with acquired brain injury* (4th ed., pp. 155-159). Thorofare, NJ: SLACK, Inc.

Domain 1: Multiple Choice Answers, Rationales, and References

47. A client who has schizophrenia is participating in OT to improve functional living skills. The client's goal is to be able to independently prepare family meals. The client has successfully used a checklist strategy to gather and keep track of items while preparing a simple cold snack. Which of the following tasks would present a "just right" challenge when using the checklist strategy to progress towards the client's goal?

   A. Setting the dining table for a group meal

   B. Cooking a three-course meal for the family

   C. Purchasing groceries for a pre-set weekly menu

Correct Answer: A

RATIONALE
Results from an analysis of the task the client has mastered (gathering and keeping track of items while preparing a simple cold snack) and the task of setting the table for a group meal demonstrates that the tasks have similar demands. To successfully implement the checklist strategy during meal preparation, the client will benefit from using it across multiple task components and contexts.

Reference:
Schell, B. A. B., Gillen, G., & Scaffa, M. E. (2014). *Willard & Spackman's occupational therapy* (12th ed., p. 792). Philadelphia, PA: Lippincott Williams & Wilkins.

NBCOT® Study Guide for the OTR Certification Examination

NOTES

48. Which activity involves the use of a closed kinetic chain movement of the upper extremity?

   A. Lifting a suitcase off the floor to carry by the handle

   B. **Pulling up on an overhead trapeze during bed mobility**

   C. Hand-to-mouth patterns used for self-feeding

Correct Answer: B

RATIONALE:
This closed kinetic chain movement includes the distal upper extremity being stabilized and in constant contact with the trapeze.

References:
Greene, D. P., & Roberts, S. L. (2017). *Kinesiology: Movement in the context of activity* (3rd ed., p. 93). St. Louis, MO: Mosby Elsevier.

Rybski, M. F. (2012). *Kinesiology for occupational therapy* (2nd ed., p. 33). Thorofare, NJ: SLACK, Inc.

49. An OTR is evaluating a client who has an ulnar nerve injury at the wrist level of the right dominant extremity. During which task would this injury be **MOST** evident?

   A. Carrying a briefcase

   B. **Turning a key in the car ignition**

   C. Operating a desktop calculator

   D. Holding coins in the palm of the hand

Correct Answer: B

RATIONALE:
Ulnar nerve palsy at the wrist impairs the hypothenar muscles and first dorsal interosseous muscle resulting in the difficulty turning a key or performing a lateral pinch.

Reference:
Pendleton, H. M., & Schultz-Krohn, W. (Eds.). (2018). *Pedretti's occupational therapy: Practice skills for the physical dysfunction* (8th ed., pp. 977, 983-984). St. Louis, MO: Mosby Elsevier.

Domain 1: Multiple Choice Answers, Rationales, and References

50. An older adult in an inpatient setting has moderate-severe debilitation from prolonged bed rest secondary to general medical-surgical post-operative complications. The patient's primary goal is to be as independent as possible with BADL prior to discharge home. The patient has full passive ROM and Fair minus (3-/5) functional muscle strength of the upper extremities. The patient can ambulate for several feet using a walker and contact guard assistance, but uses a wheelchair in the hospital room and depends on caregivers for wheelchair transport to various areas of the hospital. Based on the patient's current status, which dressing activity would be **MOST** difficult for this patient to complete while seated in the wheelchair?

A. Crossing one leg over the other and putting on loose-fitting slip-on shoes

B. Putting on a front-opening shirt after reaching for the shirt off a bedside stand

C. Getting a pair of pants hanging in the closet and putting them on

D. Washing hands at a sink and drying the hands using a towel placed next to the sink

Correct Answer: C

RATIONALE:
Patients with this muscle strength have low endurance and fatigue quickly. An analysis of the components (e.g., weight shift, dynamic balance, movement against gravity) of each option presented indicates this option is physically more demanding than the other three options.

Reference:
Pendleton, H. M., & Schultz-Krohn, W. (Eds.). (2018). *Pedretti's occupational therapy: Practice skills for the physical dysfunction* (8th ed., pp. 514, 520-521). St. Louis, MO: Mosby Elsevier.

Chapter 12

Domain 2: Multiple Choice Sample Questions

Practice questions with answer key and references

The following multiple choice items are samples related to Domain 2.

Analysis and Interpretation

Formulate conclusions regarding client needs and priorities to develop and monitor an intervention plan throughout the occupational therapy process.

1. An OTR has completed an evaluation of a client who has amyotrophic lateral sclerosis. When reviewing the results of upper extremity goniometric measurements, the OTR notes that the client's active ROM is significantly less than passive ROM. What should the OTR conclude is the **PRIMARY** cause for this discrepancy?

    A. Bony ankylosis

    B. Soft-tissue shortening

    C. Muscular weakness

Domain 2: Multiple Choice Sample Questions

2. An OTR is interpreting scores of a developmental test that was administered to a 3-year-old child. The child scored at the 89th percentile for the child's age and gender group. What can the OTR conclude based on this score?

A. The child has minor developmental deficits compared to the normative sample group.

B. Eleven percent of the children in the sample group scored higher than this child.

C. This child displays above-average developmental skills compared to similar children.

D. These scores are sensitive for measuring small changes in the child's overall development.

3. An OTR is evaluating the biceps strength of a client recovering from a musculocutaneous nerve injury. The OTR asks the client to fully flex the elbow while the client is seated upright with the shoulder adducted, the elbow fully extended, and the forearm in supination. The OTR observes that the client's forearm consistently moves into midposition on each attempt to flex the elbow despite prompting the client to maintain the forearm in supination. What conclusion can the OTR make based on this observation?

A. The brachioradialis muscle is substituting for the weaker prime mover.

B. The muscle strength of the biceps should be graded as Poor (2/5).

C. The pronator teres muscle should be blocked on future testing.

D. The movement should be retested with the client positioned in prone.

115

4. An inpatient who had a left CVA one week ago is participating in a dressing session. After putting on a sock during lower body dressing, the patient repeatedly attempts to pull the sock up even though it is already in place. What neurobehavioral deficit is MOST **CONSISTENT** with these actions?

   A. Spatial inattention

   B. Somatagnosia

   C. Dressing apraxia

   D. Premotor perseveration

5. An OTR administered a criterion-referenced standardized developmental checklist to a 3-year-old-child who has mild developmental delay. The child did not meet the standard for snipping with scissors. For what purpose would these results be **MOST USEFUL**?

   A. Linking outcomes measures to other typically developing children

   B. Determining developmentally appropriate activities to use in therapy

   C. Identifying functional tasks that would be most difficult for the student

   D. Comparing the child's performance to that of an age-equivalent population

Domain 2: Multiple Choice Sample Questions

6. A client sustained a severe hand injury 5 weeks ago. During an OT session, the client reports that family responsibilities make it impossible to complete the prescribed exercise and splinting program. What action should the OTR take in response to this comment in order to promote the client's successful participation in the home program?

   A. Determine a home program that closely aligns with typical performance patterns.

   B. Analyze a 24-hour log to determine time management issues the client is experiencing.

   C. Advise the client to make the home program the highest priority for the short term.

   D. Suggest transition to a compensatory approach for dealing with residual deficits.

7. A client sustained a TBI 3 months ago and is functioning at Level VIII (Purposeful, Appropriate, Stand-by Assist) on the Rancho Los Amigos scale. The client is participating in a meal preparation task. As part of the task, the client is asked to prepare vegetable soup using a five-step printed recipe. The client is able to read the recipe steps aloud but does not act on any of them. When the OTR covers over all but the first step of the recipe, the client follows through with the step. What conclusion can the OTR make about the client based on this observation?

   A. Adaptive strategies compensate for attention deficits.

   B. Anchoring techniques improve visual perception.

   C. Ideational apraxia interferes with task initiation.

117

NBCOT® Study Guide for the OTR Certification Examination

8. An inpatient had a right CVA one week ago. Prior to the CVA, the patient was relatively healthy and worked a full-time job. During a dressing assessment, the patient puts on a pull-over sweater and then realizes the need to put on a T-shirt underneath the sweater. To do this, the patient attempts to insert the T-shirt down the neck hole of the sweater, instead of removing the sweater to put on the T-shirt. Which statement **MOST ACCURATELY** describes the reason for the patient's action?

   A. Right hemispheric damage appears to have resulted in perseverative behaviors.

   B. Spatial integration deficits may be affecting the ability to recognize items.

   C. The central nervous system is not receiving complete visual information.

   D. The patient is not able to conceptualize steps of a task due to ideational apraxia.

9. An inpatient is preparing for discharge to home after completing 3 months of inpatient rehabilitation. The OTR is reviewing documentation in the patient's medical record and determines the patient is still working to achieve several short-term goals related to the current treatment plan. What **INITIAL** action should the OTR take based on this finding?

   A. Ensure durable medical equipment delivery and home health visits are scheduled in preparation for the patient's discharge.

   B. Complete a comprehensive re-evaluation to identify current function in relation to the discharge plan.

   C. Discuss options with the interprofessional team for extending inpatient rehabilitation until goals are achieved.

   D. Prepare a discharge summary providing a rationale for the goal shortcomings noted in the contact notes.

Domain 2: Multiple Choice Sample Questions

10. An OTR has completed a developmental assessment of a 6-year-old child who has Down syndrome. Results indicate the child is dependent in all self-care tasks. The parents do not place a high priority on dressing independence, but the OTR does. What action should the OTR take as part of the intervention planning process?

   A. Ask for the parents' consent to begin working on specific self-care skills with the child.

   B. Collaborate with the parents to identify mutually acceptable treatment goals for the child.

   C. Inform the parents that school-age children are expected to be independent with self-care.

   D. Talk with the parents about establishing independence in self-care skills as a primary goal.

11. A family practice physician referred a client to outpatient OT for conservative treatment of carpal tunnel syndrome of the dominant hand. The client reports a 3 month history of numbness and difficulty manipulating objects. Symptoms interfere with work as a jack-hammer operator for a road works department. Evaluation results indicate loss of protective sensation, 11 mm two-point discrimination, and thenar muscle atrophy. Active ROM of the affected hand is within normal limits. What **INITIAL** actions should the OTR take in addition to fabricating a volar wrist orthosis?

   A. Advise the client to wear the orthosis when sleeping and a padded glove when at work.

   B. Arrange an appointment with an orthopedic surgeon and begin a sensory reeducation program.

   C. Conduct Phalen's test and report findings of the overall evaluation process to the physician.

119

NBCOT® Study Guide for the OTR Certification Examination

NOTES

12. A young adult client was diagnosed with axonotmesis of the ulnar nerve secondary to a crush injury of the forearm 2 weeks ago. After obtaining baseline assessment information, which technique would be **MOST IMPORTANT** for the OTR to teach to the client as part of the intervention during the initial phase of the client's rehabilitation?

    A. Visual compensation

    B. Hand-dominance retraining

    C. Isometric strengthening

    D. Sensory re-education

13. An inpatient had a CVA with flaccid hemiplegia 8 days ago. When the OTR arrives for the scheduled session, the patient reports pain in the axillary region of the affected upper extremity. The OTR notes significant edema in the arm and that the arm is warm to the touch. Which of the following is the **BEST** option for why the OTR should alert the physician about these observations?

    A. Late effect of cerebrovascular disease

    B. Subluxation of the shoulder

    C. Deep vein thrombosis

14. An OTR is completing a functional visual screening of a client who has macular degeneration. The OTR asks the client to a read a passage from a magazine. The client misses several letters and words, and has difficulty finding their place in the text when scanning. What aspect of visual function should the OTR investigate further based on the client's performance?

    A. Contrast sensitivity

    B. Visual acuity

    C. Central visual field

120

Domain 2: Multiple Choice Sample Questions

15. A patient has flaccid hemiplegia and dysphagia secondary to a CVA one month ago. The patient is participating in an interprofessional rehabilitation program. One of the intervention goals is for the patient to regain independence with self-feeding and become safe when eating. What information about the patient is **MOST IMPORTANT** for the OTR to present to the interprofessional team during each care coordination meeting?

    A. Improvements in upper extremity movement patterns used for self-feeding

    B. Specific evidence-based techniques that are being used during intervention sessions

    C. Positioning, adaptive devices and caregiver assistance needed during mealtimes

    D. Ability to select nutritious foods from the hospital dining menu that are safe to swallow

16. Which situation listed below warrants a referral to a gastroenterologist?

    A. A client who has diabetes and is experiencing more frequent episodes of hyperglycemia.

    B. A resident who recently started only eating the food placed on the right side of the plate.

    C. An adolescent who has cerebral palsy who refuses to eat and reports frequent episodes of reflux.

17. A client in an outpatient setting has hemiplegia secondary to a CVA. Over the past several weeks, there has been a decline in the client's energy level, ability to concentrate, and interest in intervention activities. When asked about the change, the client replies: "I just can't sleep at night thinking about the burden I am to my family." What **INITIAL** action should the OTR take based on this observed change?

    A. Consult with the client's primary physician

    B. Advise the client to consult with a psychiatrist

    C. Adjust the timeframes for achieving short term goals

121

NBCOT® Study Guide for the OTR Certification Examination

18. A client who has chronic low back pain is participating in an interprofessional pain management program. The focus of the program is for the client to learn mechanisms for coping with pain and reducing injury risk during work-related tasks as a manual laborer. The client has been making progress since starting the program 3 weeks ago. What information is **MOST IMPORTANT** for the OTR to report about the client's progress at the next weekly team meeting?

   A. Amount of weight the client is able to lift and carry during sessions

   B. Ability to correctly perform stretching and strengthening exercises

   C. Spontaneous use of self-management strategies during activities

   D. Length of time the client engages in specific work tasks in the clinic

19. An OTR is formulating a discharge plan for an inpatient who has dementia and is functioning at Allen Cognitive Level 4 (Goal-Directed Actions). The patient will be living at home with assistance from family. What type of caregiver education is **MOST IMPORTANT** for the OTR to provide prior to the patient's discharge from the inpatient facility?

   A. Suggestions for modifying the environment to eliminate unnecessary household items

   B. Methods for promoting the patient's problem solving for independence during ADL

   C. Strategies for providing visual cues that will help the patient complete daily routines

   D. Techniques for establishing and posting a written emergency plan in the home environment

Domain 2: Multiple Choice Sample Questions

20. A private practice OTR is developing goals for a 4-year-old child with autism spectrum disorder who has difficulty with emotional regulation, impulse control, and problem-solving skills. The child attends preschool, and academically is meeting expectations. Socially, the child has not developed friendships at school or within the neighborhood. Which task should be included as a short-term goal in the intervention plan for this child?

A. Interact with peers during a structured play group.

B. Follow rules while playing an age-appropriate board game.

C. Play at the sand table without acquiring an injury.

21. An inpatient who has pneumonia and mild cognitive decline has been stabilized in the hospital and is medically ready for discharge. Currently, the patient requires constant supervision for ADL and IADL due to safety concerns and impulsive behavior. The patient and family have declined the treatment team recommendation that the patient move into an assistive living facility. Which option represents the **MOST IMPORTANT** discharge recommendation the OTR should provide the family?

A. Involve the patient in a structured adult day program.

B. Modify the home environment prior to discharge.

C. Provide the patient with 24-hour supervision.

22. A client who has severe depression has been participating in a partial hospitalization program. The client has made some improvements but continues to have difficulties concentrating on tasks and coping with day-to-day stressors. The interprofessional team agrees that the client has made sufficient progress to transition to the next level of care. Which type of program would **BEST** assist the client toward the goal of returning to work as a healthcare provider?

A. Impaired provider program

B. Support group for working professionals

C. Community mental health program

123

NBCOT® Study Guide for the OTR Certification Examination

23. An inpatient recovering from pneumonia has decreased strength and endurance, and functional active ROM. The patient ambulates independently for short distances with the use of a walker. Medical history indicates the patient has recently been diagnosed with moderate macular degeneration. The patient will be discharged in one day to live alone in a single-story home. Which service should the OTR recommend as part of the patient's discharge plans?

A. Extension of current hospital stay for comprehensive rehabilitation services

B. Home health services to assess ADL needs and teach compensatory strategies

C. Short-term placement in a skilled facility to maximize independence in ADL

24. An OTR is providing home health services to a 9-month-old infant who underwent surgery for a Type I Chiari malformation one month ago. The infant has been progressing without complication since the date of surgery. During a follow-up home visit, the infant's parent reports lack of progress with the home program because the infant has been extremely lethargic for the past few days and has had several episodes of vomiting within the past 12 hours. What should the OTR advise the parent to do based on the infant's current condition?

A. Monitor the infant's flu-like symptoms for the next 24 hours and ensure fluid intake.

B. Reschedule the appointment for the next week when symptoms should be resolved.

C. Report the infant's symptoms as soon as possible to the primary care physician.

25. An OTR is working with a client who has Stage 5 Alzheimer's disease and lives with a full-time caregiver. Based on this stage of the disease process, which option would be the **MOST BENEFICIAL** recommendation for the OTR to make to the caregiver?

A. Encourage the client to participate in a new hobby.

B. Post an illustrated daily schedule for the client to follow.

C. Provide assistance for dressing and grooming activities.

124

Domain 2: Multiple Choice Sample Questions

26. An inpatient has been participating in rehabilitation since having bilateral transfemoral amputations 2 months ago. The patient has good balance and Fair plus (3+/5) upper extremity strength, is independent with bed mobility and self-care using adaptive equipment, and requires stand-by assistance during wheelchair transfers and with wheelchair management. The patient is preparing for discharge to live at home with the spouse and an adult son. Modifications have been made to the main entrance of the home and the bathroom. The OTR plans to provide family education for promoting the patient's safe transition to the home environment. What information would be **MOST BENEFICIAL** to include as part of this process?

    A. Methods for improving the patient's independence with transfers

    B. Techniques the patient uses to transfer to a variety of surfaces

    C. Energy conservation techniques for the patient to use during ADL

    D. Wrapping techniques for shaping and protecting the residual limb

27. A patient who has hemiplegia and cognitive-perceptual deficits has been transferred from an acute care facility to a skilled nursing rehabilitation unit. When should discharge planning for this patient take place?

    A. Throughout the rehabilitation phase of treatment

    B. When the majority of short-term goals have been met

    C. After determining if the patient has potential to return home

28. A resident of a skilled nursing facility, who has moderately severe cognitive decline, becomes increasingly agitated during mealtime. What is the **FIRST** action the OTR should take based on this observation?

    A. Instruct the resident in relaxation exercises to use at mealtime.

    B. Arrange for the resident to eat meals in a calm, quiet location.

    C. Observe the resident at mealtime to identity behavioral triggers.

NBCOT® Study Guide for the OTR Certification Examination

29. A young adult client who has a substance use disorder has been referred to community-based OT. Although the client has maintained sobriety for the past 6 months, evaluation results indicate the client has an unrealistic self-concept, poor social skills and inadequate independent living skills. Which objective would be **MOST BENEFICIAL** to include as part of the initial intervention plan for supporting the client's participation in occupations?

   A. Transition to independent living with a supportive friend

   B. Acquisition of practical skills for basic life management

   C. Engagement in leisure activities with social acquaintances

   D. Education about work stressors that contribute to relapse

30. A client who has moderate cognitive decline lives in a skilled nursing facility. The client's spouse visits every morning after breakfast. The spouse informs the OTR that the client's frequency of interacting during the visits has decreased over the past few weeks, and the client now has intermittent verbal outbursts that disrupt the social interaction. In addition to informing the care team, what action should the OTR take based on this observation?

   A. Sit with client and the spouse during a visit, and ask the client direct questions to facilitate appropriate communication.

   B. Ask the spouse open-ended questions about the situation, and identify possible triggers for the change in level of interaction.

   C. Provide the spouse with information about providing immediate feedback to the client when there are signs of agitation.

31. A client in the outpatient setting recently underwent plastic surgery to correct facial disfigurement. During a grooming session, the client states, "I will never look in the mirror again." What action should the OTR take in response to the client's concern?

   A. Provide positive affirmations and encourage the client to seek reassurance from close friends.

   B. Validate the client's concerns and transition to the next intervention that does not require a mirror.

   C. Provide support and ask open-ended questions to gain insight into the client's view on their body image.

126

Domain 2: Multiple Choice Sample Questions

32. An outpatient OTR is working with an adult client who has spastic diplegia. One of the client's goals is to drive a car. The client has the necessary process skills to drive but requires adapted driving controls to access the gas and brake pedals. What is the **FIRST** action the OTR should take in this situation?

    A. Research funding options to pay for vehicle adaptations.

    B. Refer the client to a driving rehabilitation specialist.

    C. Arrange for a trial of specialized equipment from a reputable vendor.

33. An inpatient had a total hip replacement 3 days ago. During an intervention session, neither the patient nor the spouse appear interested in learning about the assistive devices for improving the patient's independence with BADL. What **INITIAL** action should the OTR take based on this observation?

    A. Explore the couple's feelings about using the equipment.

    B. Explain that assistive devices are essential to the patient's recovery.

    C. Document the reactions in the client's record and inform the care coordinator.

34. A patient in an inpatient rehabilitation setting is in the recovery phase of intervention after an acute onset of Guillain-Barré syndrome one month ago. The OTR advises the patient that using assistive devices will improve independence, but the patient refuses to use the devices stating: "My wife is happy to help me whenever I need it." How should the OTR respond to the patient's comment?

    A. Convince the patient to try the devices at least once.

    B. Discuss the patient's comment with family members.

    C. Focus intervention sessions on strengthening and ROM activities.

    D. Identify other strategies for improving occupational performance.

35. An OTR working in a community mental health setting is using dialectical behavior therapy to guide intervention planning for a client who has a borderline personality disorder. The client works in a university setting and is at risk of losing the job due to verbal outbursts and erratic mood swings. The client is aware that behavioral changes are needed and reports a willingness to work toward these changes. Which type of intervention would the OTR include in therapy sessions for supporting progress toward this objective when using this approach?

A. Individual sessions focusing on Socratic questioning and guided discovery for addressing problematic situations and emotions

B. Group skills training modules in mindfulness, interpersonal effectiveness, emotion modulation, and distress tolerance

C. Role-play sessions using prepared scripts for practicing problem-solving and decision-making related to workplace situations

36. A young adult client is participating in a community-based OT program after completing inpatient treatment for an acute episode of major depression. Evaluation results indicate the client has difficulty concentrating on simple tasks, has poor personal hygiene, and has limited insight about the impact of the depression on areas of occupation. The client states the primary goal for attending OT is "to get a job." What should be the **INITIAL** focus of sessions with this client?

A. Assigning the client to a job in a highly supervised sheltered work environment

B. Finding the client, a transitional job involving routine and repetitive work tasks

C. Determining the client's work habits and current abilities for job readiness

D. Teaching the client how to locate job opportunities and submit job applications

Domain 2: Multiple Choice Sample Questions

37. An adolescent was recently admitted to an inpatient psychiatric unit due to symptoms associated with a conduct disorder. Evaluation results indicate the adolescent has a poor self-concept, decreased fine and gross motor coordination, and is socially aggressive. What should be the focus of the **INITIAL** sessions with this adolescent?

A. Presenting options for pre vocational exploration and practice

B. Encouraging participation in self-expression group activities

C. Providing opportunities for success in a consistent structured environment

D. Enhancing physical abilities for completing responsibilities at home

38. An OTR has completed an evaluation of a patient who is experiencing complications from pneumonia and was recently admitted to a Medicare funded skilled nursing facility. The patient was living independently prior to hospitalization and wants to return home. Evaluation results indicate the patient is generally deconditioned and fatigues quickly during activity. The patient ambulates slowly using a walker, and requires frequent verbal and physical cueing for safety when using the walker during ADL. What criteria should the OTR use to prioritize the goals for this patient's intervention plan?

A. Skilled services the patient currently requires for completion of basic functional tasks.

B. Amount of assistance that will be available to the patient to maintain progress after discharge.

C. Patient's desire to improve strength, ROM, and endurance prior to discharge from the facility.

D. Amount of time the patient will need to maximize strength and endurance prior to returning independent living.

129

NBCOT® Study Guide for the OTR Certification Examination

39. An OTR is planning intervention for an outpatient client who had a CMC thumb arthroplasty one week ago. What should the OTR include as part of the **INITIAL** intervention plan at this stage of recovery?

    A. Provide the client with a ROM program for the shoulder, elbow, fingers and thumb IP joints.

    B. Educate the client to complete a progressive strengthening program of the affected hand.

    C. Teach the client to pinch resistive putty between the tip of the thumb and the index finger.

40. An outpatient client has an acute flare-up of stage I rheumatoid arthritis. Initial evaluation results indicate the client's MCP joints bilaterally are red and swollen. The client lacks 10° active extension of the MCP joints on the second through fifth digits bilaterally. The client works as a florist and reports pain as 9 out of 10 on a visual analog scale when completing activities requiring grasp and prehensile patterns. The client will be participating in OT twice weekly. Which therapeutic exercise should be included as part of the intervention plan for the client to complete by the end of the first week of therapy?

    A. Passive motion and stretch of the MCP joints through the full arc of motion

    B. Pinching and gripping a soft sponge in warm water within pain tolerance

    C. Isotonic and isometric exercises of both hands within pain-free ranges of motion

    D. Tendon gliding exercises of the fingers against light resistance therapy putty

Domain 2: Multiple Choice Sample Questions

41. An 8-year-old child sustained second-degree burns to the first web space of both hands one month ago. Results of a reevaluation indicate the child's web space is contracting despite wearing pressure garments, using night orthotics and completing home program activities. What additional action should the OTR take based on these findings?

   A. Advise the caregiver to increase the intensity and frequency of passive ROM exercises.

   B. Begin serial splinting that incorporates a polymer gel sheet over the affected areas.

   C. Provide the caregiver with a list of age-appropriate games that will promote hand use.

   D. Use a paraffin modality during OT sessions to soften the scar prior to functional activity.

42. An OTR working in an outpatient setting is planning intervention for a client who has a 12-month history of fibromyalgia. The client reports symptoms associated with this condition are limiting the ability to participate in social activities. This has led to significant frustration and progressive social isolation over the past few months. The client wants to reverse this trend. What should the OTR include as part of the **INITIAL** intervention planning process with this client?

   A. Recommend the client maintain a journal as a means of venting frustration.

   B. Explore hobbies the client can try at home that do not exacerbate pain.

   C. Identify options for modifying the client's preferred community activities.

131

NBCOT® Study Guide for the OTR Certification Examination

43. An OTR is preparing for an **INITIAL** intervention session with an inpatient who is in the acute manic phase of bipolar disorder. Which general strategy should the OTR include as part of this session?

A. Structure the environment to encourage creativity and self-expression.

B. Minimize distractions in the environment during task performance.

C. Ensure the patient is aware of the influence of mania on participation.

D. Provide the patient with an opportunity to select an activity of interest.

44. An OTR is planning an intervention session for a 6-year-old child who has fetal alcohol syndrome. The child has difficulty coping when frustrated and frequently refuses to speak in social situations and during therapy. The OTR has attempted to engage the child using play therapy and sensory-based approaches, but the child refuses to participate. How should the OTR modify the intervention approach based on the child's responses during previous interventions?

A. Engage the child in computer games that promote positive feedback.

B. Use role-play scenarios about interacting with superheroes.

C. Include expressive media using cartoon character puppetry.

132

Domain 2: Multiple Choice Sample Questions

45. An inpatient is undergoing treatment in an acute rehabilitation facility after sustaining bilateral ankle fractures one week ago. Medical records indicate the patient will be non-weight-bearing for at least 6 weeks. Currently, the patient is independent with upper body dressing; requires moderate assistance with lower body dressing, bathing, and transfers; and independently propels a standard wheelchair. One of the intervention priorities is for the patient to be independent with IADL prior to discharge. Which action is **MOST IMPORTANT** for the OTR to take in advance of scheduling intervention activities for this patient?

    A. Discuss the projected timeline for recovery with the interprofessional team.

    B. Ensure the hospital bathroom is equipped with durable medical equipment.

    C. Identify the patient's expected discharge context and available resources.

46. An OTR working in a community hospital is contributing discharge recommendations for a patient who is generally deconditioned secondary to complications from a septic episode. The patient has been participating in OT for the past 3 weeks. Currently, the patient requires moderate assistance with transfers and tolerates up to 10 minutes of seated ADL activity prior to needing a rest break. The patient's goal is to return home to live independently. Which discharge setting would be **MOST BENEFICIAL** for the OTR to recommend for the patient's next level of care?

    A. Home health with skilled services

    B. Subacute rehabilitation facility

    C. Inpatient rehabilitation hospital

NBCOT® Study Guide for the OTR Certification Examination

47. An OTR wants to measure the effectiveness of a pre-vocational group at a mental health day program. What data is **MOST IMPORTANT** to collect for this purpose?

   A. Attendance levels and completion rate of homework assignments

   B. Client satisfaction ratings completed by participants after discharge

   C. Quality of the client's interview responses during role-play activities with peers

   D. Number of clients who successfully enter employment positions following the group

48. An OTR who works in an outpatient hand therapy clinic fabricated a forearm orthosis for a client. The OTR is providing instructions to the client on the wearing schedule and care of the orthosis. Which is the **MOST EFFECTIVE** method for the OTR to use in the education session to promote the client's understanding of the information presented?

   A. Ask the patient an open-ended question that invites a descriptive response.

   B. Provide a detailed written handout with illustrations to reinforce key points.

   C. Encourage the client to independently place the orthosis on and off during the session.

49. An OTR who works in a home health setting is developing educational handouts for clients who have low vision. Which guidelines are **MOST BENEFICIAL** for the OTR to use when developing educational handouts for this population?

   A. Many different colors to highlight important information printed on high-gloss paper

   B. Large print with a minimum of 16-point font with high contrast between the text and the paper

   C. Pictorial illustrations and written information placed in columns on the page

Domain 2: Multiple Choice Sample Questions

50. An OTR who works in an outpatient setting is providing assistive technology recommendations to a client who has amyotrophic lateral sclerosis. Which is the **MOST EFFECTIVE** method for the OTR to use during the intervention session to evaluate the client's understanding of the information presented?

    A. Provide the client with the written information from the manufacturers of the devices.

    B. Engage the client in a discussion to allow the opportunity for questions to be answered.

    C. Explain to the client evidence that supports benefits and outcomes associated with each device.

NBCOT® Study Guide for the OTR Certification Examination

Answer Key

Domain 2 Sample Items

Item Number	Key
1.	C
2.	B
3.	A
4.	D
5.	B
6.	A
7.	A
8.	D
9.	B
10.	B
11.	C
12.	A
13.	C
14.	C
15.	C
16.	C
17.	A
18.	C
19.	C
20.	A
21.	C
22.	C
23.	B
24.	C
25.	C

Item Number	Key
26.	B
27.	A
28.	C
29.	B
30.	B
31.	C
32.	B
33.	A
34.	D
35.	B
36.	C
37.	C
38.	A
39.	A
40.	C
41.	B
42.	C
43.	B
44.	C
45.	C
46.	B
47.	D
48.	B
49.	B
50.	B

NBCOT® Study Guide for the OTR Certification Examination

Multiple Choice Answers, Rationales, and References

1. An OTR has completed an evaluation of a client who has amyotrophic lateral sclerosis. When reviewing the results of upper extremity goniometric measurements, the OTR notes that the client's active ROM is significantly less than passive ROM. What should the OTR conclude is the **PRIMARY** cause for this discrepancy?

    A. Bony ankylosis

    B. Soft-tissue shortening

    C. Muscular weakness

Correct Answer: C

RATIONALE:
Limitations in active ROM in the presence of full passive ROM indicate weakness or a lack of power generated by the muscle or muscle group.

Reference:
Pendleton, H. M., & Schultz-Krohn, W. (Eds.). (2018). *Pedretti's occupational therapy: Practice skills for the physical dysfunction* (8th ed., pp. 515-516, 873-876). St. Louis, MO: Mosby Elsevier.

NBCOT® Study Guide for the OTR Certification Examination

NOTES

2. An OTR is interpreting scores of a developmental test that was administered to a 3-year-old child. The child scored at the 89th percentile for the child's age and gender group. What can the OTR conclude based on this score?

A. The child has minor developmental deficits compared to the normative sample group.

B. Eleven percent of the children in the sample group scored higher than this child.

C. This child displays above-average developmental skills compared to similar children.

D. These scores are sensitive for measuring small changes in the child's overall development.

Correct Answer: B

RATIONALE:
The percentile score is the percentage of subjects that score at or below a particular raw score.

Reference:
Case-Smith, J., & O'Brien, J. C. (2015). *Occupational therapy for children and adolescents* (7th ed., p. 176). St. Louis, MO: Mosby Elsevier.

Domain 2: Multiple Choice Answers, Rationales, and References

3. An OTR is evaluating the biceps strength of a client recovering from a musculocutaneous nerve injury. The OTR asks the client to fully flex the elbow while the client is seated upright with the shoulder adducted, the elbow fully extended, and the forearm in supination. The OTR observes that the client's forearm consistently moves into midposition on each attempt to flex the elbow despite prompting the client to maintain the forearm in supination. What conclusion can the OTR make based on this observation?

    A. The brachioradialis muscle is substituting for the weaker prime mover.

    B. The muscle strength of the biceps should be graded as Poor (2/5).

    C. The pronator teres muscle should be blocked on future testing.

    D. The movement should be retested with the client positioned in prone.

Correct Answer: A

RATIONALE:
The brachioradialis is innervated by the radial nerve and is substituting for weak biceps. This results in movement of the forearm into midposition when attempting to actively flex the elbow against gravity.

Reference:
Pendleton, H. M., & Schultz-Krohn, W. (Eds.). (2018). *Pedretti's occupational therapy: Practice skills for the physical dysfunction* (8th ed., pp. 535-536). St. Louis, MO: Mosby Elsevier.

NBCOT® Study Guide for the OTR Certification Examination

4. An inpatient who had a left CVA one week ago is participating in a dressing session. After putting on a sock during lower body dressing, the patient repeatedly attempts to pull the sock up even though it is already in place. What neurobehavioral deficit is **MOST CONSISTENT** with these actions?

    A. Spatial inattention

    B. Somatagnosia

    C. Dressing apraxia

    D. Premotor perseveration

Correct Answer: D

RATIONALE:

Premotor perseveration results in repetition of movements and difficulty transitioning from one aspect of an activity to another.

Reference:

Gillen, G. (2016). *Stroke rehabilitation: A function-based approach* (4th ed., p. 592). St. Louis, MO: Elsevier.

Domain 2: Multiple Choice Answers, Rationales, and References

5. An OTR administered a criterion-referenced standardized developmental checklist to a 3-year-old-child who has mild developmental delay. The child did not meet the standard for snipping with scissors. For what purpose would these results be **MOST USEFUL**?

A. Linking outcomes measures to other typically developing children

B. Determining developmentally appropriate activities to use in therapy

C. Identifying functional tasks that would be most difficult for the student

D. Comparing the child's performance to that of an age-equivalent population

Correct Answer: B

RATIONALE:
The purpose of a criterion-referenced test is to assess the child's performance against a specific criterion or measure rather than comparing performance to same-age peers. The OTR can use results of criterion-referenced tests to identify specific tasks to use as the focus of intervention.

Reference:
Case-Smith, J., & O'Brien, J. C. (2015). *Occupational therapy for children and adolescents* (7th ed., p. 170). St. Louis, MO: Mosby Elsevier.

NBCOT® Study Guide for the OTR Certification Examination

6. A client sustained a severe hand injury 5 weeks ago. During an OT session, the client reports that family responsibilities make it impossible to complete the prescribed exercise and splinting program. What action should the OTR take in response to this comment in order to promote the client's successful participation in the home program?

A. Determine a home program that closely aligns with typical performance patterns.

B. Analyze a 24-hour log to determine time management issues the client is experiencing.

C. Advise the client to make the home program the highest priority for the short term.

D. Suggest transition to a compensatory approach for dealing with residual deficits.

Correct Answer: A

RATIONALE:
Incorporating the home program into the client's existing performance routines will enhance the opportunities for successful completion within a busy schedule.

Reference:
Pendleton, H. M., & Schultz-Krohn, W. (Eds.). (2018). *Pedretti's occupational therapy: Practice skills for the physical dysfunction* (8th ed., pp. 158-160). St. Louis, MO: Mosby Elsevier.

Domain 2: Multiple Choice Answers, Rationales, and References

7. A client sustained a TBI 3 months ago and is functioning at Level VIII (Purposeful, Appropriate, Stand-by Assist) on the Rancho Los Amigos scale. The client is participating in a meal preparation task. As part of the task, the client is asked to prepare vegetable soup using a five-step printed recipe. The client is able to read the recipe steps aloud but does not act on any of them. When the OTR covers over all but the first step of the recipe, the client follows through with the step. What conclusion can the OTR make about the client based on this observation?

    A. Adaptive strategies compensate for attention deficits.

    B. Anchoring techniques improve visual perception.

    C. Ideational apraxia interferes with task initiation.

Correct Answer: A

RATIONALE:
A client at this level of functioning has improved to being able to attend to a familiar task for up to an hour but still has residual deficits in attention. This client's performance is enhanced when the OTR provides instruction to use an adaptive strategy.

References:
Radomski, M. V., & Trombly Latham, C. A. (Eds.). (2014). *Occupational therapy for physical dysfunction* (7th ed., p. 1049). Philadelphia, PA: Lippincott Williams & Wilkins.

Smith-Gabai, H., & Holm, S. (Eds.). (2017). *Occupational therapy in acute care* (2nd ed., p. 384). Bethesda, MD: AOTA Press.

NBCOT® Study Guide for the OTR Certification Examination

8. An inpatient had a right CVA one week ago. Prior to the CVA, the patient was relatively healthy and worked a full-time job. During a dressing assessment, the patient puts on a pull-over sweater and then realizes the need to put on a T-shirt underneath the sweater. To do this, the patient attempts to insert the T-shirt down the neck hole of the sweater, instead of removing the sweater to put on the T-shirt. Which statement **MOST ACCURATELY** describes the reason for the patient's action?

A. Right hemispheric damage appears to have resulted in perseverative behaviors.

B. Spatial integration deficits may be affecting the ability to recognize items.

C. The central nervous system is not receiving complete visual information.

D. The patient is not able to conceptualize steps of a task due to ideational apraxia.

Correct Answer: D

RATIONALE:
This patient is exhibiting ideational apraxia which involves difficulty conceptualizing, sequencing, and executing a plan using ADL items or objects.

Reference:
Gillen, G. (2016). *Stroke rehabilitation: A function-based approach* (4th ed., pp. 594-595). St. Louis, MO: Elsevier.

Domain 2: Multiple Choice Answers, Rationales, and References

9. An inpatient is preparing for discharge to home after completing 3 months of inpatient rehabilitation. The OTR is reviewing documentation in the patient's medical record and determines the patient is still working to achieve several short-term goals related to the current treatment plan. What **INITIAL** action should the OTR take based on this finding?

    A. Ensure durable medical equipment delivery and home health visits are scheduled in preparation for the patient's discharge.

    B. Complete a comprehensive re-evaluation to identify current function in relation to the discharge plan.

    C. Discuss options with the interprofessional team for extending inpatient rehabilitation until goals are achieved.

    D. Prepare a discharge summary providing a rationale for the goal shortcomings noted in the contact notes.

Correct Answer: B

RATIONALE:
The OTR should complete a re-evaluation prior to discussing other options with the interprofessional team or writing the discharge summary.

Reference:
Pendleton, H. M., & Schultz-Krohn, W. (Eds.). (2018). *Pedretti's occupational therapy: Practice skills for the physical dysfunction* (8th ed., pp. 128, 130-131). St. Louis, MO: Mosby Elsevier.

NBCOT® Study Guide for the OTR Certification Examination

10. An OTR has completed a developmental assessment of a 6-year-old child who has Down syndrome. Results indicate the child is dependent in all self-care tasks. The parents do not place a high priority on dressing independence, but the OTR does. What action should the OTR take as part of the intervention planning process?

A. Ask for the parents' consent to begin working on specific self-care skills with the child.

B. **Collaborate with the parents to identify mutually acceptable treatment goals for the child.**

C. Inform the parents that school-age children are expected to be independent with self-care.

D. Talk with the parents about establishing independence in self-care skills as a primary goal.

Correct Answer: B

RATIONALE:
Understanding and integrating culture values is integral to the client-centered intervention planning process.

Reference:
Case-Smith, J., & O'Brien, J. C. (2015). *Occupational therapy for children and adolescents* (7th ed., p. 148). St. Louis, MO: Mosby Elsevier.

Domain 2: Multiple Choice Answers, Rationales, and References

11. A family practice physician referred a client to outpatient OT for conservative treatment of carpal tunnel syndrome of the dominant hand. The client reports a 3 month history of numbness and difficulty manipulating objects. Symptoms interfere with work as a jack-hammer operator for a road works department. Evaluation results indicate loss of protective sensation, 11 mm two-point discrimination, and thenar muscle atrophy. Active ROM of the affected hand is within normal limits. What **INITIAL** actions should the OTR take in addition to fabricating a volar wrist orthosis?

A. Advise the client to wear the orthosis when sleeping and a padded glove when at work.

B. Arrange an appointment with an orthopedic surgeon and begin a sensory reeducation program.

C. **Conduct Phalen's test and report findings of the overall evaluation process to the physician.**

Correct Answer: C

RATIONALE:
Phalen's test is a clinical test used to determine the involvement of the median nerve. The OTR should report the evaluation results to the physician and collaborate with the physician on the overall intervention plan.

Reference:
Pendleton, H. M., & Schultz-Krohn, W. (Eds.). (2018). *Pedretti's occupational therapy: Practice skills for the physical dysfunction* (8th ed., p. 977). St. Louis, MO: Mosby Elsevier.

NBCOT® Study Guide for the OTR Certification Examination

NOTES

12. A young adult client was diagnosed with axonotmesis of the ulnar nerve secondary to a crush injury of the forearm 2 weeks ago. After obtaining baseline assessment information, which technique would be **MOST IMPORTANT** for the OTR to teach to the client as part of the intervention during the initial phase of the client's rehabilitation?

    A. Visual compensation

    B. Hand-dominance retraining

    C. Isometric strengthening

    D. Sensory re-education

Correct Answer: A

RATIONALE:

Axonotmesis results in loss of protective sensation to the affected nerve distribution. This injury does not require surgical intervention and typically resolves within 6 months from initial injury. Since sensation is impaired in the ulnar distribution, it is **MOST IMPORTANT** to teach the client to use visual skills as a compensatory means for protecting the hand from further injury.

Reference:
Pendleton, H. M., & Schultz-Krohn, W. (Eds). (2018). *Pedretti's occupational therapy: Practice skills for the physical dysfunction* (8th ed., pp. 981-983). St. Louis, MO: Mosby Elsevier.

150

13. An inpatient had a CVA with flaccid hemiplegia 8 days ago. When the OTR arrives for the scheduled session, the patient reports pain in the axillary region of the affected upper extremity. The OTR notes significant edema in the arm and that the arm is warm to the touch. Which of the following is the **BEST** option for why the OTR should alert the physician about these observations?

A. Late effect of cerebrovascular disease

B. Subluxation of the shoulder

C. **Deep vein thrombosis**

Correct Answer: C

RATIONALE:
Symptoms of edema, pain, and localized warmth in a flaccid extremity could indicate possible presence of a deep vein thrombosis.

Reference:
Smith-Gabai, H., & Holm, S. (Eds.). (2017). *Occupational therapy in acute care* (2nd ed., pp. 259-260). Bethesda, MD: AOTA Press.

NBCOT® Study Guide for the OTR Certification Examination

14. An OTR is completing a functional visual screening of a client who has macular degeneration. The OTR asks the client to a read a passage from a magazine. The client misses several letters and words, and has difficulty finding their place in the text when scanning. What aspect of visual function should the OTR investigate further based on the client's performance?

    A. Contrast sensitivity

    B. Visual acuity

    C. Central visual field

Correct Answer: C

RATIONALE:
The performance errors made by the client during the reading task is consistent with central visual field impairment.

References:
Radomski, M. V., & Trombly Latham, C. A. (Eds.). (2014). *Occupational therapy for physical dysfunction* (7th ed., p. 111). Philadelphia, PA: Lippincott Williams & Wilkins.

Zoltan, B. (2007). *Vision, perception, and cognition: A manual for the evaluation and treatment of the adult with acquired brain injury* (4th ed., pp. 64-65). Thorofare, NJ: SLACK, Inc.

Domain 2: Multiple Choice Answers, Rationales, and References

15. A patient has flaccid hemiplegia and dysphagia secondary to a CVA one month ago. The patient is participating in an interprofessional rehabilitation program. One of the intervention goals is for the patient to regain independence with self-feeding and become safe when eating. What information about the patient is **MOST IMPORTANT** for the OTR to present to the interprofessional team during each care coordination meeting?

   A. Improvements in upper extremity movement patterns used for self-feeding

   B. Specific evidence-based techniques that are being used during intervention sessions

   C. **Positioning, adaptive devices and caregiver assistance needed during mealtimes**

   D. Ability to select nutritious foods from the hospital dining menu that are safe to swallow

Correct Answer: C

RATIONALE:
The primary purpose for an interprofessional team approach is to make collaborative decisions and coordinate patient care. Presenting information about the patient's current abilities enables other team members to reinforce these skills during functional tasks (e.g., properly positioning the patient and providing appropriate assistive devices during meals).

Reference:
Pendleton, H. M., & Schultz-Krohn, W. (Eds.). (2018). *Pedretti's occupational therapy: Practice skills for the physical dysfunction* (8th ed., pp. 684-685). St. Louis, MO: Mosby Elsevier.

153

NBCOT® Study Guide for the OTR Certification Examination

NOTES

16. Which situation listed below warrants a referral to a gastroenterologist?

    A. A client who has diabetes and is experiencing more frequent episodes of hyperglycemia.

    B. A resident who recently started only eating the food placed on the right side of the plate.

    C. An adolescent who has cerebral palsy who refuses to eat and reports frequent episodes of reflux.

Correct Answer: C

RATIONALE:
Gastroenterology is a specialty of medicine that address conditions in the gastrointestinal tract and the digestive system.

Reference:
Smith-Gabai, H., & Holm, S. (Eds.). (2017). *Occupational therapy in acute care* (2nd ed., p. 102). Bethesda, MD: AOTA Press.

17. A client in an outpatient setting has hemiplegia secondary to a CVA. Over the past several weeks, there has been a decline in the client's energy level, ability to concentrate, and interest in intervention activities. When asked about the change, the client replies: "I just can't sleep at night thinking about the burden I am to my family." What **INITIAL** action should the OTR take based on this observed change?

    A. Consult with the client's primary physician

    B. Advise the client to consult with a psychiatrist

    C. Adjust the timeframes for achieving short term goals

Correct Answer: A

RATIONALE:
The client is demonstrating signs and symptoms typically associated with depression that warrant a consultation with the client's primary care physician.

Reference:
Pendleton, H. M., & Schultz-Krohn, W. (Eds.). (2018). *Pedretti's occupational therapy: Practice skills for the physical dysfunction* (8th ed., p. 1156). St. Louis, MO: Mosby Elsevier.

154

Domain 2: Multiple Choice Answers, Rationales, and References

18. A client who has chronic low back pain is participating in an interprofessional pain management program. The focus of the program is for the client to learn mechanisms for coping with pain and reducing injury risk during work-related tasks as a manual laborer. The client has been making progress since starting the program 3 weeks ago. What information is **MOST IMPORTANT** for the OTR to report about the client's progress at the next weekly team meeting?

    A. Amount of weight the client is able to lift and carry during sessions

    B. Ability to correctly perform stretching and strengthening exercises

    C. Spontaneous use of self-management strategies during activities

    D. Length of time the client engages in specific work tasks in the clinic

Correct Answer: C

RATIONALE:
The client's spontaneous use of self-management strategies indicates progress toward the program goals of helping the client learn ways to cope with pain and reduce injury risk during work tasks.

Reference:
Pendleton, H. M., & Schultz-Krohn, W. (Eds.). (2018). *Pedretti's occupational therapy: Practice skills for the physical dysfunction* (8th ed., pp. 703, 706-708). St. Louis, MO: Mosby Elsevier.

NBCOT® Study Guide for the OTR Certification Examination

19. An OTR is formulating a discharge plan for an inpatient who has dementia and is functioning at Allen Cognitive Level 4 (Goal-Directed Actions). The patient will be living at home with assistance from family. What type of caregiver education is **MOST IMPORTANT** for the OTR to provide prior to the patient's discharge from the inpatient facility?

    A. Suggestions for modifying the environment to eliminate unnecessary household items

    B. Methods for promoting the patient's problem solving for independence during ADL

    C. Strategies for providing visual cues that will help the patient complete daily routines

    D. Techniques for establishing and posting a written emergency plan in the home environment

Correct Answer: C

RATIONALE:
A person who is functioning at Allen Cognitive Level 4 (Goal-Directed Actions) is able to complete basic ADL with visual cues.

References:
Brown, C., & Stoffel V. C. (2011). *Occupational therapy in mental health: A vision for participation.* (p. 235) Philadelphia, PA: F.A. Davis Company.

Cole, M. B. (2018). *Group dynamics in occupational therapy: The theoretical basis and practice application of group intervention* (5th ed., p. 202). Thorofare, NJ: SLACK, Inc.

Domain 2: Multiple Choice Answers, Rationales, and References

20. A private practice OTR is developing goals for a 4-year-old child with autism spectrum disorder who has difficulty with emotional regulation, impulse control, and problem-solving skills. The child attends preschool, and academically is meeting expectations. Socially, the child has not developed friendships at school or within the neighborhood. Which task should be included as a short-term goal in the intervention plan for this child?

    A. Interact with peers during a structured play group.

    B. Follow rules while playing an age-appropriate board game.

    C. Play at the sand table without acquiring an injury.

Correct Answer: A

RATIONALE:
This is a developmentally appropriate goal for a 4-year-old child who has difficulty developing friendships.

Reference:
Case-Smith, J., & O'Brien, J. C. (2015). *Occupational therapy for children and adolescents* (7th ed., pp. 89-90, 490). St. Louis, MO: Mosby Elsevier.

21. An inpatient who has pneumonia and mild cognitive decline has been stabilized in the hospital and is medically ready for discharge. Currently, the patient requires constant supervision for ADL and IADL due to safety concerns and impulsive behavior. The patient and family have declined the treatment team recommendation that the patient move into an assistive living facility. Which option represents the **MOST IMPORTANT** discharge recommendation the OTR should provide the family?

    A. Involve the patient in a structured adult day program.

    B. Modify the home environment prior to discharge.

    C. Provide the patient with 24-hour supervision.

Correct Answer: C

RATIONALE:
The patient requires 24-hour supervision to ensure safety due to mild cognitive decline and impulsive behaviors.

Reference:
Smith-Gabai, H., & Holm, S. (Eds.). (2017). *Occupational therapy in acute care* (2nd ed., pp. 84, 87-91). Bethesda, MD: AOTA Press.

NBCOT® Study Guide for the OTR Certification Examination

NOTES

22. A client who has severe depression has been participating in a partial hospitalization program. The client has made some improvements but continues to have difficulties concentrating on tasks and coping with day-to-day stressors. The interprofessional team agrees that the client has made sufficient progress to transition to the next level of care. Which type of program would **BEST** assist the client toward the goal of returning to work as a healthcare provider?

A. Impaired provider program

B. Support group for working professionals

C. Community mental health program

Correct Answer: C

RATIONALE:
A referral to a community mental health program is the best option for this client who continues to make progress toward return-to-work goals but has persisting difficulties with process skills and mood.

Reference:
Brown, C., & Stoffel V. C. (2011). *Occupational therapy in mental health: A vision for participation.* (p. 587) Philadelphia, PA: F.A. Davis Company.

Domain 2: Multiple Choice Answers, Rationales, and References

23. An inpatient recovering from pneumonia has decreased strength and endurance, and functional active ROM. The patient ambulates independently for short distances with the use of a walker. Medical history indicates the patient has recently been diagnosed with moderate macular degeneration. The patient will be discharged in one day to live alone in a single-story home. Which service should the OTR recommend as part of the patient's discharge plans?

    A. Extension of current hospital stay for comprehensive rehabilitation services

    B. Home health services to assess ADL needs and teach compensatory strategies

    C. Short-term placement in a skilled facility to maximize independence in ADL

Correct Answer: B

RATIONALE:
Since the patient can ambulate independently for short distances with the use of a walker, the patient will benefit from home health services in the natural environment of the home to further assess needs and teach compensatory strategies.

Reference:
Smith-Gabai, H., & Holm, S. (Eds.). (2017). *Occupational therapy in acute care* (2nd ed., p. 89). Bethesda, MD: AOTA Press.

NBCOT® Study Guide for the OTR Certification Examination

24. An OTR is providing home health services to a 9-month-old infant who underwent surgery for a Type I Chiari malformation one month ago. The infant has been progressing without complication since the date of surgery. During a follow-up home visit, the infant's parent reports lack of progress with the home program because the infant has been extremely lethargic for the past few days and has had several episodes of vomiting within the past 12 hours. What should the OTR advise the parent to do based on the infant's current condition?

A. Monitor the infant's flu-like symptoms for the next 24 hours and ensure fluid intake.

B. Reschedule the appointment for the next week when symptoms should be resolved.

C. Report the infant's symptoms as soon as possible to the primary care physician.

Correct Answer: C

RATIONALE:
Possible complications associated with the surgical procedure for Chiari malformation that warrant immediate contact with the physician include decreased alertness, increased drowsiness, and vomiting.

Reference:
Smith-Gabai, H., & Holm, S. (Eds.). (2017). *Occupational therapy in acute care* (2nd ed., pp. 321-322). Bethesda, MD: AOTA Press.

Domain 2: Multiple Choice Answers, Rationales, and References

25. An OTR is working with a client who has Stage 5 Alzheimer's disease and lives with a full-time caregiver. Based on this stage of the disease process, which option would be the **MOST BENEFICIAL** recommendation for the OTR to make to the caregiver?

    A. Encourage the client to participate in a new hobby.

    B. Post an illustrated daily schedule for the client to follow.

    C. Provide assistance for dressing and grooming activities.

Correct Answer: C

RATIONALE:
A client with stage 5 Alzheimer's disease has moderately severe cognitive decline and would benefit from assistance for ADL such as dressing and grooming.

Reference:
Cara, E., & MacRae, A. (2013). *Psychosocial occupational therapy: An evolving practice* (3rd ed., p. 481). Clifton Park, NY: Delmar Cengage Learning.

NBCOT® Study Guide for the OTR Certification Examination

26. An inpatient has been participating in rehabilitation since having bilateral transfemoral amputations 2 months ago. The patient has good balance and Fair plus (3+/5) upper extremity strength, is independent with bed mobility and self-care using adaptive equipment, and requires stand-by assistance during wheelchair transfers and with wheelchair management. The patient is preparing for discharge to live at home with the spouse and an adult son. Modifications have been made to the main entrance of the home and the bathroom. The OTR plans to provide family education for promoting the patient's safe transition to the home environment. What information would be **MOST BENEFICIAL** to include as part of this process?

A. Methods for improving the patient's independence with transfers

B. Techniques the patient uses to transfer to a variety of surfaces

C. Energy conservation techniques for the patient to use during ADL

D. Wrapping techniques for shaping and protecting the residual limb

Correct Answer: B

RATIONALE:

To provide safe transition to the home environment, it is important for the OTR to provide 1:1 instruction based on the needs of both the patient and the caregiver. In this case, the caregivers need to be competent in techniques the patient uses to transfer to a variety of surfaces prior to discharge.

Reference:
Schell, B. A. B., Gillen, G., & Scaffa, M. E. (2014). *Willard & Spackman's occupational therapy* (12th ed., pp. 645-647). Philadelphia, PA: Lippincott Williams & Wilkins.

Domain 2: Multiple Choice Answers, Rationales, and References

27. A patient who has hemiplegia and cognitive-perceptual deficits has been transferred from an acute care facility to a skilled nursing rehabilitation unit. When should discharge planning for this patient take place?

    A. Throughout the rehabilitation phase of treatment

    B. When the majority of short-term goals have been met

    C. After determining if the patient has potential to return home

Correct Answer: A

RATIONALE:
The OTR should formulate the intervention plan based on the outcomes of the initial assessment and in relation to the intended discharge environment. The discharge plans should be reassessed, as needed, based on the functional progress the patient demonstrates throughout the rehabilitation process.

Reference:
Smith-Gabai, H., & Holm, S. (Eds.). (2017). *Occupational therapy in acute care* (2nd ed., p. 86). Bethesda, MD: AOTA Press.

28. A resident of a skilled nursing facility, who has moderately severe cognitive decline, becomes increasingly agitated during mealtime. What is the **FIRST** action the OTR should take based on this observation?

    A. Instruct the resident in relaxation exercises to use at mealtime.

    B. Arrange for the resident to eat meals in a calm, quiet location.

    C. Observe the resident at mealtime to identity behavioral triggers.

Correct Answer: C

RATIONALE:
In order to provide the most effective intervention strategy, the OTR would first need to identify the stimuli that triggered the behavior during mealtime.

References:
Brown, C., & Stoffel V. C. (2011). *Occupational therapy in mental health: A vision for participation* (p. 236). Philadelphia, PA: F.A. Davis Company.

NBCOT® Study Guide for the OTR Certification Examination

29. A young adult client who has a substance use disorder has been referred to community-based OT. Although the client has maintained sobriety for the past 6 months, evaluation results indicate the client has an unrealistic self-concept, poor social skills and inadequate independent living skills. Which objective would be **MOST BENEFICIAL** to include as part of the initial intervention plan for supporting the client's participation in occupations?

A. Transition to independent living with a supportive friend

B. Acquisition of practical skills for basic life management

C. Engagement in leisure activities with social acquaintances

D. Education about work stressors that contribute to relapse

Correct Answer: B

RATIONALE:
The acquisition of practical life management skills is essential for enabling the client to develop a sense of control and autonomy that will support participation in meaningful occupations.

References:
Cara, E., & MacRae, A. (2013). *Psychosocial occupational therapy: An evolving practice* (3rd ed., pp. 841-869). Clifton Park, NY: Delmar Cengage Learning.

Schell, B. A. B., Gillen, G., & Scaffa, M. E. (2014). *Willard & Spackman's occupational therapy* (12th ed., p. 1183). Philadelphia, PA: Lippincott Williams & Wilkins.

164

Domain 2: Multiple Choice Answers, Rationales, and References

30. A client who has moderate cognitive decline lives in a skilled nursing facility. The client's spouse visits every morning after breakfast. The spouse informs the OTR that the client's frequency of interacting during the visits has decreased over the past few weeks, and the client now has intermittent verbal outbursts that disrupt the social interaction. In addition to informing the care team, what action should the OTR take based on this observation?

   A. Sit with client and the spouse during a visit, and ask the client direct questions to facilitate appropriate communication.

   B. Ask the spouse open-ended questions about the situation, and identify possible triggers for the change in level of interaction.

   C. Provide the spouse with information about providing immediate feedback to the client when there are signs of agitation.

Correct Answer: B

RATIONALE:
Prior to initiating intervention, the OTR first acquires additional information to understand possible triggers for the change in behavior.

Reference:
Bonder, B. R., & Dal Bello-Haas, V. (2018). *Functional performance in older adults* (4th ed., p. 377). Philadelphia, PA: F.A. Davis Company.

NBCOT® Study Guide for the OTR Certification Examination

31. A client in the outpatient setting recently underwent plastic surgery to correct facial disfigurement. During a grooming session, the client states, "I will never look in the mirror again." What action should the OTR take in response to the client's concern?

    A. Provide positive affirmations and encourage the client to seek reassurance from close friends.

    B. Validate the client's concerns and transition to the next intervention that does not require a mirror.

    C. Provide support and ask open-ended questions to gain insight into the client's view on their body image.

Correct Answer: C

RATIONALE:
The client is expressing concerns regarding body image that warrants further assessment by the OTR prior to determining the need for consultation with the physician or modifying the intervention plan.

Reference:
Smith-Gabai, H., & Holm, S. (Eds.). (2017). *Occupational therapy in acute care* (2nd ed., p. 497). Bethesda, MD: AOTA Press.

32. An outpatient OTR is working with an adult client who has spastic diplegia. One of the client's goals is to drive a car. The client has the necessary process skills to drive but requires adapted driving controls to access the gas and brake pedals. What is the **FIRST** action the OTR should take in this situation?

    A. Research funding options to pay for vehicle adaptations.

    B. Refer the client to a driving rehabilitation specialist.

    C. Arrange for a trial of specialized equipment from a reputable vendor.

Correct Answer: B

RATIONALE:
A referral to a driving rehabilitation specialist is warranted to evaluate the specialized needs for this client and to provide recommendations for vehicle modifications.

Reference:
Cook, A. M., & Polgar, J. M. (2015). *Assistive technologies: Principles & practice* (4th ed., p. 279). St. Louis, MO: Mosby Elsevier.

166

Domain 2: Multiple Choice Answers, Rationales, and References

33. An inpatient had a total hip replacement 3 days ago. During an intervention session, neither the patient nor the spouse appear interested in learning about the assistive devices for improving the patient's independence with BADL. What **INITIAL** action should the OTR take based on this observation?

    A. Explore the couple's feelings about using the equipment.

    B. Explain that assistive devices are essential to the patient's recovery.

    C. Document the reactions in the client's record and inform the care coordinator.

Correct Answer: A

RATIONALE:
One of the key features of client-centered practice is to collaborate with the client to establish a meaningful intervention plan.

Reference:
Pendleton, H. M., & Schultz-Krohn, W. (Eds.). (2018). *Pedretti's occupational therapy: Practice skills for the physical dysfunction* (8th ed., pp. 1012-1016). St. Louis, MO: Mosby Elsevier.

NBCOT® Study Guide for the OTR Certification Examination

34. A patient in an inpatient rehabilitation setting is in the recovery phase of intervention after an acute onset of Guillain-Barré syndrome one month ago. The OTR advises the patient that using assistive devices will improve independence, but the patient refuses to use the devices stating: "My wife is happy to help me whenever I need it." How should the OTR respond to the patient's comment?

    A. Convince the patient to try the devices at least once.

    B. Discuss the patient's comment with family members.

    C. Focus intervention sessions on strengthening and ROM activities.

    D. Identify other strategies for improving occupational performance.

Correct Answer: D

RATIONALE:

Use of assistive devices should be determined based on the patient's needs and priorities. If the patient does not want to use assistive devices, the OTR can work with the patient to teach energy conservation and other compensatory strategies tailored to predetermined needs and priorities.

Reference:
Pendleton, H. M., & Schultz-Krohn, W. (Eds.). (2018). *Pedretti's occupational therapy: Practice skills for the physical dysfunction* (8th ed., pp. 193-194, 931-932). St. Louis, MO: Mosby Elsevier.

Domain 2: Multiple Choice Answers, Rationales, and References

35. An OTR working in a community mental health setting is using dialectical behavior therapy to guide intervention planning for a client who has a borderline personality disorder. The client works in a university setting and is at risk of losing the job due to verbal outbursts and erratic mood swings. The client is aware that behavioral changes are needed and reports a willingness to work toward these changes. Which type of intervention would the OTR include in therapy sessions for supporting progress toward this objective when using this approach?

A. Individual sessions focusing on Socratic questioning and guided discovery for addressing problematic situations and emotions

B. Group skills training modules in mindfulness, interpersonal effectiveness, emotion modulation, and distress tolerance

C. Role-play sessions using prepared scripts for practicing problem-solving and decision-making related to workplace situations

Correct Answer: B

RATIONALE:

These interventions should be prioritized when an OTR is using the dialectical behavior treatment protocol to guide the therapeutic process.

Reference:
Brown, C., & Stoffel V. C. (2011). *Occupational therapy in mental health: A vision for participation.* (pp. 247, 271, 350-351) Philadelphia, PA: F.A. Davis Company.

NBCOT® Study Guide for the OTR Certification Examination

36. A young adult client is participating in a community-based OT program after completing inpatient treatment for an acute episode of major depression. Evaluation results indicate the client has difficulty concentrating on simple tasks, has poor personal hygiene, and has limited insight about the impact of the depression on areas of occupation. The client states the primary goal for attending OT is "to get a job." What should be the **INITIAL** focus of sessions with this client?

    A. Assigning the client to a job in a highly supervised sheltered work environment

    B. Finding the client a transitional job involving routine and repetitive work tasks

    C. Determining the client's work habits and current abilities for job readiness

    D. Teaching the client how to locate job opportunities and submit job applications

Correct Answer: C

RATIONALE:

Prior to selecting a specific employment placement, the initial step in the intervention planning process is to understand the client's work habits and current abilities.

Reference:

Cara, E., & MacRae, A. (2013). *Psychosocial occupational therapy: An evolving practice* (3rd ed., pp. 815-819). Clifton Park, NY: Delmar Cengage Learning.

37. An adolescent was recently admitted to an inpatient psychiatric unit due to symptoms associated with a conduct disorder. Evaluation results indicate the adolescent has a poor self-concept, decreased fine and gross motor coordination, and is socially aggressive. What should be the focus of the **INITIAL** sessions with this adolescent?

   A. Presenting options for pre-vocational exploration and practice

   B. Encouraging participation in self-expression group activities

   C. Providing opportunities for success in a consistent structured environment

   D. Enhancing physical abilities for completing responsibilities at home

Correct Answer: C

RATIONALE:
Since a symptom of this disorder includes poor impulse control, providing structure and consistency should be inherent in each treatment session with this adolescent. Additionally, successful experiences help to build self-concept.

Reference:
Bonder, B. R. (2015). *Psychopathology and function* (5th ed., pp. 306-308). Thorofare, NJ: SLACK, Inc.

NBCOT® Study Guide for the OTR Certification Examination

38. An OTR has completed an evaluation of a patient who is experiencing complications from pneumonia and was recently admitted to a Medicare funded skilled nursing facility. The patient was living independently prior to hospitalization and wants to return home. Evaluation results indicate the patient is generally deconditioned and fatigues quickly during activity. The patient ambulates slowly using a walker, and requires frequent verbal and physical cueing for safety when using the walker during ADL. What criteria should the OTR use to prioritize the goals for this patient's intervention plan?

A. Skilled services the patient currently requires for completion of basic functional tasks.

B. Amount of assistance that will be available to the patient to maintain progress after discharge.

C. Patient's desire to improve strength, ROM, and endurance prior to discharge from the facility.

D. Amount of time the patient will need to maximize strength and endurance prior to returning independent living.

Correct Answer: A

RATIONALE:

In a Medicare funded facility, the OTR must prioritize goals based on medical necessity and skilled services needed for function.

Reference:
Gateley, C. A., & Borcherding, S. (2017). *Documentation manual for occupational therapy: Writing SOAP notes* (4th ed., pp. 16, 25-26). Thorofare, NJ: SLACK, Inc.

Domain 2: Multiple Choice Answers, Rationales, and References

39. An OTR is planning intervention for an outpatient client who had a CMC thumb arthroplasty one week ago. What should the OTR include as part of the **INITIAL** intervention plan at this stage of recovery?

    A. Provide the client with a ROM program for the shoulder, elbow, fingers and thumb IP joints.

    B. Teach the client to complete a progressive strengthening program of the affected hand.

    C. Teach the client to pinch resistive putty between the tip of the thumb and the index finger.

Correct Answer: A

RATIONALE:
At this stage of recovery, the initial intervention plan for a CMC thumb arthroplasty one week after surgery includes immobilizing the wrist and thumb CMC while allowing AROM at the IP joint and providing the client with a ROM program for the shoulder, elbow, fingers, and thumb IP joints.

Reference:
Cooper, C. (2014). *Fundamentals of hand therapy: Clinical reasoning and treatment guidelines for common diagnoses of the upper extremity* (2nd ed., pp. 463-464, 475). St. Louis, MO: Mosby Elsevier.

173

NBCOT® Study Guide for the OTR Certification Examination

NOTES

40. An outpatient client has an acute flare-up of stage I rheumatoid arthritis. Initial evaluation results indicate the client's MCP joints bilaterally are red and swollen. The client lacks 10° active extension of the MCP joints on the second through fifth digits bilaterally. The client works as a florist and reports pain as 9 out of 10 on a visual analog scale when completing activities requiring grasp and prehensile patterns. The client will be participating in OT twice weekly. Which therapeutic exercise should be included as part of the intervention plan for the client to complete by the end of the first week of therapy?

- **A.** Passive motion and stretch of the MCP joints through the full arc of motion

- **B.** Pinching and gripping a soft sponge in warm water within pain tolerance

- **C. Isotonic and isometric exercises of both hands within pain-free ranges of motion**

- **D.** Tendon gliding exercises of the fingers against light resistance therapy putty

Correct Answer: C

RATIONALE:
During an acute flare up, exercises are important for preserving joint mobility and preventing deformities. Exercises should be completed with caution especially in the presence of painful and swollen joints.

Reference:
Pendleton, H. M., & Schultz-Krohn, W. (Eds.). (2018). *Pedretti's occupational therapy: Practice skills for the physical dysfunction* (8th ed., pp. 958-960). St. Louis, MO: Mosby Elsevier.

174

Domain 2: Multiple Choice Answers, Rationales, and References

41. An 8-year-old child sustained second-degree burns to the first web space of both hands one month ago. Results of a reevaluation indicate the child's web space is contracting despite wearing pressure garments, using night orthotics and completing home program activities. What additional action should the OTR take based on these findings?

    A. Advise the caregiver to increase the intensity and frequency of passive ROM exercises.

    B. Begin serial splinting that incorporates a polymer gel sheet over the affected areas.

    C. Provide the caregiver with a list of age-appropriate games that will promote hand use.

    D. Use a paraffin modality during OT sessions to soften the scar prior to functional activity.

Correct Answer: B

RATIONALE:
Intervention that includes serial static orthoses and polymer gel sheeting is effective for contractures of the thumb web space.

References:
Cooper, C. (2014). *Fundamentals of hand therapy: Clinical reasoning and treatment guidelines for common diagnoses of the upper extremity* (2nd ed., pp. 486-487). St. Louis, MO: Mosby Elsevier.

Pendleton, H. M., & Schultz-Krohn, W. (Eds.). (2018). *Pedretti's occupational therapy: Practice skills for the physical dysfunction* (8th ed., p. 769). St. Louis, MO: Mosby Elsevier.

NBCOT® Study Guide for the OTR Certification Examination

42. An OTR working in an outpatient setting is planning intervention for a client who has a 12-month history of fibromyalgia. The client reports symptoms associated with this condition are limiting the ability to participate in social activities. This has led to significant frustration and progressive social isolation over the past few months. The client wants to reverse this trend. What should the OTR include as part of the **INITIAL** intervention planning process with this client?

A. Recommend the client maintain a journal as a means of venting frustration.

B. Explore hobbies the client can try at home that do not exacerbate pain.

C. Identify options for modifying the client's preferred community activities.

Correct Answer: C

RATIONALE:
This option is an effective client-centered intervention to address the client's goal and allow for participation in activities outside the home.

Reference:
Lundy-Ekman, L. (2013). *Neuroscience: Fundamentals for rehabilitation* (4th ed., pp. 228-229). St. Louis, MO: Saunders Elsevier.

Domain 2: Multiple Choice Answers, Rationales, and References

43. An OTR is preparing for an **INITIAL** intervention session with an inpatient who is in the acute manic phase of bipolar disorder. Which general strategy should the OTR include as part of this session?

    A. Structure the environment to encourage creativity and self-expression.

    B. Minimize distractions in the environment during task performance.

    C. Ensure the patient is aware of the influence of mania on participation.

    D. Provide the patient with an opportunity to select an activity of interest.

Correct Answer: B

RATIONALE:
It is important to provide a structured environment with minimal distractions during the initial phase of intervention.

Reference:
Cara, E., & MacRae, A. (2013). *Psychosocial occupational therapy: An evolving practice* (3rd ed., pp. 231-232, 238.). Clifton Park, NY: Delmar Cengage Learning.

NBCOT® Study Guide for the OTR Certification Examination

44. An OTR is planning an intervention session for a 6-year-old child who has fetal alcohol syndrome. The child has difficulty coping when frustrated and frequently refuses to speak in social situations and during therapy. The OTR has attempted to engage the child using play therapy and sensory-based approaches, but the child refuses to participate. How should the OTR modify the intervention approach based on the child's responses during previous interventions?

A. Engage the child in computer games that promote positive feedback.

B. Use role-play scenarios about interacting with superheroes.

C. **Include expressive media using cartoon character puppetry.**

Correct Answer: C

RATIONALE:
Expressive media such as puppetry is an effective intervention approach to support the child's engagement in the therapeutic process.

Reference:
Brown, C., & Stoffel V. C. (2011). *Occupational therapy in mental health: A vision for participation* (p. 325). Philadelphia, PA: F.A. Davis Company.

Domain 2: Multiple Choice Answers, Rationales, and References

45. An inpatient is undergoing treatment in an acute rehabilitation facility after sustaining bilateral ankle fractures one week ago. Medical records indicate the patient will be non-weight-bearing for at least 6 weeks. Currently, the patient is independent with upper body dressing; requires moderate assistance with lower body dressing, bathing, and transfers; and independently propels a standard wheelchair. One of the intervention priorities is for the patient to be independent with IADL prior to discharge. Which action is **MOST IMPORTANT** for the OTR to take in advance of scheduling intervention activities for this patient?

   A. Discuss the projected timeline for recovery with the interprofessional team.

   B. Ensure the hospital bathroom is equipped with durable medical equipment.

   C. Identify the patient's expected discharge context and available resources.

Correct Answer: C

RATIONALE:
A key feature of client-centered care is to select and implement interventions that align with the available resources and the patient's expected discharge site.

Reference:
Schell, B. A. B., Gillen, G., & Scaffa, M. E. (2014). *Willard & Spackman's occupational therapy* (12th ed., p. 637). Philadelphia, PA: Lippincott Williams & Wilkins.

NBCOT® Study Guide for the OTR Certification Examination

46. An OTR working in a community hospital is contributing discharge recommendations for a patient who is generally deconditioned secondary to complications from a septic episode. The patient has been participating in OT for the past 3 weeks. Currently, the patient requires moderate assistance with transfers and tolerates up to 10 minutes of seated ADL activity prior to needing a rest break. The patient's goal is to return home to live independently. Which discharge setting would be **MOST BENEFICIAL** for the OTR to recommend for the patient's next level of care?

A. Home health with skilled services

B. **Subacute rehabilitation facility**

C. Inpatient rehabilitation hospital

Correct Answer: B

RATIONALE:

The **MOST BENEFICIAL** discharge recommendation based on the patient's current level of function and rate of recovery is a subacute rehabilitation facility.

Reference:

Smith-Gabai, H., & Holm, S. (Eds.). (2017). *Occupational therapy in acute care* (2nd ed., p. 89). Bethesda, MD: AOTA Press.

Domain 2: Multiple Choice Answers, Rationales, and References

47. An OTR wants to measure the effectiveness of a pre-vocational group at a mental health day program. What data is **MOST IMPORTANT** to collect for this purpose?

    A. Attendance levels and completion rate of homework assignments

    B. Client satisfaction ratings completed by participants after discharge

    C. Quality of the client's interview responses during role-play activities with peers

    D. Number of clients who successfully enter employment positions following the group

Correct Answer: D

RATIONALE:
Quantitative data, such as measuring the number of clients who successfully enter employment positions after participating in the group, is **MOST IMPORTANT** to contribute to the understanding about the effectiveness of the group.

Reference:
Brown, C., & Stoffel V. C. (2011). *Occupational therapy in mental health: A vision for participation.* (p. 605) Philadelphia, PA: F.A. Davis Company.

NBCOT® Study Guide for the OTR Certification Examination

48. An OTR who works in an outpatient hand therapy clinic fabricated a forearm orthosis for a client. The OTR is providing instructions to the client on the wearing schedule and care of the orthosis. Which is the **MOST EFFECTIVE** method for the OTR to use in the education session to promote the client's understanding of the information presented?

A. Ask the patient an open-ended question that invites a descriptive response.

B. Provide a detailed written handout with illustrations to reinforce key points.

C. Encourage the client to independently place the orthosis on and off during the session.

Correct Answer: B

RATIONALE:
Written documentation allows the patient to review the instructions after the session and refer to the handout when needed.

Reference:
Smith-Gabai, H., & Holm, S. (Eds.). (2017). *Occupational therapy in acute care* (2nd ed., p. 647). Bethesda, MD: AOTA Press.

Domain 2: Multiple Choice Answers, Rationales, and References

49. An OTR who works in a home health setting is developing educational handouts for clients who have low vision. Which guidelines are **MOST BENEFICIAL** for the OTR to use when developing educational handouts for this population?

    A. Many different colors to highlight important information printed on high-gloss paper

    B. Large print with a minimum of 16-point font with high contrast between the text and the paper

    C. Pictorial illustrations and written information placed in columns on the page

Correct Answer: B

RATIONALE:
These features will increase the readability of educational materials for clients who have low vision.

References:
Barney, K. F., & Perkinson, M. A. (2016). *Occupational therapy with aging adults: Promoting quality of life through collaborative practice* (p. 158). St. Louis, MO: Elsevier Mosby.

Smith-Gabai, H., & Holm, S. (Eds.). (2017). *Occupational therapy in acute care* (2nd ed., p. 636). Bethesda, MD: AOTA Press.

NBCOT® Study Guide for the OTR Certification Examination

50. An OTR who works in an outpatient setting is providing assistive technology recommendations to a client who has amyotrophic lateral sclerosis. Which is the **MOST EFFECTIVE** method for the OTR to use during the intervention session to evaluate the client's understanding of the information presented?

    A. Provide the client with the written information from the manufacturers of the devices.

    B. Engage the client in a discussion to allow the opportunity for questions to be answered.

    C. Explain to the client evidence that supports benefits and outcomes associated with each device.

Correct Answer: B

RATIONALE:
An important part of assessing health literacy is to discuss the recommendations with the client and ensure all questions are answered.

Reference:
Cook, A. M., & Polgar, J. M. (2015). *Assistive technologies: Principles & practice* (4th ed., pp. 107-108). St. Louis, MO: Mosby Elsevier.

Domain 2: Multiple Choice Answers, Rationales, and References

Chapter 13

Domain 3: Multiple Choice Sample Questions

Practice questions with answer key and references

The following multiple choice items are samples related to Domain 3.

Intervention Management

Select interventions for managing a client-centered plan throughout the occupational therapy process.

NOTES

1. A high school student has spastic diplegia and cognitive delay. The student self-propels a wheelchair and requires moderate assistance for functional transfers. The student has been the target of peer-bullying in school and has been attending OT to help increase social participation. One of the student's goals is to attend a dance being planned by the dance committee of student volunteers. During a role-play session, the student tells the OTR, "I really want to go to the dance, but I am worried that I won't fit in." Which recommendation should the OTR suggest for addressing the student's concern?

   A. Ask the committee to recruit parent volunteers willing to attend the dance as facilitators of social inclusion.

   B. Require the committee leader to provide inclusion training for all students at a school assembly prior to the dance.

   C. Have the student partner with the committee to select a music playlist for the dance that includes modified line dances.

2. An OTR plans to use a sensorimotor approach to improve the handwriting skills of a 6-year-old student who has a mild learning disability. The student maintains a very tight grip on a pencil when writing, consistently uses a palmar grasp when holding the pencil, and has directional confusion when forming letters. Which activity would be effective to include as part of the **INITIAL** intervention when using this approach?

   A. Painting letters using a wide-barrel brush on paper attached to an upright easel

   B. Rolling out colored modeling dough and making cookie cutter shapes on a tabletop

   C. Using spring-opening blunt-edge scissors to cut out geometric paper shapes

   D. Providing hand-over-hand assistance during writing assignments

3. An inpatient had a TBI one month ago and is functioning at Level VII (Automatic-appropriate) on the Rancho Los Amigos scale. Currently, the patient is able to follow two-step instructions and attends to a familiar task for up to 15 minutes at a time. The patient wants to return home to resume homemaking roles. One of the patient's short-term goals is to independently bake cookies for a family member's upcoming birthday. How should the activity be graded to support the patient's successful participation in this task?

   A. Have the patient prepare cookies using slice and bake packaged cookie dough.

   B. Provide the patient with a recipe of ingredients for mixing and baking cookies.

   C. Have the patient prepare cookies using a boxed cookie mix with pre-measured ingredients.

   D. Mix the ingredients together and have the patient drop the cookies onto the cookie sheet.

NBCOT® Study Guide for the OTR Certification Examination

NOTES

4. A 5-year-old child sustained partial and full thickness burns on the volar surfaces of both wrists and forearms 3 months ago. Although the child wears pressure garments, scarring across the wrist is limiting wrist mobility. Which activity could be graded to **MOST EFFECTIVELY** help with increasing the child's wrist motion?

    A. Tossing a bean bag at a target placed at varying distances from the child

    B. Moving a parachute up and down during parachute games with peers

    C. Bouncing a medium-size therapy ball from one hand to the other

    D. Creeping on hands and knees through a play tunnel maze

5. An inpatient sustained a complete T_5 spinal cord injury one month ago and has been in the intensive care unit on extended bed-rest. The OTR recently initiated a program of graded bed mobility in preparation for beginning transfer training. The patient is now able to sit in bed with the head of the bed elevated to 45o for one-hour intervals without experiencing any dizziness. Which position is safest for the patient to be placed in **NEXT**?

    A. Upright in a standard wheelchair with close monitoring

    B. Upright on a tilt-table at 90° while wearing an abdominal binder and elastic stockings

    C. Seated in a semi-reclining wheelchair with legs elevated

    D. Seated on the edge of the bed with both legs unsupported and knees flexed to 90°

Domain 3: Multiple Choice Sample Questions

6. A patient with a borderline personality disorder was admitted to an inpatient facility 4 days ago secondary to an exacerbation of suicidal and self-mutilating behavior. The patient's condition is now stable and the patient is functioning at Allen Cognitive Level 5 (Exploratory Actions). The patient reports being overwhelmed by a new personal relationship, experiencing job dissatisfaction, and feeling a lack of control in most daily situations. Which intervention would be **MOST BENEFICIAL** for addressing problems in performance skills and patterns secondary to the concurrent symptoms?

  A. Coping skills groups that address a variety of adaptive strategies

  B. One-on-one sessions to encourage the patient to contract for safety

  C. Daily self-care sessions that focus on structured BADL

  D. Structured one-step craft activities to promote successful outcomes

7. An inpatient had a TBI 3 weeks ago and is functioning at Level II (Generalized response) on the Rancho Los Amigos scale. Which intervention should be a priority to include in treatment sessions during this phase of the patient's rehabilitation?

  A. Personal hygiene tasks using cueing to minimize outbursts

  B. Simple life skills tasks using compensatory cognitive strategies

  C. Self-feeding program using assistive devices and hand-over-hand cues

  D. Sensory stimulation program using graded and consistent stimuli

8. Which activity represents an effective sensory-based approach for improving tolerance to touch for a 5-year-old child who has mild tactile defensiveness?

  A. Swinging in a prone position in a net swing

  B. Spinning in a seated position on a scooter board

  C. Playing with a feather boa during a dress-up activity

  D. Log-rolling to snuggly wrap the body in a blanket

NBCOT® Study Guide for the OTR Certification Examination

NOTES

9. An adolescent client who has a moderate traumatic brain injury is participating in an initial BADL session. During the session, the client frequently seeks physical contact with the OTR. What action should the OTR take in response to the client's behavior?

A. Provide the client with alternate methods for obtaining proprioceptive input.

B. Advise the client of generally accepted distances for personal space.

C. Inform the client that the behavior is inappropriate and set reasonable limits.

10. An inpatient has a TBI and is functioning at Level V (Confused-inappropriate) on the Rancho Los Amigos scale. Which approach would be **MOST EFFECTIVE** for facilitating the patient's success with grooming tasks based on the patient's current cognitive level?

A. Provide repeated verbal instructions until the patient completes the task.

B. Use forward chaining techniques if the patient is distracted from the task.

C. Demonstrate a portion of the activity then ask the patient to return demonstration.

D. Give one-step instructions and hand-over-hand cueing throughout the task.

11. A client with schizophrenia is being discharged from a long term care facility to a group home. The client is independent with self-care and enjoys cooking, but requires assistance during meal preparation tasks due to a disregard for safety. The group home staff is willing to assist the client during meal preparation activities. What recommendations should the OTR provide the staff to maximize the client's participation in meal preparation?

A. Allow the client to prepare meals using recipes familiar to the client.

B. Limit the client's meal preparation activities to pre-made microwaveable meals.

C. Provide step-by-step verbal cues throughout a cooking task.

190

Domain 3: Multiple Choice Sample Questions

12. A client who is legally blind reports having difficulty locating grooming items in the bathroom every morning, resulting in being late for work. Which recommendation should the OTR suggest for improving the client's occupational performance?

A. Complete the majority of bathing and grooming tasks the night before.

B. Wake-up at least one hour earlier so that grooming will not be rushed.

C. Organize items in the bathroom so that there is a specific place for each item.

D. Discuss with the employer options for implementing a later start time at work.

13. A client who has low vision is learning methods for handling money when shopping for personal items in a store. The client is able to identify coins using touch, but wants suggestions for handling paper monetary denominations. Which recommendation should be included as part of the **INITIAL** intervention with this client?

A. Use a consistent method of folding individual denominations.

B. Pay for purchases using a bank debit card instead of paper money.

C. Consistently place money denominations in a specific order in a wallet.

191

NBCOT® Study Guide for the OTR Certification Examination

NOTES

14. An inpatient with relapsing-remitting multiple sclerosis has been making steady progress during morning BADL. For the past 3 mornings, the patient reportedly completed the morning self-care routine independently. During a reevaluation of BADL, the patient becomes physically exhausted while dressing after taking a shower and asks to return to bed. In addition to talking with the patient about energy conservation, what action should the OTR take based on the patient's physical response?

A. Ask the patient to identify the BADL tasks that typically take the most time to complete.

B. Talk with the patient about pacing self-care tasks throughout the day.

C. Teach the patient to monitor symptoms while incorporating appropriate rest-activity ratios into self-care tasks.

D. Advise the patient to complete self-care while seated upright in bed in order to reduce energy expenditure.

15. An OTR is teaching medication management strategies to an older adult client who has diabetes and low vision. One of the intervention goals for the client is to increase compliance in adhering to the prescribed medication regimen. In addition to teaching the client to combine the medication schedule with familiar ADL routines, what would be the **MOST EFFECTIVE** approach in improving medication adherence in this client?

A. Establish a habit of counting the remaining pills in each bottle.

B. Dedicate set periods of time in the day for taking medication.

C. Trial several types of adaptive aides for medication management.

16. Which of the following joint protection techniques should a client with rheumatoid arthritis use when completing kitchen tasks?

A. Grasp cookware with the fingertips.

B. Transport items using a wheeled cart.

C. Stir foods with weighted long-handled utensils.

D. Twist a jar lid open with the least affected hand.

192

Domain 3: Multiple Choice Sample Questions

17. A resident of a skilled nursing facility has Wernicke's aphasia secondary to a left CVA and is frustrated during intervention sessions. Which communication techniques should the OTR use to limit the resident's frustration?

    A. Alphabet and low tech communication boards

    B. Sign language and written instructions

    C. Hand gestures and tactile cues

18. A service competent OTR is completing a feeding reevaluation with an inpatient who has hemiplegia secondary to a CVA 5 days ago. A screening indicates the patient's cognitive and perceptual skills are intact. Observation during mealtime and results of a video fluoroscopy study show the patient has decreased tongue mobility, hypotonicity of the cheek and lips on the affected side, slowed swallow response, and a wet gurgly voice quality after swallowing several bites of food. Which types of food and liquid should the OTR recommend for the patient to reduce risk of aspiration?

    A. Pureed meat and vegetables and honey-thickened liquids

    B. Moistened soft foods and thin flavored liquids

    C. Normal foods cut in small pieces and nectar-thickened liquids

NBCOT® Study Guide for the OTR Certification Examination

NOTES

19. An OTR is completing a feeding evaluation of a 4-year-old child who has mild hypotonia, immature oral motor control, and oral hypersensitivity. The child sits in a standard dining chair during meals and requires moderate to maximum assistance from a caregiver for feeding. When attempting to swallow food the child hyperextends the neck, elevates both shoulders, and has poor lip closure. What information should the OTR include in the **INITIAL** caregiver instructions based on this observation?

A. Methods for using cryotherapy to stimulate facial muscles prior to feeding the child

B. Handling techniques for facilitating full forward neck flexion during feeding

C. Adaptive positioning techniques for promoting trunk alignment

D. Neuromuscular facilitation techniques for promoting head and trunk stability

20. A 12-month-old infant has moderate hypotonia resulting in developmental delay and poor oral motor control. Which position is recommended for this infant for promoting oral motor function during feeding?

A. Slightly reclined with trunk fully supported and the neck and head at midline

B. Fully upright in sitting with the head and neck resting in slight extension

C. Seated upright in a standard high chair with a lap tray positioned close to the chest

D. Semi-reclined in a position of comfort on a soft beanbag chair

194

Domain 3: Multiple Choice Sample Questions

21. A student in the first grade has moderate hypotonicity resulting in poor oral motor control. One of the student's goals is to be able to "eat the same foods as the other kids" at lunchtime in the cafeteria at school. Currently, the student requires moderate assistance when eating and eats a soft diet. What should be the **INITIAL** focus of intervention for progressing toward this goal?

    A. Asking the student to identify specific food preferences from the cafeteria menu

    B. Determining which cafeteria foods have the textures the student can eat

    C. Identifying seating and positioning options for the student in the cafeteria

    D. Providing the student with assistive devices to use when eating in the cafeteria

22. A 5-year-old child with Down syndrome and delayed motor skill development is learning to self-toilet. Over the past several months, the child has made significant progress and is now able to complete age-appropriate toileting tasks, with the exception of independently pulling up pants. Based on the child's current abilities, what is the **MOST EFFECTIVE** technique to include in the intervention plan to support this child's success with toileting?

    A. Read a social story to reinforce successful daily bowel and bladder routines.

    B. Develop a pictorial reward chart using a system of positive reinforcement.

    C. Use preferred games to increase upper extremity strength and coordination.

NBCOT® Study Guide for the OTR Certification Examination

NOTES

23. A client had an open reduction external fixation of a distal radius fracture several days ago. Evaluation results indicate moderate swelling of the hand, decreased active ROM of the digits, and protective posturing of the involved arm close to the chest at all times. Which intervention would be **MOST BENEFICIAL** to include in sessions during this initial phase of the client's recovery?

A. Education about proper positioning in a standard pouch sling to minimize swelling

B. Exercises to promote capsular gliding and ROM of the shoulder of the affected arm

C. Static splinting to prevent MCP joint collateral ligament tightness

D. Use of a dry whirlpool modality to manage edema of the affected hand

24. A client has an upper extremity flexor synergy secondary to a CVA. The client has developed a severe soft-tissue contracture of the affected elbow. Which method would be **MOST EFFECTIVE** for increasing soft tissue length for improving elbow extension?

A. Provide submaximal stretch to the contracted soft tissue for prolonged periods of time.

B. Perform passive ROM to the affected elbow with high-load stretch for brief periods of time.

C. Apply a long-arm cast while the affected elbow is being stretched to the terminal end range.

196

Domain 3: Multiple Choice Sample Questions

25. A client sustained a distal radius fracture of the dominant upper extremity 6 weeks ago. A short arm cast was applied on the day of injury and was removed one day ago. The client holds the affected arm close to the chest in a protected position due to pain, which the client rates as 6 out of 10 using a visual analog scale. The hand and forearm are moderately edematous. The client is able to flex the fingers to within one inch (2.54 cm) from each fingertip to the distal palmar crease. The client refused to move the wrist due to pain. Which intervention should be a priority to include as part of the treatment plan during the **INITIAL** phase of the client's rehabilitation?

    A. Fabrication of a dynamic finger flexion orthotic

    B. Passive ROM exercises for the wrist and fingers

    C. Manual edema mobilization of the affected extremity

    D. Gentle stress loading exercises as tolerated

26. An OTR is providing a home program to a client who has stage 1 complex regional pain syndrome. What information should be included in the home program to **MOST EFFECTIVELY** help the client with symptom management?

    A. Pictures illustrating passive ROM exercises for each joint of the affected hand

    B. Recommendations for one-handed activities to protect the affected hand during ADL

    C. Techniques for elevating the hand and completing active ROM exercises

    D. Instructions for incorporating energy conservation into daily tasks

197

NOTES

27. A client is developing pitting edema of the hand secondary to flaccid hemiplegia. What should the OTR teach the client and caregiver as part of the **INITIAL** intervention for managing this client's edema?

A. Methods for using elasticized compression wraps for the digits and hand

B. Importance of proper upper extremity positioning and elevation

C. Procedures for providing retrograde massage of the upper extremity

D. Techniques for completing passive ROM exercises of the digits

28. A patient has moderate flexor spasticity in the dominant upper extremity secondary to a TBI. During a self-care session, the OTR plans to inhibit the patient's muscle tone prior to encouraging active movement. Which method would be **MOST EFFECTIVE** to include as part of the intervention session?

A. Positioning the patient's shoulder in abduction and external rotation during the task

B. Applying resistance to the patient's maximally contracted biceps at the start of the session

C. Administering a light, quick stretch to the patient's triceps when reaching forward

D. Applying firm, prolonged manual pressure across the patient's biceps tendon prior to a BADL task

Domain 3: Multiple Choice Sample Questions

29. An OTR is working with a client who has type 1 complex regional pain syndrome (CRPS) affecting functional use of the dominant upper extremity. Pain interferes with the ability to complete ADL and tasks that involve reaching, lifting, and carrying. The client reports that pain fluctuates in intensity, but does not decrease below a 6/10 on the analogue pain scale, even after taking analgesic medication. The OTR notes that the client's affected upper extremity is cold to the touch and there are signs of muscle atrophy. Based on these results, what would be the **MOST EFFECTIVE** intervention for the OTR to include in sessions with this client?

    A. Apply ice or a cooling agent prior to initiating a therapeutic exercise program.

    B. Recommend immobilizing the affected limb in a pouch sling for 1-2 weeks.

    C. Perform active ROM exercises and functional activities that promote weight bearing.

30. An OTR is teaching stand-pivot transfers to a client who has Stage 2 Parkinson's disease and uses a wheelchair for mobility. After instructing the client to properly position the chair in relation to the transfer surface, and asking the client to lock the wheelchair brakes, what should the OTR ask the client to do **NEXT**?

    A. Scoot the hips forward to the edge of the wheelchair.

    B. Come to standing by pushing up on the wheelchair arm rests.

    C. Rock forward while reaching toward the transfer surface.

    D. Position both feet perpendicular to the transfer surface.

NBCOT® Study Guide for the OTR Certification Examination

NOTES

31. A client with stage 2 Parkinson's disease is preparing to move from sitting on a tub transfer bench in the bathtub to standing up at a walker placed outside the bathtub. Which method would be effective for the client to use at the start of the transfer?

A. Rocking rhythmically back and forth on the bench a few times

B. Using a towel to quickly rub the larger muscles of the thighs

C. Bearing weight through both arms by pressing down on the bench

D. Pulling forward on the grab bar mounted to the bathroom wall

32. An OTR, who works in the hospital setting, is starting an ADL session at the bedside of an inpatient who has mitochondrial encephalopathy and flaccid hemiplegia. The patient is lying supine in bed and is wearing a prefabricated foot drop orthosis on the affected lower extremity. What is the **PRIMARY** purpose for having the patient wear a foot drop orthosis?

A. To increase circulation in the lower extremity and prevent thromboembolism

B. To provide stability when sitting on the edge of bed and during transfer training

C. To offer pressure relief while supporting the foot in a neutral position

33. An OTR is fabricating an orthotic for a client who has a claw-hand deformity secondary to an ulnar nerve injury several months ago. Which type of orthotic is indicated for this client?

A. Dorsal-based MCP joint blocking orthotic with a dynamic component to pull the fourth and fifth digit IP joints into extension

B. Low-profile dynamic orthotic that blocks hyperextension of the second through fifth digits and has an IP joint extension outrigger

C. Volar-based forearm and hand static orthotic that blocks MCP joint hyperextension while allowing IP joint motion

D. Hand-based orthotic that positions the fourth and fifth digits in 30o-40o of MCP joint flexion while allowing IP joint motion

200

Domain 3: Multiple Choice Sample Questions

34. What is the **PRIMARY** reason for recommending an air-filled wheelchair cushion to a client with a C_5 (ASIA A) spinal cord injury?

    A. To offer low daily maintenance needs

    B. To provide even relief from pressure

    C. To provide a stable base of support

35. An OTR is fabricating a static orthotic for a client who has a partial thickness burn to the dorsum of the hand. The primary purpose of the orthotic is to maintain the length of the MCP joint collateral ligaments. How should the MCP joints, IP joints and wrist be positioned in the orthotic to achieve this goal?

	MCP Joint	IP Joint Position	Wrist Position
A.	20°–30° Flexion	20°–25° Flexion	25°–30° Extension
B.	35°–45° Flexion	30°–40° Flexion	Neutral
C.	0° Extension	45°–60° Flexion	Neutral
D.	60°–70° Flexion	0°–5° Flexion	25°–30° Extension

NBCOT® Study Guide for the OTR Certification Examination

NOTES

36. A client has relapsing-remitting multiple sclerosis and recently transitioned from assisted ambulation to using a standard wheelchair for mobility. A recent onset of fatigue, upper extremity weakness, and back and neck discomfort is beginning to interfere with job performance. The client is employed as a magazine editor, and spends much of the day sitting in the wheelchair while working at the computer monitor positioned at eye level. The client wants to continue sitting in a wheelchair to avoid having to complete transfers when moving from the desk to other parts of the work area. Which modification would be **MOST BENEFICIAL** for this client?

A. Power scooter with padded seat and electric tilt-in-space control

B. Voice-controlled computer system and telephone headset

C. Solid seat insert, lumbar support and bilateral forearm supports

D. Deltoid aid and a split design computer keyboard

37. A school-based OTR is selecting seating alternatives for a student who has moderate hypotonia and has just transitioned to a full-day kindergarten program. The student uses a wheelchair for mobility and does not tolerate an upright sitting position throughout the school day. What type of positioning system would be **MOST BENEFICIAL** for this student?

A. Lightweight chair with reclining back and reverse wheel configuration

B. Corner chair with high lateral supports that can be placed on the floor

C. Dense foam lateral supports and gel cushion for the current wheelchair

D. Modular wheelchair with tilt-in-space feature in the mobility base

Domain 3: Multiple Choice Sample Questions

38. An inpatient had a total hip replacement 2 weeks ago. The OTR is discussing home set-up and seating options with the patient as part of the discharge instructions. What type of seat should the OTR recommend the patient sit on when watching television at home?

   A. Firm raised armchair with a wedge pillow roll between the cushion and back of the chair

   B. Cushioned, armless dining chair elevated on one inch (2.54 cm) high blocks

   C. Sofa with enough length to allow the patient to elevate both legs on the seat cushions

   D. Upholstered reclining chair with extra pillows to elevate the affected leg

39. An OTR is providing information about assistive devices to a client who has osteoarthritis of the first CMC joints of both hands. Which devices would be **MOST BENEFICIAL** for protecting these joints during meal preparation?

   A. Washable universal cuff, rocker knife with contoured handle, and wall-mounted jar opener

   B. Right-angled knife with ergonomic handle, over-stove mirror, and swivel serving utensils

   C. Mixing bowls with non-slip bottom, scoop dish, and cutting board with slicing guide

   D. Built-up utensils, adjustable bowl tipper, and mountable electric can opener

NBCOT® Study Guide for the OTR Certification Examination

NOTES

40. A resident recently was admitted to a long term care facility after having an intracerebral hemorrhage secondary to a ruptured aneurysm. Currently, the resident is able to verbalize basic needs, can follow simple one-step directions, and has minimal functional movement of all extremities. The resident wants to be able to change channels on the television independently but is unable to hold the remote control device or apply enough pressure on the buttons to activate the device. The OTR is choosing a switch-activated indirect selection device that will enable the resident to complete this task. Which type of switch is **OPTIMAL** to use with this device?

   A. Pneumatic switch

   B. Plate switch

   C. Pillow switch

41. An inpatient is recovering from partial and full thickness burns on the dominant upper extremity and has recently developed heterotopic ossification (HO) at the elbow. Prior to the onset of HO symptoms, the patient was independent with self-feeding. Now the patient uses only the non-dominant hand for holding utensils. Which assistive device would be **MOST BENEFICIAL** for improving the patient's functional abilities when eating?

   A. Universal cuff with elongated utensil

   B. Swivel spoon and elongated utensils

   C. Rocker knife with a built-up handle

   D. Mechanical feeder with supinator attachment

204

Domain 3: Multiple Choice Sample Questions

42. A client with a non-operable cerebellum tumor is participating in OT to increase independence with self-feeding. Which assistive devices should the client use to promote progress toward this goal?

    A. Suction plate and cup holder

    B. Side-cutting fork and rocker knife

    C. Plastic cup and lightweight utensils

    D. Universal cuff with mobile arm support

43. An OTR is selecting a new seating system for a college student who has cerebral palsy and uses a wheelchair for all functional mobility. The client has flexible asymmetrical postures including scoliosis, kyphosis, and pelvic obliquity. The student wants to be able to sit upright for 12-14 hours per day. Which custom seating system would **BEST** support progress toward this goal?

    A. Contoured

    B. Planar

    C. Modular

44. An inpatient in a rehabilitation facility is preparing for discharge to home. The patient has hemiplegia, uses a wheelchair for mobility and completes self-care independently with assistive devices. The patient's home bathroom has a standard bathtub and a separate walk-in shower with a safety glass door and a 6-inch (15.24 cm) high doorsill. Both the shower and the tub have safety grab bars. Which piece of durable medical equipment would be **MOST BENEFICIAL** for this patient to use at home?

    A. Padded transfer bench with swivel seat for the bathtub

    B. Shower chair that can be used in the shower or bathtub

    C. Plastic bath chair with armrests and accessory caddy

    D. Transfer board and plastic shower stool with a contoured seat

NBCOT® Study Guide for the OTR Certification Examination

NOTES

45. A client with fibromyalgia reports hand pain and stiffness make it difficult to grasp a standard knife and fork during meals. Which assistive device would be **MOST BENEFICIAL** for improving the client's functional abilities when eating?

    A. Utensils with built-up handles

    B. Rocker knife and plate with raised sides

    C. Universal cuff with wrist support

    D. Lightweight utensils with non-slip grips

46. A client has an open wound on the dorsum of the dominant hand. The medical record indicates mechanical debridement to promote wound healing. Which of the following wound management options represents mechanical debridement?

    A. Wound dressings that keep the wound moist to trap the body's natural enzymes.

    B. Topical enzymes on the wound to selectively remove necrotic tissue and debris.

    C. Whirlpool as a preparatory activity to remove dead tissue from the wound.

47. A home health client had surgery for a total hip arthroplasty 2 weeks ago. During an ADL session, the OTR notes that the area near to the surgical site is warm to the touch and has new erythema. The wound has purulent drainage and a foul odor. Which of the following conditions is **TYPICALLY** associated with these reported symptoms?

    A. Venous stasis

    B. Wound infection

    C. Tissue necrosis

206

Domain 3: Multiple Choice Sample Questions

48. An OTR is providing recommendations to the caregiver of a client who has moderate severe cognitive decline secondary to Alzheimer's disease. The caregiver reports the client wanders throughout the home at night trying to find the bathroom. On several occasions the client has walked out the front door of the home thinking it was the door leading into the bathroom. Which environmental adaptation should the OTR recommend to the caregiver based on this report?

   A. Use movement sensitive audio-visual assistive technology.

   B. Place a commode chair in the client's bedroom.

   C. Install a video monitor in several locations in the house.

   D. Keep hallway and bedroom lights on at night.

49. Which of the following environmental adaptations will improve safety during meal preparation for a client who has low vision?

   A. Installing a microwave that has preprogrammed cooking options

   B. Placing tactile markings on the operating features of appliances

   C. Arranging items on the pantry and cabinet shelves in alphabetical order

   D. Using large-sized bowls and pots for mixing and stove-top cooking

50. Which of the following is the **BEST** example of a primary objective for using the universal design for learning (UDL) principles with students who attend a middle school?

   A. To provide environmental design principles to adapt the classrooms and other learning spaces to include students who have a disability.

   B. To provide all students in the school the ability to learn and the opportunity to demonstrate academic performance abilities.

   C. To recommend desk heights, ergonomic computer workstations and adapted play environments that benefit most students in the school.

207

NBCOT® Study Guide for the OTR Certification Examination

Answer Key

Domain 3 Sample Items

Item Number	Key	Item Number	Key
1.	C	26.	C
2.	A	27.	B
3.	A	28.	D
4.	D	29.	C
5.	C	30.	A
6.	A	31.	A
7.	D	32.	C
8.	D	33.	D
9.	C	34.	B
10.	D	35.	D
11.	C	36.	C
12.	C	37.	C
13.	A	38.	A
14.	C	39.	D
15.	C	40.	B
16.	B	41.	B
17.	C	42.	A
18.	A	43.	A
19.	C	44.	A
20.	A	45.	A
21.	C	46.	C
22.	C	47.	B
23.	B	48.	A
24.	A	49.	B
25.	C	50.	B

NBCOT® Study Guide for the OTR Certification Examination

Multiple Choice Answers, Rationales, and References

1. A high school student has spastic diplegia and cognitive delay. The student self-propels a wheelchair and requires moderate assistance for functional transfers. The student has been the target of peer-bullying in school and has been attending OT to help increase social participation. One of the student's goals is to attend a dance being planned by the dance committee of student volunteers. During a role-play session, the student tells the OTR, "I really want to go to the dance, but I am worried that I won't fit in." Which recommendation should the OTR suggest for addressing the student's concern?

    A. Ask the committee to recruit parent volunteers willing to attend the dance as facilitators of social inclusion.

    B. Require the committee leader to provide inclusion training for all students at a school assembly prior to the dance.

    C. Have the student partner with the committee to select a music playlist for the dance that includes modified line dances.

Correct Answer: C

RATIONALE:
This activity supports the student in social participation with peers both during the planning phase and at the school dance.

Reference:
Case-Smith, J., & O'Brien, J. C. (2015). *Occupational therapy for children and adolescents* (7th ed., pp. 122, 325, 367). St. Louis, MO: Mosby Elsevier.

NBCOT® Study Guide for the OTR Certification Examination

NOTES

2. An OTR plans to use a sensorimotor approach to improve the handwriting skills of a 6-year-old student who has a mild learning disability. The student maintains a very tight grip on a pencil when writing, consistently uses a palmar grasp when holding the pencil, and has directional confusion when forming letters. Which activity would be effective to include as part of the **INITIAL** intervention when using this approach?

A. Painting letters using a wide-barrel brush on paper attached to an upright easel

B. Rolling out colored modeling dough and making cookie cutter shapes on a tabletop

C. Using spring-opening blunt-edge scissors to cut out geometric paper shapes

D. Providing hand-over-hand assistance during writing assignments

Correct Answer: A

RATIONALE:
An upright orientation helps to decrease directional confusion, provides proprioceptive input for proximal control, and promotes a more mature grasp pattern.

Reference:
Case-Smith, J., & O'Brien, J. C. (2015). *Occupational therapy for children and adolescents* (7th ed., pp. 513-518). St. Louis, MO: Mosby Elsevier.

Domain 3: Multiple Choice Answers, Rationales, and References

3. An inpatient had a TBI one month ago and is functioning at Level VII (Automatic-appropriate) on the Rancho Los Amigos scale. Currently, the patient is able to follow two-step instructions and attends to a familiar task for up to 15 minutes at a time. The patient wants to return home to resume homemaking roles. One of the patient's short-term goals is to independently bake cookies for a family member's upcoming birthday. How should the activity be graded to support the patient's successful participation in this task?

NOTES

A. **Have the patient prepare cookies using slice and bake packaged cookie dough.**

B. Provide the patient with a recipe of ingredients for mixing and baking cookies.

C. Have the patient prepare cookies using a boxed cookie mix with pre-measured ingredients.

D. Mix the ingredients together and have the patient drop the cookies onto the cookie sheet.

Correct Answer: A

RATIONALE:
This option aligns with the patient's current functional level and short-term goal to independently bake cookies.

Reference:
Pendleton, H. M., & Schultz-Krohn, W. (Eds.). (2018). *Pedretti's occupational therapy: Practice skills for the physical dysfunction* (8th ed., pp. 713-717, 847-848, 851-852). St. Louis, MO: Mosby Elsevier.

NBCOT® Study Guide for the OTR Certification Examination

NOTES

4. A 5-year-old child sustained partial and full thickness burns on the volar surfaces of both wrists and forearms 3 months ago. Although the child wears pressure garments, scarring across the wrist is limiting wrist mobility. Which activity could be graded to **MOST EFFECTIVELY** help with increasing the child's wrist motion?

    A. Tossing a bean bag at a target placed at varying distances from the child

    B. Moving a parachute up and down during parachute games with peers

    C. Bouncing a medium-size therapy ball from one hand to the other

    D. **Creeping on hands and knees through a play tunnel maze**

Correct Answer: D

RATIONALE:

Using activity analysis methods, it is evident that this option provides opportunity for weight bearing with the wrists in extension. This will assist in elongating the soft tissue that is inhibiting motion.

References:
Case-Smith, J., & O'Brien, J. C. (2015). *Occupational therapy for children and adolescents* (7th ed., pp. 853, 856). St. Louis, MO: Mosby Elsevier.

Pendleton, H. M., & Schultz-Krohn, W. (Eds.). (2018). *Pedretti's occupational therapy: Practice skills for the physical dysfunction* (8th ed., pp. 713-715, 717-719). St. Louis, MO: Mosby Elsevier.

214

Domain 3: Multiple Choice Answers, Rationales, and References

5. An inpatient sustained a complete T_5 spinal cord injury one month ago and has been in the intensive care unit on extended bed-rest. The OTR recently initiated a program of graded bed mobility in preparation for beginning transfer training. The patient is now able to sit in bed with the head of the bed elevated to 45° for one-hour intervals without experiencing any dizziness. Which position is safest for the patient to be placed in **NEXT**?

    A. Upright in a standard wheelchair with close monitoring

    B. Upright on a tilt-table at 90° while wearing an abdominal binder and elastic stockings

    C. Seated in a semi-reclining wheelchair with legs elevated

    D. Seated on the edge of the bed with both legs unsupported and knees flexed to 90°

Correct Answer: C

RATIONALE:
To avoid adverse postural reactions, changes to the patient's position should be incremental and gradual. Positioning the patient's upper body in a more upright position while keeping the legs elevated reduces the risk of orthostatic hypotension.

References:
Radomski, M. V., & Trombly Latham, C. A. (Eds.). (2014). *Occupational therapy for physical dysfunction* (7th ed., pp. 1174-1175). Philadelphia, PA: Lippincott Williams & Wilkins.

Smith-Gabai, H., & Holm, S. (Eds.). (2017). *Occupational therapy in acute care* (2nd ed., pp. 256-257). Bethesda, MD: AOTA Press.

NBCOT® Study Guide for the OTR Certification Examination

NOTES

6. A patient with a borderline personality disorder was admitted to an inpatient facility 4 days ago secondary to an exacerbation of suicidal and self-mutilating behavior. The patient's condition is now stable and the patient is functioning at Allen Cognitive Level 5 (Exploratory Actions). The patient reports being overwhelmed by a new personal relationship, experiencing job dissatisfaction, and feeling a lack of control in most daily situations. Which intervention would be **MOST BENEFICIAL** for addressing problems in performance skills and patterns secondary to the concurrent symptoms?

   A. **Coping skills groups that address a variety of adaptive strategies**

   B. One-on-one sessions to encourage the patient to contract for safety

   C. Daily self-care sessions that focus on structured BADL

   D. Structured one-step craft activities to promote successful outcomes

Correct Answer: A

RATIONALE:
Patients functioning at this cognitive level typically are able to use problem solving and inductive reasoning. This type of group provides the patient with opportunities to learn adaptive coping strategies that can be used in a variety of situations relative to the patient's typical performance skills and patterns.

References:
Bonder, B. R. (2015). *Psychopathology and function* (5th ed., pp. 385-386). Thorofare, NJ: SLACK, Inc.

Brown, C., & Stoffel V. C. (2011). *Occupational therapy in mental health: A vision for participation* (pp. 143-153). Philadelphia, PA: F.A. Davis Company.

Domain 3: Multiple Choice Answers, Rationales, and References

7. An inpatient had a TBI 3 weeks ago and is functioning at Level II (Generalized response) on the Rancho Los Amigos scale. Which intervention should be a priority to include in treatment sessions during this phase of the patient's rehabilitation?

    A. Personal hygiene tasks using cueing to minimize outbursts

    B. Simple life skills tasks using compensatory cognitive strategies

    C. Self-feeding program using assistive devices and hand-over-hand cues

    D. Sensory stimulation program using graded and consistent stimuli

Correct Answer: D

RATIONALE:
A patient who is functioning at Level II (Generalized response) on the Rancho Los Amigos scale responds non-purposefully and inconsistently to stimuli. A sensory stimulation program is part of a comprehensive intervention plan during this phase of rehabilitation.

Reference:
Pendleton, H. M., & Schultz-Krohn, W. (Eds.). (2018). *Pedretti's occupational therapy: Practice skills for the physical dysfunction* (8th ed., pp. 847-848, 855-856). St. Louis, MO: Mosby Elsevier.

8. Which activity represents an effective sensory-based approach for improving tolerance to touch for a 5-year-old child who has mild tactile defensiveness?

    A. Swinging in a prone position in a net swing

    B. Spinning in a seated position on a scooter board

    C. Playing with a feather boa during a dress-up activity

    D. Log-rolling to snuggly wrap the body in a blanket

Correct Answer: D

RATIONALE:
Deep touch stimuli is typically more tolerable than light touch in the presence of tactile defensiveness.

Reference:
Case-Smith, J., & O'Brien, J. C. (2015). *Occupational therapy for children and adolescents* (7th ed., pp. 268-269). St. Louis, MO: Mosby Elsevier.

NBCOT® Study Guide for the OTR Certification Examination

NOTES

9. An adolescent client who has a moderate traumatic brain injury is participating in an initial BADL session. During the session, the client frequently seeks physical contact with the OTR. What action should the OTR take in response to the client's behavior?

   A. Provide the client with alternate methods for obtaining proprioceptive input.

   B. Advise the client of generally accepted distances for personal space.

   C. **Inform the client that the behavior is inappropriate and set reasonable limits.**

Correct Answer: C

RATIONALE:
Establishing clear and reasonable limits is an important part of a behavior management plan.

Reference:
Pendleton, H. M., & Schultz-Krohn, W. (Eds.). (2018). *Pedretti's occupational therapy: Practice skills for the physical dysfunction* (8th ed., pp. 854-855). St. Louis, MO: Mosby Elsevier.

218

Domain 3: Multiple Choice Answers, Rationales, and References

10. An inpatient has a TBI and is functioning at Level V (Confused-inappropriate) on the Rancho Los Amigos scale. Which approach would be **MOST EFFECTIVE** for facilitating the patient's success with grooming tasks based on the patient's current cognitive level?

A. Provide repeated verbal instructions until the patient completes the task.

B. Use forward chaining techniques if the patient is distracted from the task.

C. Demonstrate a portion of the activity then ask the patient to return demonstration.

D. Give one-step instructions and hand-over-hand cueing throughout the task.

Correct Answer: D

RATIONALE:
Patients at this level of function have most success during simplified and highly structured tasks. Providing one-step instructions and hand-over-hand assistance supports the patient's participation with the grooming task.

Reference:
Radomski, M. V., & Trombly Latham, C. A. (Eds.). (2014). *Occupational therapy for physical dysfunction* (7th ed., p. 1059). Philadelphia, PA: Lippincott Williams & Wilkins.

NBCOT® Study Guide for the OTR Certification Examination

NOTES

11. A client with schizophrenia is being discharged from a long term care facility to a group home. The client is independent with self-care and enjoys cooking, but requires assistance during meal preparation tasks due to a disregard for safety. The group home staff is willing to assist the client during meal preparation activities. What recommendations should the OTR provide the staff to maximize the client's participation in meal preparation?

A. Allow the client to prepare meals using recipes familiar to the client.

B. Limit the client's meal preparation activities to pre-made microwaveable meals.

C. Provide step-by-step verbal cues throughout a cooking task.

Correct Answer: C

RATIONALE:
Providing the group home staff with step-by-step verbal cues will promote carryover of the client's skills into everyday meal preparation routines.

Reference:
Cara, E., & MacRae, A. (2013). *Psychosocial occupational therapy: An evolving practice* (3rd ed., pp. 201, 212-214). Clifton Park, NY: Delmar Cengage Learning.

Domain 3: Multiple Choice Answers, Rationales, and References

12. A client who is legally blind reports having difficulty locating grooming items in the bathroom every morning, resulting in being late for work. Which recommendation should the OTR suggest for improving the client's occupational performance?

 A. Complete the majority of bathing and grooming tasks the night before.

 B. Wake-up at least one hour earlier so that grooming will not be rushed.

 C. Organize items in the bathroom so that there is a specific place for each item.

 D. Discuss with the employer options for implementing a later start time at work.

Correct Answer: C

RATIONALE:
This option most closely aligns with the client's current habits and routines.

Reference:
Pendleton, H. M., & Schultz-Krohn, W. (Eds.). (2018). *Pedretti's occupational therapy: Practice skills for the physical dysfunction* (8th ed., pp. 7, 223). St. Louis, MO: Mosby Elsevier.

NBCOT® Study Guide for the OTR Certification Examination

NOTES

13. A client who has low vision is learning methods for handling money when shopping for personal items in a store. The client is able to identify coins using touch, but wants suggestions for handling paper monetary denominations. Which recommendation should be included as part of the **INITIAL** intervention with this client?

A. **Use a consistent method of folding individual denominations.**

B. Pay for purchases using a bank debit card instead of paper money.

C. Consistently place money denominations in a specific order in a wallet.

Correct Answer: A

RATIONALE:
An adaptive strategy that will support independence in money management in a client who has low vision is to use a consistent method for folding each individual denomination.

Reference:
Pendleton, H. M., & Schultz-Krohn, W. (Eds.). (2018). *Pedretti's occupational therapy: Practice skills for the physical dysfunction* (8th ed., p. 224). St. Louis, MO: Mosby Elsevier.

Domain 3: Multiple Choice Answers, Rationales, and References

14. An inpatient with relapsing-remitting multiple sclerosis has been making steady progress during morning BADL. For the past 3 mornings, the patient reportedly completed the morning self-care routine independently. During a reevaluation of BADL, the patient becomes physically exhausted while dressing after taking a shower and asks to return to bed. In addition to talking with the patient about energy conservation, what action should the OTR take based on the patient's physical response?

A. Ask the patient to identify the BADL tasks that typically take the most time to complete.

B. Talk with the patient about pacing self-care tasks throughout the day.

C. Teach the patient to monitor symptoms while incorporating appropriate rest-activity ratios into self-care tasks.

D. Advise the patient to complete self-care while seated upright in bed in order to reduce energy expenditure.

Correct Answer: C

RATIONALE:
Monitoring symptoms and using appropriate work-rest ratios will minimize the likelihood of becoming physically exhausted.

Reference:
Pendleton, H. M., & Schultz-Krohn, W. (Eds.). (2018). *Pedretti's occupational therapy: Practice skills for the physical dysfunction* (8th ed., pp. 889-893). St. Louis, MO: Mosby Elsevier.

NBCOT® Study Guide for the OTR Certification Examination

NOTES

15. An OTR is teaching medication management strategies to an older adult client who has diabetes and low vision. One of the intervention goals for the client is to increase compliance in adhering to the prescribed medication regimen. In addition to teaching the client to combine the medication schedule with familiar ADL routines, what would be the **MOST EFFECTIVE** approach in improving medication adherence in this client?

   A. Establish a habit of counting the remaining pills in each bottle.

   B. Dedicate set periods of time in the day for taking medication.

   C. **Trial several types of adaptive aides for medication management.**

Correct Answer: C

RATIONALE:
Trialing several types of adaptive aides for medication management allows for the development of a client-centered recommendation.

Reference:
Pendleton, H. M., & Schultz-Krohn, W. (Eds.). (2018). *Pedretti's occupational therapy: Practice skills for the physical dysfunction* (8th ed., pp. 7, 223). St. Louis, MO: Mosby Elsevier.

16. Which of the following joint protection techniques should a client with rheumatoid arthritis use when completing kitchen tasks?

   A. Grasp cookware with the fingertips.

   B. **Transport items using a wheeled cart.**

   C. Stir foods with weighted long-handled utensils.

   D. Twist a jar lid open with the least affected hand.

Correct Answer: B

RATIONALE:
Using a wheeled cart to transport items from one area of the kitchen to another minimizes stress on small finger joints.

Reference:
Pendleton, H. M., & Schultz-Krohn, W. (Eds.). (2018). *Pedretti's occupational therapy: Practice skills for the physical dysfunction* (8th ed., pp. 966-968). St. Louis, MO: Mosby Elsevier.

17. A resident of a skilled nursing facility has Wernicke's aphasia secondary to a left CVA and is frustrated during intervention sessions. Which communication techniques should the OTR use to limit the resident's frustration?

    A. Alphabet and low tech communication boards

    B. Sign language and written instructions

    C. Hand gestures and tactile cues

Correct Answer: C

RATIONALE:
Using hand gestures and tactile cues will support a resident who has Wernicke's aphasia, difficulty comprehending spoken and written words, to understand the intention of the activity during intervention sessions.

Reference:
Gillen, G. (2016). *Stroke rehabilitation: A function-based approach* (4th ed., p.683). St. Louis, MO: Elsevier.

NBCOT® Study Guide for the OTR Certification Examination

NOTES

18. A service competent OTR is completing a feeding reevaluation with an inpatient who has hemiplegia secondary to a CVA 5 days ago. A screening indicates the patient's cognitive and perceptual skills are intact. Observation during mealtime and results of a video fluoroscopy study show the patient has decreased tongue mobility, hypotonicity of the cheek and lips on the affected side, slowed swallow response, and a wet gurgly voice quality after swallowing several bites of food. Which types of food and liquid should the OTR recommend for the patient to reduce risk of aspiration?

A. **Pureed meat and vegetables and honey-thickened liquids**

B. Moistened soft foods and thin flavored liquids

C. Normal foods cut in small pieces and nectar-thickened liquids

Correct Answer: A

RATIONALE:
The clinical presentation of this client warrants the recommendation of pureed food and honey-thickened liquids.

Reference:
Radomski, M. V., & Trombly Latham, C. A. (Eds.). (2014). *Occupational therapy for physical dysfunction* (7th ed., pp. 1338, 1341-1343). Philadelphia, PA: Lippincott Williams & Wilkins.

Domain 3: Multiple Choice Answers, Rationales, and References

19. An OTR is completing a feeding evaluation of a 4-year-old child who has mild hypotonia, immature oral motor control, and oral hypersensitivity. The child sits in a standard dining chair during meals and requires moderate to maximum assistance from a caregiver for feeding. When attempting to swallow food the child hyperextends the neck, elevates both shoulders, and has poor lip closure. What information should the OTR include in the **INITIAL** caregiver instructions based on this observation?

    A. Methods for using cryotherapy to stimulate facial muscles prior to feeding the child

    B. Handling techniques for facilitating full forward neck flexion during feeding

    C. Adaptive positioning techniques for promoting trunk alignment

    D. Neuromuscular facilitation techniques for promoting head and trunk stability

Correct Answer: C

RATIONALE:
Positioning and postural alignment impact oral motor control. The OTR should evaluate the child's sitting position during mealtimes and recommend specific feeding positions and positioning devices.

Reference:
Case-Smith, J., & O'Brien, J. C. (2015). *Occupational therapy for children and adolescents* (7th ed., pp. 400-402). St. Louis, MO: Mosby Elsevier.

NBCOT® Study Guide for the OTR Certification Examination

NOTES

20. A 12-month-old infant has moderate hypotonia resulting in developmental delay and poor oral motor control. Which position is recommended for this infant for promoting oral motor function during feeding?

A. **Slightly reclined with trunk fully supported and the neck and head at midline**

B. Fully upright in sitting with the head and neck resting in slight extension

C. Seated upright in a standard high chair with a lap tray positioned close to the chest

D. Semi-reclined in a position of comfort on a soft beanbag chair

Correct Answer: A

RATIONALE:
Improving postural alignment and stability helps promote oral motor function.

Reference:
Case-Smith, J., & O'Brien, J. C. (2015). *Occupational therapy for children and adolescents* (7th ed., pp. 400-402). St. Louis, MO: Mosby Elsevier.

Domain 3: Multiple Choice Answers, Rationales, and References

21. A student in the first grade has moderate hypotonicity resulting in poor oral motor control. One of the student's goals is to be able to "eat the same foods as the other kids" at lunchtime in the cafeteria at school. Currently, the student requires moderate assistance when eating and eats a soft diet. What should be the **INITIAL** focus of intervention for progressing toward this goal?

    A. Asking the student to identify specific food preferences from the cafeteria menu

    B. Determining which cafeteria foods have the textures the student can eat

    C. Identifying seating and positioning options for the student in the cafeteria

    D. Providing the student with assistive devices to use when eating in the cafeteria

Correct Answer: C

RATIONALE:
The first step in supporting this student to achieve the stated goal is to ensure that the student's positioning needs have been met and that the features of the environment are optimal to support the student's success.

Reference:
Case-Smith, J., & O'Brien, J. C. (2015). *Occupational therapy for children and adolescents* (7th ed., pp. 398-400). St. Louis, MO: Mosby Elsevier.

NBCOT® Study Guide for the OTR Certification Examination

NOTES

22. A 5-year-old child with Down syndrome and delayed motor skill development is learning to self-toilet. Over the past several months, the child has made significant progress and is now able to complete age-appropriate toileting tasks, with the exception of independently pulling up pants. Based on the child's current abilities, what is the **MOST EFFECTIVE** technique to include in the intervention plan to support this child's success with toileting?

A. Read a social story to reinforce successful daily bowel and bladder routines.

B. Develop a pictorial reward chart using a system of positive reinforcement.

C. **Use preferred games to increase upper extremity strength and coordination.**

Correct Answer: C

RATIONALE:

Down syndrome is associated with hypotonia and delayed motor development. Using play occupations such as games will support this child in developing the motor skills and strength needed to support progress toward independence in toileting.

Reference:
Case-Smith, J., & O'Brien, J. C. (2015). *Occupational therapy for children and adolescents* (7th ed., pp. 224-225). St. Louis, MO: Mosby Elsevier.

Domain 3: Multiple Choice Answers, Rationales, and References

23. A client had an open reduction external fixation of a distal radius fracture several days ago. Evaluation results indicate moderate swelling of the hand, decreased active ROM of the digits, and protective posturing of the involved arm close to the chest at all times. Which intervention would be **MOST BENEFICIAL** to include in sessions during this initial phase of the client's recovery?

A. Education about proper positioning in a standard pouch sling to minimize swelling

B. Exercises to promote capsular gliding and ROM of the shoulder of the affected arm

C. Static splinting to prevent MCP joint collateral ligament tightness

D. Use of a dry whirlpool modality to manage edema of the affected hand

Correct Answer: B

RATIONALE:
Insidious onset of shoulder restrictions can occur due to disuse and protective posturing. It is **MOST BENEFICIAL** to include ROM exercises of the unaffected joints in the intervention plan.

References:
Cooper, C. (2014). *Fundamentals of hand therapy: Clinical reasoning and treatment guidelines for common diagnoses of the upper extremity* (2nd ed., pp. 317-322). St. Louis, MO: Mosby Elsevier.

Radomski, M. V., & Trombly Latham, C. A. (Eds.). (2014). *Occupational therapy for physical dysfunction* (7th ed., p. 1149). Philadelphia, PA: Lippincott Williams & Wilkins.

NBCOT® Study Guide for the OTR Certification Examination

NOTES

24. A client has an upper extremity flexor synergy secondary to a CVA. The client has developed a severe soft-tissue contracture of the affected elbow. Which method would be **MOST EFFECTIVE** for increasing soft tissue length for improving elbow extension?

   A. Provide submaximal stretch to the contracted soft tissue for prolonged periods of time.

   B. Perform passive ROM to the affected elbow with high-load stretch for brief periods of time.

   C. Apply a long-arm cast while the affected elbow is being stretched to the terminal end range.

Correct Answer: A

RATIONALE:
Low load prolonged stress is an effective technique for increasing the length of contracted soft tissue.

Reference:
Gillen, G. (2016). *Stroke rehabilitation: A function-based approach* (4th ed., pp. 541-542). St. Louis, MO: Elsevier.

Domain 3: Multiple Choice Answers, Rationales, and References

25. A client sustained a distal radius fracture of the dominant upper extremity 6 weeks ago. A short arm cast was applied on the day of injury and was removed one day ago. The client holds the affected arm close to the chest in a protected position due to pain, which the client rates as 6 out of 10 using a visual analog scale. The hand and forearm are moderately edematous. The client is able to flex the fingers to within one inch (2.54 cm) from each fingertip to the distal palmar crease. The client refused to move the wrist due to pain. Which intervention should be a priority to include as part of the treatment plan during the **INITIAL** phase of the client's rehabilitation?

A. Fabrication of a dynamic finger flexion orthotic

B. Passive ROM exercises for the wrist and fingers

C. **Manual edema mobilization of the affected extremity**

D. Gentle stress loading exercises as tolerated

Correct Answer: C

RATIONALE:
Edema reduction must be a priority of the intervention.

Reference:
Pendleton, H. M., & Schultz-Krohn, W. (Eds.). (2018). *Pedretti's occupational therapy: Practice skills for the physical dysfunction* (8th ed., pp. 981, 991-992). St. Louis, MO: Mosby Elsevier.

NBCOT® Study Guide for the OTR Certification Examination

NOTES

26. An OTR is providing a home program to a client who has stage 1 complex regional pain syndrome. What information should be included in the home program to **MOST EFFECTIVELY** help the client with symptom management?

A. Pictures illustrating passive ROM exercises for each joint of the affected hand

B. Recommendations for one-handed activities to protect the affected hand during ADL

C. **Techniques for elevating the hand and completing active ROM exercises**

D. Instructions for incorporating energy conservation into daily tasks

Correct Answer: C

RATIONALE:

In the presence of complex regional pain syndrome (CRPS), vasospasm and vasodilation results in an abnormal persistence of edema. Edema control is important to include in a home program. If edema is not controlled, the protein-rich exudates that cause swelling will result in collagen formation, which will cause joint stiffness and decreased functional mobility.

Reference:
Pendleton, H. M., & Schultz-Krohn, W. (Eds.). (2018). *Pedretti's occupational therapy: Practice skills for the physical dysfunction* (8th ed., pp. 994-995). St. Louis, MO: Mosby Elsevier.

Domain 3: Multiple Choice Answers, Rationales, and References

27. A client is developing pitting edema of the hand secondary to flaccid hemiplegia. What should the OTR teach the client and caregiver as part of the **INITIAL** intervention for managing this client's edema?

    A. Methods for using elasticized compression wraps for the digits and hand

    B. Importance of proper upper extremity positioning and elevation

    C. Procedures for providing retrograde massage of the upper extremity

    D. Techniques for completing passive ROM exercises of the digits

Correct Answer: B

RATIONALE:
The OTR should teach the client and caregiver to position the distal end of the client's extremity approximately 3.5 inches (9 cm) above the heart. Elevation to this height allows gravity to assist with hemodynamic fluid transport.

References:
Gillen, G. (2016). *Stroke rehabilitation: A function-based approach* (4th ed., pp. 516-524). St. Louis, MO: Elsevier.

Radomski, M. V., & Trombly Latham, C. A. (Eds.). (2014). *Occupational therapy for physical dysfunction* (7th ed., p. 1137). Philadelphia, PA: Lippincott Williams & Wilkins.

NBCOT® Study Guide for the OTR Certification Examination

NOTES

28. A patient has moderate flexor spasticity in the dominant upper extremity secondary to a TBI. During a self-care session, the OTR plans to inhibit the patient's muscle tone prior to encouraging active movement. Which method would be **MOST EFFECTIVE** to include as part of the intervention session?

A. Positioning the patient's shoulder in abduction and external rotation during the task

B. Applying resistance to the patient's maximally contracted biceps at the start of the session

C. Administering a light, quick stretch to the patient's triceps when reaching forward

D. Applying firm, prolonged manual pressure across the patient's biceps tendon prior to a BADL task

Correct Answer: D

RATIONALE:
Applying firm, prolonged manual pressure across the patient's biceps tendon is an inhibition technique.

Reference:
Meriano, C., & Latella, D. (2016). *Occupational therapy interventions: function and occupations* (2nd ed., pp. 95-98). Thorofare, NJ: SLACK Inc.

236

Domain 3: Multiple Choice Answers, Rationales, and References

29. An OTR is working with a client who has type 1 complex regional pain syndrome (CRPS) affecting functional use of the dominant upper extremity. Pain interferes with the ability to complete ADL and tasks that involve reaching, lifting, and carrying. The client reports that pain fluctuates in intensity, but does not decrease below a 6/10 on the analogue pain scale, even after taking analgesic medication. The OTR notes that the client's affected upper extremity is cold to the touch and there are signs of muscle atrophy. Based on these results, what would be the **MOST EFFECTIVE** intervention for the OTR to include in sessions with this client?

    A. Apply ice or a cooling agent prior to initiating a therapeutic exercise program.

    B. Recommend immobilizing the affected limb in a pouch sling for 1-2 weeks.

    C. Perform active ROM exercises and functional activities that promote weight bearing.

Correct Answer: C

RATIONALE:
Interventions for type 1 complex regional pain syndrome (CRPS) include performing active ROM exercises and functional activities that promote weight bearing.

Reference:
Smith-Gabai, H., & Holm, S. (Eds.). (2017). *Occupational therapy in acute care* (2nd ed., pp. 356-357). Bethesda, MD: AOTA Press.

NBCOT® Study Guide for the OTR Certification Examination

NOTES

30. An OTR is teaching stand-pivot transfers to a client who has Stage 2 Parkinson's disease and uses a wheelchair for mobility. After instructing the client to properly position the chair in relation to the transfer surface, and asking the client to lock the wheelchair brakes, what should the OTR ask the client to do **NEXT**?

   A. Scoot the hips forward to the edge of the wheelchair.

   B. Come to standing by pushing up on the wheelchair arm rests.

   C. Rock forward while reaching toward the transfer surface.

   D. Position both feet perpendicular to the transfer surface.

Correct Answer: A

RATIONALE:
After positioning the wheelchair and locking the brakes, the client should scoot both hips forward to the edge of the chair. Prior to standing, the client's feet should be positioned firmly on the floor and both knees should be flexed to 90°. This position provides a safe base of support to enable the client to come to standing position and then pivot toward the transfer surface.

Reference:
Pendleton, H. M., & Schultz-Krohn, W. (Eds.). (2018). *Pedretti's occupational therapy: Practice skills for the physical dysfunction* (8th ed., p. 249). St. Louis, MO: Mosby Elsevier.

Domain 3: Multiple Choice Answers, Rationales, and References

31. A client with stage 2 Parkinson's disease is preparing to move from sitting on a tub transfer bench in the bathtub to standing up at a walker placed outside the bathtub. Which method would be effective for the client to use at the start of the transfer?

    A. Rocking rhythmically back and forth on the bench a few times

    B. Using a towel to quickly rub the larger muscles of the thighs

    C. Bearing weight through both arms by pressing down on the bench

    D. Pulling forward on the grab bar mounted to the bathroom wall

Correct Answer: A

RATIONALE:
This is a technique used with clients who have difficulty initiating motion due to rigidity associated with this stage of Parkinson's disease.

Reference:
Pendleton, H. M., & Schultz-Krohn, W. (Eds.). (2018). *Pedretti's occupational therapy: Practice skills for the physical dysfunction* (8th ed., pp. 464, 896-897). St. Louis, MO: Mosby Elsevier.

NBCOT® Study Guide for the OTR Certification Examination

NOTES

32. An OTR, who works in the hospital setting, is starting an ADL session at the bedside of an inpatient who has mitochondrial encephalopathy and flaccid hemiplegia. The patient is lying supine in bed and is wearing a prefabricated foot drop orthosis on the affected lower extremity. What is the **PRIMARY** purpose for having the patient wear a foot drop orthosis?

A. To increase circulation in the lower extremity and prevent thromboembolism

B. To provide stability when sitting on the edge of bed and during transfer training

C. **To offer pressure relief while supporting the foot in a neutral position**

Correct Answer: C

RATIONALE:
The **PRIMARY** purpose for having the patient wear a foot drop orthosis is to offer pressure relief while supporting the foot in a neutral position.

Reference:
Smith-Gabai, H., & Holm, S. (Eds.). (2017). *Occupational therapy in acute care* (2nd ed., pp. 195-196, 649). Bethesda, MD: AOTA Press.

Domain 3: Multiple Choice Answers, Rationales, and References

33. An OTR is fabricating an orthotic for a client who has a claw-hand deformity secondary to an ulnar nerve injury several months ago. Which type of orthotic is indicated for this client?

    A. Dorsal-based MCP joint blocking orthotic with a dynamic component to pull the fourth and fifth digit IP joints into extension

    B. Low-profile dynamic orthotic that blocks hyperextension of the second through fifth digits and has an IP joint extension outrigger

    C. Volar-based forearm and hand static orthotic that blocks MCP joint hyperextension while allowing IP joint motion

    D. Hand-based orthotic that positions the fourth and fifth digits in 30°- 40° of MCP joint flexion while allowing IP joint motion

Correct Answer: D

RATIONALE:

A claw-hand deformity is characterized by hyperextension of the fourth and fifth digits and is typically secondary to an ulnar nerve injury. Blocking the fourth and fifth MCP joints in slight flexion allows the extensor digitorum communis tendon to extend the IP joints in the absence of the ulnar innervated intrinsic muscles. The orthotic will enable the client to have a more functional grasp.

References:

Coppard, B. M., & Lohman, H. (2015). *Introduction to orthotics: A clinical reasoning and problem-solving approach* (4th ed., pp. 306-307). St. Louis, MO: Mosby Elsevier.

Pendleton, H. M., & Schultz-Krohn, W. (Eds.). (2018). *Pedretti's occupational therapy: Practice skills for the physical dysfunction* (8th ed., p. 984). St. Louis, MO: Mosby Elsevier.

NBCOT® Study Guide for the OTR Certification Examination

NOTES

34. What is the **PRIMARY** reason for recommending an air-filled wheelchair cushion to a client with a C_5 (ASIA A) spinal cord injury?

A. To offer low daily maintenance needs

B. To provide even relief from pressure

C. To provide a stable base of support

Correct Answer: B

RATIONALE:

One advantage of an air-filled cushion is that it provides even pressure relief.

References:

Cook, A. M., & Polgar, J. M. (2015). *Assistive technologies: Principles & practice* (4th ed., p. 209). St. Louis, MO: Mosby Elsevier.

Radomski, M. V., & Trombly Latham, C. A. (Eds.). (2014). *Occupational therapy for physical dysfunction* (7th ed., p. 500). Philadelphia, PA: Lippincott Williams & Wilkins.

Domain 3: Multiple Choice Answers, Rationales, and References

35. An OTR is fabricating a static orthotic for a client who has a partial thickness burn to the dorsum of the hand. The primary purpose of the orthotic is to maintain the length of the MCP joint collateral ligaments. How should the MCP joints, IP joints and wrist be positioned in the orthotic to achieve this goal?

	MCP Joint	IP Joint Position	Wrist Position
A.	20°–30° Flexion	20°–25° Flexion	25°–30° Extension
B.	35°–45° Flexion	30°–40° Flexion	Neutral
C.	0° Extension	45°–60° Flexion	Neutral
D.	60°–70° Flexion	0°–5° Flexion	25°–30° Extension

Correct Answer: D

RATIONALE:
Due to the irregular shape of the metacarpal head, the MCP joint collateral ligaments are tight when the MCP joint is in flexion. By positioning the MCP joints between 60°-70° of flexion, the MCP joint collateral ligaments will be taut and the formation of MCP flexion contractures minimized. Positioning the IP joints in 0°- 5° flexion discourages the formation of IP joint flexion contractures caused by shortening of the volar plate, collateral ligaments, and adhesions of the lateral bands.

Reference:
Pendleton, H. M., & Schultz-Krohn, W. (Eds.). (2018). *Pedretti's occupational therapy: Practice skills for the physical dysfunction* (8th ed., pp. 1065-1067). St. Louis, MO: Mosby Elsevier.

NBCOT® Study Guide for the OTR Certification Examination

NOTES

36. A client has relapsing-remitting multiple sclerosis and recently transitioned from assisted ambulation to using a standard wheelchair for mobility. A recent onset of fatigue, upper extremity weakness, and back and neck discomfort is beginning to interfere with job performance. The client is employed as a magazine editor, and spends much of the day sitting in the wheelchair while working at the computer monitor positioned at eye level. The client wants to continue sitting in a wheelchair to avoid having to complete transfers when moving from the desk to other parts of the work area. Which modification would be **MOST BENEFICIAL** for this client?

A. Power scooter with padded seat and electric tilt-in-space control

B. Voice-controlled computer system and telephone headset

C. **Solid seat insert, lumbar support and bilateral forearm supports**

D. Deltoid aid and a split design computer keyboard

Correct Answer: C

RATIONALE:
Modifying the wheelchair by adding a solid seat insert helps to establish and maintain pelvic alignment for improved postural support. Forearm supports provide external support for the weak upper extremities. These modifications aid in reducing postural discomfort and muscular fatigue.

Reference:
Pendleton, H. M., & Schultz-Krohn, W. (Eds.). (2018). *Pedretti's occupational therapy: Practice skills for the physical dysfunction* (8th ed., pp. 242-244, 348-350). St. Louis, MO: Mosby Elsevier.

Domain 3: Multiple Choice Answers, Rationales, and References

37. A school-based OTR is selecting seating alternatives for a student who has moderate hypotonia and has just transitioned to a full-day kindergarten program. The student uses a wheelchair for mobility and does not tolerate an upright sitting position throughout the school day. What type of positioning system would be **MOST BENEFICIAL** for this student?

    A. Lightweight chair with reclining back and reverse wheel configuration

    B. Corner chair with high lateral supports that can be placed on the floor

    C. Dense foam lateral supports and gel cushion for the current wheelchair

    D. Modular wheelchair with tilt-in-space feature in the mobility base

Correct Answer: C

RATIONALE:
This allows positioning of the trunk posterior to the pelvis and accommodates for the forces of gravity against upright positioning.

Reference:
Case-Smith, J., & O'Brien, J. C. (2015). *Occupational therapy for children and adolescents* (7th ed., pp. 579-587). St. Louis, MO: Mosby Elsevier.

NBCOT® Study Guide for the OTR Certification Examination

NOTES

38. An inpatient had a total hip replacement 2 weeks ago. The OTR is discussing home set-up and seating options with the patient as part of the discharge instructions. What type of seat should the OTR recommend the patient sit on when watching television at home?

A. **Firm raised armchair with a wedge pillow roll between the cushion and back of the chair**

B. Cushioned, armless dining chair elevated on one inch (2.54 cm) high blocks

C. Sofa with enough length to allow the patient to elevate both legs on the seat cushions

D. Upholstered reclining chair with extra pillows to elevate the affected leg

Correct Answer: A

RATIONALE:
This allows optimal positioning for designated hip precautions.

References:
Pendleton, H. M., & Schultz-Krohn, W. (Eds.). (2018). *Pedretti's occupational therapy: Practice skills for the physical dysfunction* (8th ed., p. 1014). St. Louis, MO: Mosby Elsevier.

Radomski, M. V., & Trombly Latham, C. A. (Eds.). (2014). *Occupational therapy for physical dysfunction* (7th ed., pp. 1115-1117). Philadelphia, PA: Lippincott Williams & Wilkins.

Domain 3: Multiple Choice Answers, Rationales, and References

39. An OTR is providing information about assistive devices to a client who has osteoarthritis of the first CMC joints of both hands. Which devices would be **MOST BENEFICIAL** for protecting these joints during meal preparation?

    A. Washable universal cuff, rocker knife with contoured handle, and wall-mounted jar opener

    B. Right-angled knife with ergonomic handle, over-stove mirror, and swivel serving utensils

    C. Mixing bowls with non-slip bottom, scoop dish, and cutting board with slicing guide

    D. Built-up utensils, adjustable bowl tipper, and mountable electric can opener

Correct Answer: D

RATIONALE:
These assistive devices will reduce the stress on first CMC joints during meal preparation activities.

Reference:
Pendleton, H. M., & Schultz-Krohn, W. (Eds.). (2018). *Pedretti's occupational therapy: Practice skills for the physical dysfunction* (8th ed., pp. 964-965). St. Louis, MO: Mosby Elsevier.

NBCOT® Study Guide for the OTR Certification Examination

NOTES

40. A resident recently was admitted to a long term care facility after having an intracerebral hemorrhage secondary to a ruptured aneurysm. Currently, the resident is able to verbalize basic needs, can follow simple one-step directions, and has minimal functional movement of all extremities. The resident wants to be able to change channels on the television independently but is unable to hold the remote control device or apply enough pressure on the buttons to activate the device. The OTR is choosing a switch-activated indirect selection device that will enable the resident to complete this task. Which type of switch is **OPTIMAL** to use with this device?

A. Pneumatic switch

B. Plate switch

C. Pillow switch

Correct Answer: B

RATIONALE:
A plate switch responds to minimal force, so it will allow this resident to independently access the channels on the television.

Reference:
Radomski, M. V., & Trombly Latham, C. A. (Eds.). (2014). *Occupational therapy for physical dysfunction* (7th ed., pp. 533-534). Philadelphia, PA: Lippincott Williams & Wilkins.

248

Domain 3: Multiple Choice Answers, Rationales, and References

41. An inpatient is recovering from partial and full thickness burns on the dominant upper extremity and has recently developed heterotopic ossification (HO) at the elbow. Prior to the onset of HO symptoms, the patient was independent with self-feeding. Now the patient uses only the non-dominant hand for holding utensils. Which assistive device would be **MOST BENEFICIAL** for improving the patient's functional abilities when eating?

NOTES

   A. Universal cuff with elongated utensil

   B. Swivel spoon and elongated utensils

   C. Rocker knife with a built-up handle

   D. Mechanical feeder with supinator attachment

Correct Answer: B

RATIONALE:
Heterotopic bone formation results in loss of active ROM of the elbow. Flexion, extension, and supination are typically affected.

Reference:
Pendleton, H. M., & Schultz-Krohn, W. (Eds.). (2018). *Pedretti's occupational therapy: Practice skills for the physical dysfunction* (8th ed., pp. 197, 1075). St. Louis, MO: Mosby Elsevier.

249

NBCOT® Study Guide for the OTR Certification Examination

NOTES

42. A client with a non-operable cerebellum tumor is participating in OT to increase independence with self-feeding. Which assistive devices should the client use to promote progress toward this goal?

A. Suction plate and cup holder

B. Side-cutting fork and rocker knife

C. Plastic cup and lightweight utensils

D. Universal cuff with mobile arm support

Correct Answer: A

RATIONALE:
Cerebellar lesions result in ataxia and dysmetria. These assistive devices will help the client stabilize the plate and hold the cup during a meal.

Reference:
Pendleton, H. M., & Schultz-Krohn, W. (Eds.). (2018). *Pedretti's occupational therapy: Practice skills for the physical dysfunction* (8th ed., pp. 201-202, 459-460). St. Louis, MO: Mosby Elsevier.

43. An OTR is selecting a new seating system for a college student who has cerebral palsy and uses a wheelchair for all functional mobility. The client has flexible asymmetrical postures including scoliosis, kyphosis, and pelvic obliquity. The student wants to be able to sit upright for 12-14 hours per day. Which custom seating system would **BEST** support progress toward this goal?

A. Contoured

B. Planar

C. Modular

Correct Answer: A

RATIONALE:
A contoured cushion is beneficial for this client who is at-risk for skin breakdown and has moderate positioning and seating needs.

Reference:
Cook, A. M., & Polgar, J. M. (2015). *Assistive technologies: Principles & practice* (4th ed., pp. 206-207, 213). St. Louis, MO: Mosby Elsevier.

250

Domain 3: Multiple Choice Answers, Rationales, and References

44. An inpatient in a rehabilitation facility is preparing for discharge to home. The patient has hemiplegia, uses a wheelchair for mobility and completes self-care independently with assistive devices. The patient's home bathroom has a standard bathtub and a separate walk-in shower with a safety glass door and a 6-inch (15.24 cm) high doorsill. Both the shower and the tub have safety grab bars. Which piece of durable medical equipment would be **MOST BENEFICIAL** for this patient to use at home?

    A. Padded transfer bench with swivel seat for the bathtub

    B. Shower chair that can be used in the shower or bathtub

    C. Plastic bath chair with armrests and accessory caddy

    D. Transfer board and plastic shower stool with a contoured seat

Correct Answer: A

RATIONALE:
The tub transfer bench provides the patient with the safest method for transferring from/to the wheelchair and bathtub.

Reference:
Pendleton, H. M., & Schultz-Krohn, W. (Eds.). (2018). *Pedretti's occupational therapy: Practice skills for the physical dysfunction* (8th ed., p. 181). St. Louis, MO: Mosby Elsevier.

NBCOT® Study Guide for the OTR Certification Examination

NOTES

45. A client with fibromyalgia reports hand pain and stiffness make it difficult to grasp a standard knife and fork during meals. Which assistive device would be **MOST BENEFICIAL** for improving the client's functional abilities when eating?

    A. Utensils with built-up handles

    B. Rocker knife and plate with raised sides

    C. Universal cuff with wrist support

    D. Lightweight utensils with non-slip grips

Correct Answer: A

RATIONALE:
This is recommended for clients who have limited motion for gripping small handles.

Reference:
Pendleton, H. M., & Schultz-Krohn, W. (Eds.). (2018). *Pedretti's occupational therapy: Practice skills for the physical dysfunction* (8th ed., p. 197). St. Louis, MO: Mosby Elsevier.

46. A client has an open wound on the dorsum of the dominant hand. The medical record indicates mechanical debridement to promote wound healing. Which of the following wound management options represents mechanical debridement?

    A. Wound dressings that keep the wound moist to trap the body's natural enzymes.

    B. Topical enzymes on the wound to selectively remove necrotic tissue and debris.

    C. Whirlpool as a preparatory activity to remove dead tissue from the wound.

Correct Answer: C

RATIONALE:
Mechanical debridement involves the removal of necrotic tissue using methods such as fluid irrigation and whirlpool.

Reference:
Cooper, C. (2014). *Fundamentals of hand therapy: Clinical reasoning and treatment guidelines for common diagnoses of the upper extremity* (2nd ed., pp. 208-209). St. Louis, MO: Mosby Elsevier.

Domain 3: Multiple Choice Answers, Rationales, and References

47. A home health client had surgery for a total hip arthroplasty
2 weeks ago. During an ADL session, the OTR notes that the
area near to the surgical site is warm to the touch and has new
erythema. The wound has purulent drainage and a foul odor. Which
of the following conditions is **TYPICALLY** associated with these
reported symptoms?

    A. Venous stasis

    B. Wound infection

    C. Tissue necrosis

Correct Answer: B

RATIONALE:
Signs and symptoms of infection include red skin and warmth near the
wound and purulent exudate with a foul odor.

Reference:
Cooper, C. (2014). *Fundamentals of hand therapy: Clinical reasoning
and treatment guidelines for common diagnoses of the upper extremity*
(2nd ed., p. 215). St. Louis, MO: Mosby Elsevier.

NBCOT® Study Guide for the OTR Certification Examination

NOTES

48. An OTR is providing recommendations to the caregiver of a client who has moderate severe cognitive decline secondary to Alzheimer's disease. The caregiver reports the client wanders throughout the home at night trying to find the bathroom. On several occasions the client has walked out the front door of the home thinking it was the door leading into the bathroom. Which environmental adaptation should the OTR recommend to the caregiver based on this report?

A. Use movement sensitive audio-visual assistive technology.

B. Place a commode chair in the client's bedroom.

C. Install a video monitor in several locations in the house.

D. Keep hallway and bedroom lights on at night.

Correct Answer: A

RATIONALE:

Using motion sensitive audio-visual assistive technology is the safest option for promoting a safe home environment that contains the least restrictions. Caregivers will be alerted to the client's movements if the client wanders at night.

References:

Brown, C., & Stoffel V. C. (2011). *Occupational therapy in mental health: A vision for participation* (pp. 234-235). Philadelphia, PA: F.A. Davis Company.

Pendleton, H. M., & Schultz-Krohn, W. (Eds.). (2018). *Pedretti's occupational therapy: Practice skills for the physical dysfunction* (8th ed., pp. 878-885). St. Louis, MO: Mosby Elsevier.

Domain 3: Multiple Choice Answers, Rationales, and References

49. Which of the following environmental adaptations will improve safety during meal preparation for a client who has low vision?

    A. Installing a microwave that has preprogrammed cooking options

    B. **Placing tactile markings on the operating features of appliances**

    C. Arranging items on the pantry and cabinet shelves in alphabetical order

    D. Using large-sized bowls and pots for mixing and stove-top cooking

Correct Answer: B

RATIONALE:
Tactile markings will enable the client to monitor the settings on appliances. This will improve kitchen safety, especially with meal preparations.

Reference:
Pendleton, H. M., & Schultz-Krohn, W. (Eds.). (2018). *Pedretti's occupational therapy: Practice skills for the physical dysfunction* (8th ed., p. 224). St. Louis, MO: Mosby Elsevier.

NBCOT® Study Guide for the OTR Certification Examination

NOTES

50. Which of the following is the **BEST** example of a primary objective for using the universal design for learning (UDL) principles with students who attend a middle school?

A. To provide environmental design principles to adapt the classrooms and other learning spaces to include students who have a disability.

B. To provide all students in the school the ability to learn and the opportunity to demonstrate academic performance abilities.

C. To recommend desk heights, ergonomic computer workstations and adapted play environments that benefit most students in the school.

Correct Answer: B

RATIONALE:
The primary objective of applying the universal design for learning principles is to establish the conditions to support all students in mastering the skill of learning.

Reference:
Case-Smith, J., & O'Brien, J. C. (2015). *Occupational therapy for children and adolescents* (7th ed., p. 549). St. Louis, MO: Mosby Elsevier.

Domain 3: Multiple Choice Answers, Rationales, and References

Chapter 14

Domain 4: Multiple Choice Sample Questions

Practice questions with answer key and references

The following multiple choice items are samples related to Domain 4.

Competency and Practice Management

Manage professional activities of self and relevant others as guided by evidence, regulatory compliance, and standards of practice to promote quality care.

NOTES

1. An OTR is using the principles of evidence-based practice (EBP) to guide professional decision making. The OTR knows the first step of EBP involves generating a pertinent question and identifying a need. Which option represents the **MOST BENEFICAL** source for identifying a relevant topic for investigation?

    A. Clinical issues encountered during everyday practice

    B. Quantitative results of a randomized control trial

    C. Analysis of practice trends in a scholarly database

2. An OTR working in a pediatric hospital-based clinic wants to begin using a newly developed listening device as part of the OT intervention for children diagnosed with autism. What information is **MOST IMPORTANT** for the OTR to determine prior to using this device with these children?

   A. Standard protocol to use with each child who will use the device.

   B. Clinical practice guidelines and evidence related to using the device.

   C. Plan to monitor the effectiveness of the new intervention.

   D. Third-party payers reimburse the device as a therapeutic modality.

3. An OTR is critically reviewing evidence to provide recommendations for a client who has rheumatoid arthritis and who wants to know if attending a water aerobics class would be beneficial. The OTR searches a scholarly database and finds 14 relevant studies. What action should the OTR take to determine the **MOST BENEFICIAL** evidence to support water aerobics recommendations for this client?

   A. Share the results of the search with the client and ask the client to select their preferred studies.

   B. Evaluate the studies using an organized methodology designed to appraise the evidence.

   C. Ask experienced practitioners on a social media site to recommend the best study.

NBCOT® Study Guide for the OTR Certification Examination

NOTES

4. An OTR is reviewing the results of a single-subject case study. The study investigates the therapeutic effectiveness of sensory stories in children with autism spectrum disorder to influence target behaviors. The OTR wants to integrate sensory stories into daily clinical practice. Using the principles of evidenced-based practice, what action should the OTR take **NEXT** to inform clinical decisions for practice?

A. Locate the conclusions for several relevant pre- and post-tests and single-subject studies.

B. Search an evidenced-based database for a meta-analysis or systematic review on the topic.

C. Interview multiple experts in the field whose opinions on sensory approaches are valued.

5. An OTR, who works in an inpatient rehabilitation setting, completes a critical appraisal of outcome measures for patients with TBI. The OTR wants to propose including these measures in the department's clinical protocols but finds that the fast pace of the setting is a barrier to communicating with colleagues. What is the **MOST BENEFICIAL** method for the OTR to present the benefits of modifying the department's clinical protocols for the TBI population?

A. Encourage each therapist to read scholarly articles that support a change in protocol.

B. Discuss the evidence with colleagues intermittently throughout the workday.

C. Ask the supervisor to include program planning on the agenda during a staff meeting.

260

Domain 4: Multiple Choice Sample Questions

6. An OTR, who works with children who have cerebral palsy, wants to stay abreast of research relevant to the practice area but is overwhelmed by the amount of evidence available. What is the **MOST BENEFICIAL** strategy for the OTR to use to integrate evidence into practice-based decisions?

A. Utilize systematic reviews and resources that synthesize study results.

B. Test various search methods and analyze the effectiveness of each approach.

C. Locate a scholarly database that includes all levels of evidence (Level I - Level V).

7. An OTR is reviewing a research article investigating the role of peer support among members living in a retirement community. Data collection methods included observation, note- taking and semi-structured interviews conducted with members over a 6-month period. Constant comparison and open coding were undertaken to categorize core concepts. A conceptual model identifying 5 tiers of peer support was constructed based on members' experience. Which type of qualitative research design does this investigation represent?

A. Grounded theory study

B. Participatory action research

C. Critical theory study

D. Phenomenological study

8. An OTR, who works in a hospital setting, is investigating the perceptions of patients with neurodegenerative disease who have had several hospitalizations over a 3-month period. What type of research method would be **MOST BENEFICIAL** for this purpose?

A. Quantitative

B. Qualitative

C. Meta-analysis

261

NBCOT® Study Guide for the OTR Certification Examination

NOTES

9. An OTR has been leading discussions about evidence-based practice during monthly rehabilitation team meetings. The discussion at the next meeting will focus on reviewing the final step associated with this systematic process of searching and appraising literature. What information should the OTR include in the presentation when summarizing the final step in the evidence-based practice process?

   A. Appraising and synthesizing the evidence

   B. Evaluating the effectiveness of each step in the process

   C. Applying best evidence to guide practice decisions

10. A hospital-wide interprofessional continuous quality improvement (CQI) committee has identified reduction in pressure sores related to hospitalizations as an opportunity for improvement. After discussing the initiative with the rehabilitation manager, what should the OTR do **NEXT** to contribute to this process?

   A. Explain to all rehabilitation staff the Department of Health and Human Services (DHHS) initiative to decrease the incidence of pressure sores related to hospitalizations.

   B. Develop a survey for the rehabilitation staff to determine the frequency of assessment and provision of interventions related to wound management and care.

   C. Develop an in-service education program for all rehabilitation staff including information about pressure sores being preventable and a major concern of health care.

Domain 4: Multiple Choice Sample Questions

11. After becoming initially certified as an OTR, an individual worked in an outpatient OT clinic for 4 years. After that time, the individual did not work as an OT and has not participated in occupational therapy professional development activities for the past 6 years. The individual wants to resume OT clinical practice. What ethical responsibility does the individual have prior to obtaining a job in an outpatient setting?

A. Identify professional development units that can be carried over from the previous job.

B. Volunteer as an OT in a clinical setting to establish service competence.

C. Create an effective learning plan related to skills needed for the desired practice setting.

D. Submit an application to renew national certification as an OTR.

12. An OTR is designing a process improvement plan to reduce the use of patient restraints in a skilled nursing facility. What is the **INITIAL** step toward promoting corrective actions?

A. Use incident reports to track staff members who most frequently use restraints.

B. Develop procedures for tracking and monitoring restraint use within the facility.

C. Survey other skilled nursing facilities to identify typical reasons for use of patient restraints.

D. Implement an operating procedure for the correct application of patient restraints.

NOTES

263

NBCOT® Study Guide for the OTR Certification Examination

NOTES

13. An OTR is providing supervision to a home health aide, who assists a client with bathing. During the initial OT evaluation, the patient identified independence in bathing as a priority goal and was assessed to require 25% assistance. However, the aide tells the OTR that the patient wants total assistance during bathing sessions and frequently asks the aide to complete tasks that the patient can perform. What is the **FIRST** action the OTR should take to support progress toward the patient's bathing goal?

   A. Document the discrepancy in the patient's performance level between the OTR and the aide.

   B. Plan to re-evaluate the client's level of assistance for bathing during the next scheduled session.

   C. Conduct a joint session with the client and the aide to review goals for bathing.

14. An OTR is developing a program for clients who are considering bariatric surgery as a weight-loss option. Which type of program represents a comprehensive client-centered approach that would be effective for improving surgical outcomes or potentially eliminating the need for surgery?

   A. Self-actualization education

   B. Stress management classes

   C. Lifestyle modification program

   D. Weekly support groups

264

Domain 4: Multiple Choice Sample Questions

15. An OTR is developing a client-centered fall prevention program for community-dwelling older adults. The objective of the program is to reduce the participants' risk of falling. Topics the OTR plans to cover include the benefits of having a health care provider review a list of prescribed medications, the advantages of routinely completing an exercise program, and the purpose of having a regular vision examination. Which additional topic would be **MOST BENEFICIAL** to include in this type of fall prevention program?

A. Methods and tips to modify the home environment to increase personal safety

B. Resources to enhance social involvement and engagement in the community

C. Reviews of healthy eating habits and nutritional information on prepared foods

16. An OTR wants to measure the effectiveness of a leisure education program for clients who attend an outpatient chemical dependency unit. What method should the OTR use to obtain a valid measure of the program's effectiveness?

A. Track the number of clients referred to the program with the number of clients who complete the program.

B. Compare a measurement of client leisure involvement at the start of the program with leisure involvement upon completion of the program.

C. Administer a questionnaire about the perceived importance of leisure activities to clients who complete the program.

D. Monitor the frequency of client attendance and level of participation during each session of the program.

265

NBCOT® Study Guide for the OTR Certification Examination

NOTES

17. An OTR working in a skilled nursing facility frequently teaches residents how to use adaptive devices during BADL. The OTR wants to evaluate if the instruction methods and devices are effective in helping to improve the residents' functional performance. Which method would be **MOST EFFECTIVE** to use for gathering this information?

   A. Note the number of times the residents bring the devices to BADL sessions.

   B. Ask the residents how often during the week they use the devices for BADL.

   C. Have the residents demonstrate the use of the devices during a session.

   D. Track how many times the residents spontaneously use the devices during BADL.

18. An OTR has been asked by the director of nursing in an acute-care hospital to provide an in-service to the nursing staff to describe the role of OT in preventing deep venous thrombosis and pulmonary embolus. Which intervention is **MOST IMPORTANT** to include as part of this presentation to explain the role of OT in thromboembolic disease prevention?

   A. Prescribe anticoagulation therapy to thin the blood and prevent clots from forming.

   B. Recommend mechanical interventions such as compression stockings and pumps.

   C. Support early mobilization to facilitate patient engagement in self-care activities.

Domain 4: Multiple Choice Sample Questions

19. An OTR is providing consultative services to develop a wellness program at a community senior center. A needs assessment survey indicates center participants have a fear of falling, feel they are at risk for falls, and want to age in place for as long as possible. In addition to including fall prevention education, which topic should the OTR recommend as part of the educational programming offered at the center?

A. Benefits of participating in socially stimulating activities

B. Value of identifying effective home modifications

C. Influence of aging on immediate and delayed memory

20. Which of the following is the **BEST** example of a primary objective for a health promotion program for people with chronic conditions?

A. Prevention of secondary conditions to enhance overall quality of life

B. Facilitate healing and recovery from existing disease processes

C. Teach information about medical interventions and service providers

21. An OTR who works in a hospital setting is evaluating an inpatient who recently had a severe stroke. The patient currently requires a ventilator for respiratory support and is not able to verbalize goals. To complete the evaluation process, what ethical obligation does the OTR have for upholding professional responsibilities?

A. Acquire information for the occupational profile from other sources.

B. Conclude the patient is not eligible for services until medically stable.

C. Document that the patient has poor potential for rehabilitation.

NOTES

267

NBCOT® Study Guide for the OTR Certification Examination

NOTES

22. An OTR who works in a hospital setting has been asked by the Readmission Prevention committee to provide an in-service to the team about OT services in the care of a patient with diabetes. Which intervention is **MOST IMPORTANT** to include in this presentation to explain the role of OT in maintaining glycemic control?

    A. Support the development of healthy routines and participation in activities.

    B. Explain how food composition and portion size affect blood sugar.

    C. Provide instructions for correctly timing and measuring medication dosages.

23. An OTR working in a pediatric outpatient setting approaches the therapy manager and states, "I believe my colleague is billing for interventions that are not being provided during client sessions." After acknowledging the practitioner's concern, what actions should the manager take **NEXT**?

    A. Develop a remediation program for resolving future billing issues.

    B. Initiate a review of internal clinical service coding and billing practices.

    C. Ask the OTR to provide supporting proof of the colleague's misconduct.

24. An OTR is employed at a skilled nursing facility on an hourly basis and is typically scheduled to work 2 shifts each month. The facility-specific clinical protocol directs the OTR to use a standardized assessment tool that is unfamiliar to the OTR. What is the **FIRST** action the OTR should take in this situation?

    A. Alert the therapy supervisor that additional training is needed.

    B. Follow the step-by-step procedural instructions on the test form.

    C. Request a colleague administer the assessment tool when needed.

268

Domain 4: Multiple Choice Sample Questions

25. An OTR has been providing home health services for 2 weeks to a patient who has had cardiac bypass surgery. The OTR determines that the patient could benefit from an outpatient cardiac rehabilitation program. The OTR informs the supervisor of these conclusions, but the supervisor recommends that the patient continue with home health services to maintain Medicare reimbursement. What action should the OTR take in this situation?

A. Ask the patient and family about their service preference.

B. Continue to provide services based on the initial plan.

C. Contact the patient's physician to discuss a referral to the program.

D. Provide justification for the referral in a discharge summary.

26. An OTR working in an industrial setting is documenting the success of a wellness program. One of the program goals is to reduce the number of job-related injuries among workers in a warehouse shipping and receiving department. The initial assessment cited risks related to poor worker fitness, improper lifting techniques, and inadequate work routines. What information about the program should be documented in the program reports to management to provide the **MOST BENEFICIAL** information about the effectiveness of the program?

A. Evidence of improved body mechanics among workers during lifting tasks

B. Number of new or recurring injuries during the reporting period

C. Pre- and post-test results from a worker questionnaire about job-related ergonomics

269

NBCOT® Study Guide for the OTR Certification Examination

NOTES

27. An inpatient had a total hip arthroplasty 2 days ago with post-operative precautions that include touchdown weight-bearing (TDWB). Which option **BEST** represents instructions an OTR should provide to reinforce the touchdown weight-bearing (TDWB) precaution?

    A. Use pain as the limiting factor and place up to 100% of body weight through the operative extremity.

    B. Learn to apply up to 50% of body weight through the operative extremity.

    C. Place the toes of the operative extremity on the floor to maintain balance but do not bear weight.

28. An adolescent is in an acute setting after sustaining a recent C_6 (ASIA B) spinal cord injury. The adolescent underwent surgery 4 days ago for cervical stabilization and is recovering from the surgery as expected. The adolescent has been on bedrest since the surgery, but now has medical clearance to transfer out of bed with assistance. One of the goals for the adolescent is to sit in a bedside chair for BADL. Prior to transferring the adolescent out of bed, what action **MUST** the OTR take?

    A. Evaluate sensation at key dermatomal segments.

    B. Measure the adolescent's resting vital signs.

    C. Complete a comprehensive manual muscle test.

29. An inpatient had coronary artery bypass graft (CABG) surgery 3 days ago. While sitting on the edge of the bed during a grooming session, the patient's heart rate increases 10 beats per minute above the patient's resting heart rate. What **INITIAL** action should the OTR take based on this observation?

    A. Discontinue the activity and help the patient transfer to a side-lying position in bed.

    B. Document this response and other clinical observations in the client's medical record.

    C. Continue to monitor vital signs and proceed with the planned intervention session.

270

Domain 4: Multiple Choice Sample Questions

30. An OTR is providing home-based services to an adult client who had an open reduction and internal fixation of a tibia fracture. The client lives at home and can ambulate for short distances in the house using crutches. The client's short-term goal is to be able to take a bath independently. What should the OTR teach to the client during the **INITIAL** bathing session?

A. Proper method for setting up an inflatable bed bath with the assistance of a caregiver

B. Positioning of the affected leg over the side of the tub after transferring to a tub bench

C. Methods for wrapping the affected leg in a moisture barrier prior to transferring to a tub bench

D. Sterile techniques for using hydrogen peroxide to clean the skin surrounding the pin sites

31. A client who had a CVA one month ago now has moderate-severe flexor spasticity and scapular immobility of the involved upper extremity. Which technique is **CONTRAINDICATED** to use for minimizing the impact of the spasticity on passive mobility for dressing and hygiene?

A. Self-ROM exercises in supine several times per day

B. Reciprocal overhead pulley exercises using wall mounted pulleys

C. Upper extremity weight-bearing during functional tasks

D. Long-arm air splinting prior to completing a self-care task

271

NBCOT® Study Guide for the OTR Certification Examination

NOTES

32. An OTR working in a children's hospital has been providing services daily for the past several weeks to a school-age child hospitalized for treatment of a systemic congenital condition. When the OTR arrives at the child's room for the next scheduled session, there is a sign posted on the door indicating enteric contact precautions are in place. What action **MUST** the OTR take based on this observation?

   A. Follow transmission precaution procedures when interacting with the child.

   B. Cancel sessions with the child until these precautions are no longer in place.

   C. Rub hands with an alcohol-based hand sanitizer at the end of sessions with the child.

33. What is the **FIRST** action the OTR should take when a patient who has schizophrenia exhibits an increase in lip smacking, tongue protrusion, and facial grimacing?

   A. Request that the patient stop the behavior.

   B. Suggest that the patient change medications.

   C. Inform the patient's physician.

34. An OTR who works in a home health setting is providing an intervention to address BADL of a client who had a stroke. At first, the client actively participates in the intervention activity, but begins to perseverate on the same action while brushing teeth. The client's level of arousal declines, and the client starts to drool and then vomit. What action should the OTR take **FIRST** in this situation?

   A. Determine if the client has a history of adverse reactions to medication.

   B. Activate emergency medical services by calling 911.

   C. Contact a family member to receive consent for medical intervention.

272

Domain 4: Multiple Choice Sample Questions

35. An inpatient who has COPD is participating in a dressing session while seated at bedside. While putting on a pair of pants, the patient begins to have dyspnea. Pulse oximetry indicates the patient's oxygen saturation level is 93%. After stopping the activity, what should the OTR have the patient do **NEXT**?

   A. Take several short shallow breaths through the mouth.

   B. Breathe in deeply through the nose and slowly exhale through pursed lips.

   C. Inhale through pursed lips and quickly exhale through the nose.

   D. Breathe through a nasal cannula using supplemental oxygen.

36. A client is in the early stages of a slow, progressive upper motor neuron disease. Mild intention tremors and fatigue interfere with completion of typical daily tasks and ability to work a full day as an accountant. Currently, the client ambulates with a cane in the home and uses a wheelchair for community mobility. The client's goal is to remain working as long as possible. Which work accommodation meets the employer's obligation for this client as required by the Americans with Disabilities Act?

   A. Consideration for modifying the client's current work schedule

   B. Employee review to change the essential elements of the job description

   C. Modification of doorways throughout the workplace for maximal accessibility

37. Which federal law in the United States regulates the provision of early intervention, special education, and related services to children with disabilities from birth to two years of age?

   A. Individuals with Disabilities Education Act (IDEA) Part C

   B. Section 504 of the Vocational Rehabilitation Act

   C. Individuals with Disabilities Education Act (IDEA) Part B

NOTES

NBCOT® Study Guide for the OTR Certification Examination

NOTES

38. An OTR is a contract employee at a preschool and works 2-3 shifts each month. During a scheduled shift, the OTR receives a call from a student's physician asking for a progress update for a student. The therapist locates the student's file but is unsure of the school's confidentiality policy. What action should the OTR take **NEXT**?

   A. Provide the physician with a summary of functional gains made by the student.

   B. Consult with the therapy supervisor to understand the privacy restrictions.

   C. Request that the family provide written consent for consultation with team members.

39. An OTR working in a home health setting receives a phone call about a new referral for a patient who has Parkinson's disease and whose primary insurance is Medicare Part A. The physician has only requested OT services on the referral. What action **MUST** the OTR take prior to scheduling a home visit with this patient?

   A. Determine how many visits are authorized based on the diagnosis.

   B. Ensure the appropriate disciplines have opened the case.

   C. Identify which procedural codes will be reimbursed by the payer.

40. A rheumatologist has prescribed bilateral nighttime resting hand orthotics for a child who has early stage juvenile rheumatoid arthritis. The parents ask the OTR who works at the child's school to fabricate the orthotics. Despite having this condition, the child is functioning at grade-level and is not on the OT caseload. What action should the OTR take in response to the parents' request?

   A. Schedule a time after school hours to fabricate the orthotics for the child.

   B. Initiate an IEP indicating the child's needs for school-based OT.

   C. Inform the parents to schedule an appointment at an outpatient OT clinic.

   D. Provide the parents with catalog information for ordering pre-fabricated orthotics.

274

Domain 4: Multiple Choice Sample Questions

41. An OTR is leading a community-based class for self-referred clients who have rheumatoid arthritis. Through class discussion and observation, the OTR determines that one of the clients in the class would benefit from bilateral hand orthotics. After discussing this observation with the client and determining the client intends to pay for services using insurance benefits, what action should the OTR take **NEXT** to address the client's needs?

A. Contact the insurance company to obtain reimbursement authorization for the orthotics.

B. Arrange a clinic appointment time to fabricate the orthotics for the client.

C. Understand the state regulatory requirements for direct access to OT services.

D. Complete a comprehensive evaluation to justify the need for the orthotics to the primary care physician.

42. A patient who has global aphasia and flaccid hemiplegia secondary to a CVA has been participating in OT. During an employee safety in-service, a customer service employee, who is a distant relative of this patient, asks the OTR about the patient's progress in OT. Which statement represents an appropriate response for the OTR to provide to this inquiry?

A. "Based on the recent evaluation, the patient has a long way to go."

B. "I can't talk about the patient without the patient's approval."

C. "The patient seems to be satisfied with the overall progress."

D. "I think the patient will have a difficult time returning home."

NOTES

43. A client who is recovering from a severe hand injury uses Medicaid as the primary source of reimbursement for OT services provided at a hand therapy clinic. The client plans to relocate to an adult child's home in another state even though the client requires continuation of OT services. Upon learning this information, what recommendation regarding transitional services should the OTR make to the client?

    A. Determine the Medicaid benefits that will be authorized based on the new address.

    B. Notify the current Medicaid provider to transfer benefits based on the new address.

    C. Have a family member locate a comparable hand therapy clinic near the new address.

44. A third-party payer has denied reimbursement of pre-authorized occupational therapy services based on "insufficient information to substantiate payment." The OTR is writing a letter to appeal the denial. What type of client-related information is **MOST IMPORTANT** to include to increase the likelihood of reimbursement?

    A. Outline of functional tasks used during each intervention session

    B. Summary of progress based on functional goals and medical necessity

    C. Annotated reference list indicating evidence-based best practice guidelines

    D. Rate of progress compared to other clients who have the same diagnosis

Domain 4: Multiple Choice Sample Questions

45. An inpatient in a Medicare funded rehabilitation facility recently had transtibial amputations of both legs. The patient participates in 3 hours of therapy per day and is currently scheduled for discharge in 2 weeks. During the weekly interprofessional meeting the OTR reports the patient has met the OT intervention goals. The physical therapist reports the patient will continue to require physical therapy 2 hours per day until discharge from the facility in 2 weeks. The prosthetist will also be working with the patient during this time. What action should the OTR take based on the meeting reports?

A. Complete a discharge summary and discontinue the patient from OT services.

B. Determine if there are any other activities in which the patient would like to participate.

C. Schedule the patient for at least one hour of OT per day to meet the 3-hour therapy rule.

D. Continue to schedule OT sessions to maintain the progress the patient has made thus far.

46. An OTR who works in a Medicare-funded inpatient rehabilitation unit is completing an evaluation of a patient who had bilateral total knee arthroplasties 3 days ago. The patient is in generally good health, plans to live independently at home, and wants to resume volunteer work in the community. The patient currently requires OT services to increase independence in bathing, dressing, and toileting. What **MUST** the OTR consider when scheduling the patient for OT?

A. Availability of caregivers to participate in daily sessions for caregiver education and training

B. Impact of the patient's prior level of function on frequency and duration of sessions

C. Minimum number of therapy hours required for reimbursement by the third-party payer

D. Patient's physical endurance for completing activities according to a clinical pathway

277

NBCOT® Study Guide for the OTR Certification Examination

NOTES

47. A client sustained a hand injury 8 weeks ago and has been participating in an outpatient OT program several times a week for the past 3 weeks. The OTR has just fabricated a dynamic orthotic to correct a PIP joint contracture. What information is **MOST IMPORTANT** to include in the contact note for this visit?

   A. Results of a sensory evaluation of the affected hand

   B. Goniometric measurements of the affected hand

   C. Thickness and type of material used for the orthotic

   D. Orthotic construction methods and care instructions

48. An OTR has completed the initial evaluation of an inpatient who has leukemia. The OTR plans to work with the patient on a daily basis prior to the patient's planned discharge to home in one week. What information is **MOST IMPORTANT** to include in the initial evaluation report?

   A. Summary data as it relates to the occupational profile

   B. Details about interventions for promoting goal attainment

   C. Descriptions of community support services available

   D. Recommendations for post-discharge OT services

49. An inpatient has been participating in ADL, social skills, and prevocational groups as part of a multidisciplinary program for the treatment of anorexia. What information about the patient's participation should be documented in the "A" section of the SOAP note to provide the **MOST BENEFICIAL** information about the patient's progress?

   A. Patient reports of compliance with caloric intake requirements

   B. Evidence of specific decision-making skills the patient uses during assigned group tasks

   C. Examples of patient's conformity with strict limits set on personal behavior

   D. Impressions about the patient's ability to use appropriate judgment related to own skills and assets

278

Domain 4: Multiple Choice Sample Questions

50. A client who sustained a Colles' fracture of the dominant extremity has been participating in OT. Reevaluation results indicate that the client's active wrist extension and supination increased by 5°, grip strength increased by 5 lbs (2.27kg), and pinch strength improved by 1 lb (0.45kg). The client is able to touch fingertips to palm, but stiffness and swelling limit tight gripping. Pain interferes with the client's ability to complete typical work tasks using the affected hand, but the client compensates for most tasks, except writing, by using the non-dominant hand. Which statement is **BEST** to include in the assessment section of the client's weekly progress note?

A. Improvements are noted in ROM and strength, but persistent stiffness, swelling, and pain interfere with full functional use of the affected hand for completion of daily tasks.

B. ROM and strength of the affected hand and wrist are improved slightly compared to previous evaluation. Pain and swelling interferes with ability to make a full fist.

C. Client is able to complete work tasks by using the non-dominant extremity. Recommend continuation of OT for pain management and to improve ROM and strength of the dominant hand.

D. Decreased ROM and strength interfere with client's ability to write at work. Client would benefit from training activities to improve fine motor skills.

NBCOT® Study Guide for the OTR Certification Examination

Answer Key

Domain 4 Sample Items

Item Number	Key
1.	A
2.	B
3.	B
4.	B
5.	C
6.	A
7.	A
8.	B
9.	B
10.	B
11.	C
12.	B
13.	C
14.	C
15.	A
16.	B
17.	D
18.	C
19.	B
20.	A
21.	A
22.	A
23.	B
24.	A
25.	D

Item Number	Key
26.	B
27.	C
28.	B
29.	C
30.	C
31.	B
32.	A
33.	C
34.	B
35.	B
36.	A
37.	A
38.	B
39.	B
40.	C
41.	C
42.	B
43.	A
44.	B
45.	A
46.	C
47.	B
48.	A
49.	D
50.	A

NBCOT® Study Guide for the OTR Certification Examination

Multiple Choice Answers, Rationales, and References

1. An OTR is using the principles of evidence-based practice (EBP) to guide professional decision making. The OTR knows the first step of EBP involves generating a pertinent question and identifying a need. Which option represents the **MOST BENEFICAL** source for identifying a relevant topic for investigation?

   A. **Clinical issues encountered during everyday practice**

   B. Quantitative results of a randomized control trial

   C. Analysis of practice trends in a scholarly database

Correct Answer: A

RATIONALE:
Reflecting on issues or challenging clinical situations that occur during everyday practice will guide the OTR in identifying meaningful questions for investigation.

Reference:
Smith-Gabai, H., & Holm, S. (Eds.). (2017). *Occupational therapy in acute care* (2nd ed., p. 28). Bethesda, MD: AOTA Press.

NBCOT® Study Guide for the OTR Certification Examination

NOTES

2. An OTR working in a pediatric hospital-based clinic wants to begin using a newly developed listening device as part of the OT intervention for children diagnosed with autism. What information is **MOST IMPORTANT** for the OTR to determine prior to using this device with these children?

   A. Standard protocol to use with each child who will use the device.

   B. **Clinical practice guidelines and evidence related to using the device.**

   C. Plan to monitor the effectiveness of the new intervention.

   D. Third-party payers reimburse the device as a therapeutic modality.

Correct Answer: B

RATIONALE:
This type of appraisal relates to evidence-based practice (EBP) procedures and should be completed prior to using this device or implementing a new clinical procedure related to the use of this device.

Reference:
Jacobs, K., & McCormack, G. L. (Eds.). (2011). *The occupational therapy manager* (5th ed., pp. 331-340). Bethesda, MD: AOTA Press.

Domain 4: Multiple Choice Answers, Rationales, and References

3. An OTR is critically reviewing evidence to provide recommendations for a client who has rheumatoid arthritis and who wants to know if attending a water aerobics class would be beneficial. The OTR searches a scholarly database and finds 14 relevant studies. What action should the OTR take to determine the **MOST BENEFICIAL** evidence to support water aerobics recommendations for this client?

A. Share the results of the search with the client and ask the client to select their preferred studies.

B. Evaluate the studies using an organized methodology designed to appraise the evidence.

C. Ask experienced practitioners on a social media site to recommend the best study.

Correct Answer: B

RATIONALE:

Using an organized methodology such as a checklist, structured form, or a critical appraisal scale supports a systematic approach to determining best evidence.

Reference:

Law, M., & MacDermid, J. (Eds.). (2014). *Evidence-based rehabilitation: A guide to practice* (3rd ed., pp. 41-42). Thorofare, NJ: SLACK, Inc.

NBCOT® Study Guide for the OTR Certification Examination

NOTES

4. An OTR is reviewing the results of a single-subject case study. The study investigates the therapeutic effectiveness of sensory stories in children with autism spectrum disorder to influence target behaviors. The OTR wants to integrate sensory stories into daily clinical practice. Using the principles of evidenced-based practice, what action should the OTR take **NEXT** to inform clinical decisions for practice?

    A. Locate the conclusions for several relevant pre- and post-tests and single-subject studies.

    B. **Search an evidenced-based database for a meta-analysis or systematic review on the topic.**

    C. Interview multiple experts in the field whose opinions on sensory approaches are valued.

Correct Answer: B

RATIONALE:
A meta-analysis or systematic review is considered Level I evidence and is the highest level of evidence to inform practice decisions.

Reference:
Brown, C., & Stoffel V. C. (2011). *Occupational therapy in mental health: A vision for participation* (pp. 57-61). Philadelphia, PA: F.A. Davis Company.

Domain 4: Multiple Choice Answers, Rationales, and References

5. An OTR, who works in an inpatient rehabilitation setting, completes a critical appraisal of outcome measures for patients with TBI. The OTR wants to propose including these measures in the department's clinical protocols but finds that the fast pace of the setting is a barrier to communicating with colleagues. What is the **MOST BENEFICIAL** method for the OTR to present the benefits of modifying the department's clinical protocols for the TBI population?

A. Encourage each therapist to read scholarly articles that support a change in protocol.

B. Discuss the evidence with colleagues intermittently throughout the workday.

C. Ask the supervisor to include program planning on the agenda during a staff meeting.

Correct Answer: C

RATIONALE:
This approach allows for the dissemination of information and subsequent discussion of it with multiple staff members.

Reference:
Law, M., & MacDermid, J. (Eds.). (2014). *Evidence-based rehabilitation: A guide to practice* (3rd ed., pp. 300-301). Thorofare, NJ: SLACK, Inc.

NBCOT® Study Guide for the OTR Certification Examination

6. An OTR, who works with children who have cerebral palsy, wants to stay abreast of research relevant to the practice area but is overwhelmed by the amount of evidence available. What is the **MOST BENEFICIAL** strategy for the OTR to use to integrate evidence into practice-based decisions?

A. Utilize systematic reviews and resources that synthesize study results.

B. Test various search methods and analyze the effectiveness of each approach.

C. Locate a scholarly database that includes all levels of evidence (Level I - Level V).

Correct Answer: A

RATIONALE:
Referring to systematic reviews and using available resources that synthesize study results are strategies that can help an OTR stay current on relevant research.

Reference:
Law, M., & MacDermid, J. (Eds.). (2014). *Evidence-based rehabilitation: A guide to practice* (3rd ed., p. 211). Thorofare, NJ: SLACK, Inc.

Domain 4: Multiple Choice Answers, Rationales, and References

7. An OTR is reviewing a research article investigating the role of peer support among members living in a retirement community. Data collection methods included observation, note- taking and semi-structured interviews conducted with members over a 6-month period. Constant comparison and open coding were undertaken to categorize core concepts. A conceptual model identifying 5 tiers of peer support was constructed based on members' experience. Which type of qualitative research design does this investigation represent?

A. Grounded theory study

B. Participatory action research

C. Critical theory study

D. Phenomenological study

Correct Answer: A

RATIONALE:
Grounded theory is a research method in which there is continuous comparison between collected data and interpretation, which results in a set of categories and emerging theory.

Reference:
DePoy, E., & Gitlin, L. N. (2016). *Introduction to research: Understanding and applying multiple strategies* (5th ed., pp. 161-164, 169-170). St. Louis, MO: Mosby Elsevier.

NBCOT® Study Guide for the OTR Certification Examination

NOTES

8. An OTR, who works in a hospital setting, is investigating the perceptions of patients with neurodegenerative disease who have had several hospitalizations over a 3-month period. What type of research method would be **MOST BENEFICIAL** for this purpose?

 A. Quantitative

 B. Qualitative

 C. Meta-analysis

Correct Answer: B

RATIONALE:
A qualitative research method will allow for the collection of data and meaningful information that will inform the OTR on the perceptions of patients with neurodegenerative disease.

Reference:
Smith-Gabai, H., & Holm, S. (Eds.). (2017). *Occupational therapy in acute care* (2nd ed., pp. 24-25). Bethesda, MD: AOTA Press.

9. An OTR has been leading discussions about evidence-based practice during monthly rehabilitation team meetings. The discussion at the next meeting will focus on reviewing the final step associated with this systematic process of searching and appraising literature. What information should the OTR include in the presentation when summarizing the final step in the evidence-based practice process?

 A. Appraising and synthesizing the evidence

 B. Evaluating the effectiveness of each step in the process

 C. Applying best evidence to guide practice decisions

Correct Answer: B

RATIONALE:
The final step in the evidence-based practice process is to evaluate the effectiveness of each step in the process.

Reference:
Smith-Gabai, H., & Holm, S. (Eds.). (2017). *Occupational therapy in acute care* (2nd ed., p. 28). Bethesda, MD: AOTA Press.

Domain 4: Multiple Choice Answers, Rationales, and References

10. A hospital-wide interprofessional continuous quality improvement (CQI) committee has identified reduction in pressure sores related to hospitalizations as an opportunity for improvement. After discussing the initiative with the rehabilitation manager, what should the OTR do **NEXT** to contribute to this process?

A. Explain to all rehabilitation staff the Department of Health and Human Services (DHHS) initiative to decrease the incidence of pressure sores related to hospitalizations.

B. Develop a survey for the rehabilitation staff to determine the frequency of assessment and provision of interventions related to wound management and care.

C. Develop an in-service education program for all rehabilitation staff including information about pressure sores being preventable and a major concern of health care.

Correct Answer: B

RATIONALE:
This step in the continuous quality improvement (CQI) process allows for data collection that can help assess the current situation prior to developing solutions.

Reference:
Braveman, B. (2016). *Leading and managing occupational therapy services: An evidence-based approach* (2nd ed., pp. 335-336, 341). Philadelphia, PA: F.A. Davis Company.

NBCOT® Study Guide for the OTR Certification Examination

NOTES

11. After becoming initially certified as an OTR, an individual worked in an outpatient OT clinic for 4 years. After that time, the individual did not work as an OT and has not participated in occupational therapy professional development activities for the past 6 years. The individual wants to resume OT clinical practice. What ethical responsibility does the individual have prior to obtaining a job in an outpatient setting?

    A. Identify professional development units that can be carried over from the previous job.

    B. Volunteer as an OT in a clinical setting to establish service competence.

    C. Create an effective learning plan related to skills needed for the desired practice setting.

    D. Submit an application to renew national certification as an OTR.

Correct Answer: C

RATIONALE:
OT practitioners have the ethical responsibility of perceiving their current level of professional competence. Creating an effective learning plan that is based on the skills needed for the desired practice setting is a good start in this process.

Reference:
Jacobs, K., & McCormack, G. L. (Eds.). (2011). *The occupational therapy manager* (5th ed., pp. 485-496). Bethesda, MD: AOTA Press.

292

Domain 4: Multiple Choice Answers, Rationales, and References

12. An OTR is designing a process improvement plan to reduce the use of patient restraints in a skilled nursing facility. What is the **INITIAL** step toward promoting corrective actions?

    A. Use incident reports to track staff members who most frequently use restraints.

    B. Develop procedures for tracking and monitoring restraint use within the facility.

    C. Survey other skilled nursing facilities to identify typical reasons for use of patient restraints.

    D. Implement an operating procedure for the correct application of patient restraints.

Correct Answer: B

RATIONALE:
The **INITIAL** step an OTR should take when designing a process improvement plan is to assess and measure the current performance of the facility associated with the issue that has been identified.

Reference:
Braveman, B. (2016). *Leading and managing occupational therapy services: An evidence-based approach* (2nd ed., pp. 335-336, 341). Philadelphia, PA: F.A. Davis Company.

NBCOT® Study Guide for the OTR Certification Examination

NOTES

13. An OTR is providing supervision to a home health aide, who assists a client with bathing. During the initial OT evaluation, the patient identified independence in bathing as a priority goal and was assessed to require 25% assistance. However, the aide tells the OTR that the patient wants total assistance during bathing sessions and frequently asks the aide to complete tasks that the patient can perform. What is the **FIRST** action the OTR should take to support progress toward the patient's bathing goal?

   A. Document the discrepancy in the patient's performance level between the OTR and the aide.

   B. Plan to re-evaluate the client's level of assistance for bathing during the next scheduled session.

   C. Conduct a joint session with the client and the aide to review goals for bathing.

Correct Answer: C

RATIONALE:
It is the responsibility of the supervising OTR to provide adequate supervision and training to ensure the effectiveness of the intervention.

Reference:
Schell, B. A. B., Gillen, G., & Scaffa, M. E. (2014). *Willard & Spackman's occupational therapy* (12th ed., pp. 1086-1087). Philadelphia, PA: Lippincott Williams & Wilkins.

294

Domain 4: Multiple Choice Answers, Rationales, and References

14. An OTR is developing a program for clients who are considering bariatric surgery as a weight-loss option. Which type of program represents a comprehensive client-centered approach that would be effective for improving surgical outcomes or potentially eliminating the need for surgery?

    A. Self-actualization education

    B. Stress management classes

    C. Lifestyle modification program

    D. Weekly support groups

Correct Answer: C

RATIONALE:

A lifestyle modification program addresses performance patterns to influence outcomes related to weight management and obesity prevention.

Reference:

Scaffa, M. E., Reitz, S. M., & Pizzi, M. A. (2010). *Occupational therapy in the promotion of health and wellness.* (pp. 270-271). Philadelphia, PA: F.A. Davis Company.

NBCOT® Study Guide for the OTR Certification Examination

NOTES

15. An OTR is developing a client-centered fall prevention program for community-dwelling older adults. The objective of the program is to reduce the participants' risk of falling. Topics the OTR plans to cover include the benefits of having a health care provider review a list of prescribed medications, the advantages of routinely completing an exercise program, and the purpose of having a regular vision examination. Which additional topic would be **MOST BENEFICIAL** to include in this type of fall prevention program?

A. **Methods and tips to modify the home environment to increase personal safety**

B. Resources to enhance social involvement and engagement in the community

C. Reviews of healthy eating habits and nutritional information on prepared foods

Correct Answer: A

RATIONALE:
Important features of a comprehensive fall prevention program include: medication review by a healthcare provider, engagement in physical activity, routine vision examinations, and ensuring a safe home environment.

Reference:
Smith-Gabai, H., & Holm, S. (Eds.). (2017). *Occupational therapy in acute care* (2nd ed., p. 110). Bethesda, MD: AOTA Press.

Domain 4: Multiple Choice Answers, Rationales, and References

16. An OTR wants to measure the effectiveness of a leisure education program for clients who attend an outpatient chemical dependency unit. What method should the OTR use to obtain a valid measure of the program's effectiveness?

A. Track the number of clients referred to the program with the number of clients who complete the program.

B. Compare a measurement of client leisure involvement at the start of the program with leisure involvement upon completion of the program.

C. Administer a questionnaire about the perceived importance of leisure activities to clients who complete the program.

D. Monitor the frequency of client attendance and level of participation during each session of the program.

Correct Answer: B

RATIONALE:
This method provides measurable performance-based information for evaluating program effectiveness.

Reference:
Fazio, L. S. (2017). *Developing occupation-centered programs with the community* (3rd ed., pp. 260-266). Upper Saddle River, NJ: Pearson Education, Inc.

NBCOT® Study Guide for the OTR Certification Examination

NOTES

17. An OTR working in a skilled nursing facility frequently teaches residents how to use adaptive devices during BADL. The OTR wants to evaluate if the instruction methods and devices are effective in helping to improve the residents' functional performance. Which method would be **MOST EFFECTIVE** to use for gathering this information?

   A. Note the number of times the residents bring the devices to BADL sessions.

   B. Ask the residents how often during the week they use the devices for BADL.

   C. Have the residents demonstrate the use of the devices during a session.

   D. Track how many times the residents spontaneously use the devices during BADL.

Correct Answer: D

RATIONALE:

Tracking spontaneous use of the devices during BADL provides the best indication of transfer of learning and the impact of the devices on residents' functional performance.

References:
Fazio, L. S. (2017). *Developing occupation-centered programs with the community* (3rd ed., pp. 260-266). Upper Saddle River, NJ: Pearson Education, Inc.

Pendleton, H. M., & Schultz-Krohn, W. (Eds.). (2018). *Pedretti's occupational therapy: Practice skills for the physical dysfunction* (8th ed., p. 94). St. Louis, MO: Mosby Elsevier.

Domain 4: Multiple Choice Answers, Rationales, and References

18. An OTR has been asked by the director of nursing in an acute-care hospital to provide an in-service to the nursing staff to describe the role of OT in preventing deep venous thrombosis and pulmonary embolus. Which intervention is **MOST IMPORTANT** to include as part of this presentation to explain the role of OT in thromboembolic disease prevention?

   A. Prescribe anticoagulation therapy to thin the blood and prevent clots from forming.

   B. Recommend mechanical interventions such as compression stockings and pumps.

   C. **Support early mobilization to facilitate patient engagement in self-care activities.**

Correct Answer: C

RATIONALE:
The **MOST IMPORTANT** role for OT in thromboembolic disease prevention is to support early mobilization to facilitate patient engagement in self-care activities.

Reference:
Smith-Gabai, H., & Holm, S. (Eds.). (2017). *Occupational therapy in acute care* (2nd ed., pp. 259-260). Bethesda, MD: AOTA Press.

299

NBCOT® Study Guide for the OTR Certification Examination

NOTES

19. An OTR is providing consultative services to develop a wellness program at a community senior center. A needs assessment survey indicates center participants have a fear of falling, feel they are at risk for falls, and want to age in place for as long as possible. In addition to including fall prevention education, which topic should the OTR recommend as part of the educational programming offered at the center?

   A. Benefits of participating in socially stimulating activities

   B. Value of identifying effective home modifications

   C. Influence of aging on immediate and delayed memory

Correct Answer: B

RATIONALE:
An effective person-environment fit promotes safe aging-in-place. By including the value of identifying effective home modifications in the educational program, the client will be able to determine if changes will be beneficial in the home.

Reference:
Pendleton, H. M., & Schultz-Krohn, W. (Eds.). (2018). *Pedretti's occupational therapy: Practice skills for the physical dysfunction* (8th ed., pp. 1144-1145). St. Louis, MO: Mosby Elsevier.

20. Which of the following is the **BEST** example of a primary objective for a health promotion program for people with chronic conditions?

    A. Prevention of secondary conditions to enhance overall quality of life

    B. Facilitate healing and recovery from existing disease processes

    C. Teach information about medical interventions and service providers

Correct Answer: A

RATIONALE:
One of the goals of a wellness program is to enhance quality of life by addressing lifestyle factors that prevent secondary conditions.

Reference:
Scaffa, M. E., Reitz, S. M., & Pizzi, M. A. (2010). *Occupational therapy in the promotion of health and wellness.* (p. 386). Philadelphia, PA: F.A. Davis Company.

21. An OTR who works in a hospital setting is evaluating an inpatient who recently had a severe stroke. The patient currently requires a ventilator for respiratory support and is not able to verbalize goals. To complete the evaluation process, what ethical obligation does the OTR have for upholding professional responsibilities?

    A. Acquire information for the occupational profile from other sources.

    B. Conclude the patient is not eligible for services until medically stable.

    C. Document that the patient has poor potential for rehabilitation.

Correct Answer: A

RATIONALE:
It is the responsibility of the OTR to obtain an accurate picture of the client in order to complete the evaluation process.

Reference:
Hinojosa, J., & Kramer, P. (Eds.). (2014). *Evaluation in occupational therapy: Obtaining and interpreting data* (4th ed., pp. 9-11). Bethesda, MD: AOTA Press.

NBCOT® Study Guide for the OTR Certification Examination

NOTES

22. An OTR who works in a hospital setting has been asked by the Readmission Prevention committee to provide an in-service to the team about OT services in the care of a patient with diabetes. Which intervention is **MOST IMPORTANT** to include in this presentation to explain the role of OT in maintaining glycemic control?

    A. Support the development of healthy routines and participation in activities.

    B. Explain how food composition and portion size affect blood sugar.

    C. Provide instructions for correctly timing and measuring medication dosages.

Correct Answer: A

RATIONALE:
The unique role of occupational therapy in maintaining glycemic control and management of diabetes is to support the patient in developing healthy performance patterns.

Reference:
Smith-Gabai, H., & Holm, S. (Eds.). (2017). *Occupational therapy in acute care* (2nd ed., pp. 85, 403). Bethesda, MD: AOTA Press.

Domain 4: Multiple Choice Answers, Rationales, and References

23. An OTR working in a pediatric outpatient setting approaches the therapy manager and states, "I believe my colleague is billing for interventions that are not being provided during client sessions." After acknowledging the practitioner's concern, what actions should the manager take **NEXT**?

    A. Develop a remediation program for resolving future billing issues.

    B. Initiate a review of internal clinical service coding and billing practices.

    C. Ask the OTR to provide supporting proof of the colleague's misconduct.

Correct Answer: B

RATIONALE:
The manager is responsible for the oversight of billing practices utilized by occupational therapy staff.

Reference:
Jacobs, K., & McCormack, G. L. (Eds.). (2011). *The occupational therapy manager* (5th ed., pp. 478, 511-513). Bethesda, MD: AOTA Press.

NOTES

303

NBCOT® Study Guide for the OTR Certification Examination

NOTES

24. An OTR is employed at a skilled nursing facility on an hourly basis and is typically scheduled to work 2 shifts each month. The facility-specific clinical protocol directs the OTR to use a standardized assessment tool that is unfamiliar to the OTR. What is the **FIRST** action the OTR should take in this situation?

A. **Alert the therapy supervisor that additional training is needed.**

B. Follow the step-by-step procedural instructions on the test form.

C. Request a colleague administer the assessment tool when needed.

Correct Answer: A

RATIONALE:
It is the responsibility of the OTR to be adequately qualified and prepared to complete all components of the job.

Reference:
Hinojosa, J., & Kramer, P. (Eds.). (2014). *Evaluation in occupational therapy: Obtaining and interpreting data* (4th ed., p. 43). Bethesda, MD: AOTA Press.

Domain 4: Multiple Choice Answers, Rationales, and References

25. An OTR has been providing home health services for 2 weeks to a patient who has had cardiac bypass surgery. The OTR determines that the patient could benefit from an outpatient cardiac rehabilitation program. The OTR informs the supervisor of these conclusions, but the supervisor recommends that the patient continue with home health services to maintain Medicare reimbursement. What action should the OTR take in this situation?

    A. Ask the patient and family about their service preference.

    B. Continue to provide services based on the initial plan.

    C. Contact the patient's physician to discuss a referral to the program.

    D. Provide justification for the referral in a discharge summary.

Correct Answer: D

RATIONALE:
For home health services to be covered under Medicare, the interventions provided must be medically necessary with the expectation of achieving performance outcomes.

References:
Jacobs, K., & McCormack, G. L. (Eds.). (2011). *The occupational therapy manager* (5th ed., pp. 390-391). Bethesda, MD: AOTA Press.

Schell, B. A. B., Gillen, G., & Scaffa, M. E. (2014). *Willard & Spackman's occupational therapy* (12th ed., pp. 1055-1062). Philadelphia, PA: Lippincott Williams & Wilkins.

NBCOT® Study Guide for the OTR Certification Examination

NOTES

26. An OTR working in an industrial setting is documenting the success of a wellness program. One of the program goals is to reduce the number of job-related injuries among workers in a warehouse shipping and receiving department. The initial assessment cited risks related to poor worker fitness, improper lifting techniques, and inadequate work routines. What information about the program should be documented in the program reports to management to provide the **MOST BENEFICIAL** information about the effectiveness of the program?

   A. Evidence of improved body mechanics among workers during lifting tasks

   B. Number of new or recurring injuries during the reporting period

   C. Pre- and post-test results from a worker questionnaire about job-related ergonomics

Correct Answer: B

RATIONALE:
Tracking the number of new or recurring injuries during the reporting period is a quantitative metric to evaluate the effectiveness of the program.

References:
Fazio, L. S. (2017). *Developing occupation-centered programs with the community* (3rd ed., pp. 260-266). Upper Saddle River, NJ: Pearson Education, Inc.

Law, M., & MacDermid, J. (Eds.). (2014). *Evidence-based rehabilitation: A guide to practice* (3rd ed., p. 80). Thorofare, NJ: SLACK, Inc.

Domain 4: Multiple Choice Answers, Rationales, and References

27. An inpatient had a total hip arthroplasty 2 days ago with post-operative precautions that include touchdown weight-bearing (TDWB). Which option **BEST** represents instructions an OTR should provide to reinforce the touchdown weight-bearing (TDWB) precaution?

   A. Use pain as the limiting factor and place up to 100% of body weight through the operative extremity.

   B. Learn to apply up to 50% of body weight through the operative extremity.

   C. **Place the toes of the operative extremity on the floor to maintain balance but do not bear weight.**

Correct Answer: C

RATIONALE:

Touch-down weight bearing (TDWB), also referred to as toe-touch weight bearing (TTWB), involves only touching the floor for balance and not placing any weight on the affected leg during walking and standing.

Reference:

Smith-Gabai, H., & Holm, S. (Eds.). (2017). *Occupational therapy in acute care* (2nd ed., p. 452). Bethesda, MD: AOTA Press.

NBCOT® Study Guide for the OTR Certification Examination

NOTES

28. An adolescent is in an acute setting after sustaining a recent C_6 (ASIA B) spinal cord injury. The adolescent underwent surgery 4 days ago for cervical stabilization and is recovering from the surgery as expected. The adolescent has been on bedrest since the surgery, but now has medical clearance to transfer out of bed with assistance. One of the goals for the adolescent is to sit in a bedside chair for BADL. Prior to transferring the adolescent out of bed, what action **MUST** the OTR take?

   A. Evaluate sensation at key dermatomal segments.

   B. Measure the adolescent's resting vital signs.

   C. Complete a comprehensive manual muscle test.

Correct Answer: B

RATIONALE:
Measuring the adolescent's resting vital signs prior to movement is essential to maintain the patient's safety and to guide the OTR's clinical decisions before and during activity.

Reference:
Case-Smith, J., & O'Brien, J. C. (2015). *Occupational therapy for children and adolescents* (7th ed., pp. 845-846). St. Louis, MO: Mosby Elsevier.

Domain 4: Multiple Choice Answers, Rationales, and References

29. An inpatient had coronary artery bypass graft (CABG) surgery 3 days ago. While sitting on the edge of the bed during a grooming session, the patient's heart rate increases 10 beats per minute above the patient's resting heart rate. What **INITIAL** action should the OTR take based on this observation?

    A. Discontinue the activity and help the patient transfer to a side-lying position in bed.

    B. Document this response and other clinical observations in the client's medical record.

    C. Continue to monitor vital signs and proceed with the planned intervention session.

Correct Answer: C

RATIONALE:
An increase in heart rate by 10 beats per minute above the patient's resting heart rate is an appropriate cardiovascular response to activity.

Reference:
Pendleton, H. M., & Schultz-Krohn, W. (Eds.). (2018). *Pedretti's occupational therapy: Practice skills for the physical dysfunction* (8th ed., p. 1130). St. Louis, MO: Mosby Elsevier.

NBCOT® Study Guide for the OTR Certification Examination

NOTES

30. An OTR is providing home-based services to an adult client who had an open reduction and internal fixation of a tibia fracture. The client lives at home and can ambulate for short distances in the house using crutches. The client's short-term goal is to be able to take a bath independently. What should the OTR teach to the client during the **INITIAL** bathing session?

   A. Proper method for setting up an inflatable bed bath with the assistance of a caregiver

   B. Positioning of the affected leg over the side of the tub after transferring to a tub bench

   C. **Methods for wrapping the affected leg in a moisture barrier prior to transferring to a tub bench**

   D. Sterile techniques for using hydrogen peroxide to clean the skin surrounding the pin sites

Correct Answer: C

RATIONALE:
The client should be instructed on how to keep the surgical site dry and covered during showering to prevent risk of infection.

Reference:
Smith-Gabai, H., & Holm, S. (Eds.). (2017). *Occupational therapy in acute care* (2nd ed., pp. 460, 468). Bethesda, MD: AOTA Press.

310

Domain 4: Multiple Choice Answers, Rationales, and References

31. A client who had a CVA one month ago now has moderate-severe flexor spasticity and scapular immobility of the involved upper extremity. Which technique is **CONTRAINDICATED** to use for minimizing the impact of the spasticity on passive mobility for dressing and hygiene?

NOTES

    A. Self-ROM exercises in supine several times per day

    B. Reciprocal overhead pulley exercises using wall mounted pulleys

    C. Upper extremity weight-bearing during functional tasks

    D. Long-arm air splinting prior to completing a self-care task

Correct Answer: B

RATIONALE:
Reciprocal overhead pulley exercises that use wall mounted pulleys is contraindicated for this client due to the risk of causing impingement syndrome and increasing the client's pain.

Reference:
Pendleton, H. M., & Schultz-Krohn, W. (Eds.). (2018). *Pedretti's occupational therapy: Practice skills for the physical dysfunction* (8th ed., pp. 832-834). St. Louis, MO: Mosby Elsevier.

NBCOT® Study Guide for the OTR Certification Examination

NOTES

32. An OTR working in a children's hospital has been providing services on a daily basis for the past several weeks to a school-age child hospitalized for treatment of a systemic congenital condition. When the OTR arrives at the child's room for the next scheduled session, there is a sign posted on the door indicating enteric contact precautions are in place. What action **MUST** the OTR take based on this observation?

A. **Follow transmission precaution procedures when interacting with the child.**

B. Cancel sessions with the child until these precautions are no longer in place.

C. Rub hands with an alcohol-based hand sanitizer at the end of sessions with the child.

Correct Answer: A

RATIONALE:
To prevent the spread of the infectious agent, the OTR in this circumstance should use transmission precaution procedures when interacting with the child.

Reference:
Smith-Gabai, H., & Holm, S. (Eds.). (2017). *Occupational therapy in acute care* (2nd ed., pp. 486-487). Bethesda, MD: AOTA Press.

312

Domain 4: Multiple Choice Answers, Rationales, and References

33. What is the **FIRST** action the OTR should take when a patient who has schizophrenia exhibits an increase in lip smacking, tongue protrusion, and facial grimacing?

    A. Request that the patient stop the behavior.

    B. Suggest that the patient change medications.

    C. Inform the patient's physician.

Correct Answer: C

RATIONALE:

Extrapyramidal symptoms such as lip smacking, tongue protrusion, and facial grimacing are potential adverse effects of antipsychotic medications often prescribed for schizophrenia.

Reference:

Bonder, B. R. (2015). *Psychopathology and function* (5th ed., pp. 421-422). Thorofare, NJ: SLACK, Inc.

NOTES

NBCOT® Study Guide for the OTR Certification Examination

NOTES

34. An OTR who works in a home health setting is providing an intervention to address BADL of a client who had a stroke. At first, the client actively participates in the intervention activity, but begins to perseverate on the same action while brushing teeth. The client's level of arousal declines, and the client starts to drool and then vomit. What action should the OTR take **FIRST** in this situation?

A. Determine if the client has a history of adverse reactions to medication.

B. **Activate emergency medical services by calling 911.**

C. Contact a family member to receive consent for medical intervention.

Correct Answer: B

RATIONALE:
This client is showing signs of a medical situation that requires urgent medical attention.

References:
Pendleton, H. M., & Schultz-Krohn, W. (Eds.). (2018). *Pedretti's occupational therapy: Practice skills for the physical dysfunction* (8th ed., pp. 149-150). St. Louis, MO: Mosby Elsevier.

Smith-Gabai, H., & Holm, S. (Eds.). (2017). *Occupational therapy in acute care* (2nd ed., pp. 310-311). Bethesda, MD: AOTA Press.

314

Domain 4: Multiple Choice Answers, Rationales, and References

35. An inpatient who has COPD is participating in a dressing session while seated at bedside. While putting on a pair of pants, the patient begins to have dyspnea. Pulse oximetry indicates the patient's oxygen saturation level is 93%. After stopping the activity, what should the OTR have the patient do **NEXT**?

    A. Take several short shallow breaths through the mouth.

    B. Breathe in deeply through the nose and slowly exhale through pursed lips.

    C. Inhale through pursed lips and quickly exhale through the nose.

    D. Breathe through a nasal cannula using supplemental oxygen.

Correct Answer: B

RATIONALE:
Pursed lip breathing is an intervention technique that assists in mitigating the effects of dyspnea.

Reference:
Pendleton, H. M., & Schultz-Krohn, W. (Eds.). (2018). *Pedretti's occupational therapy: Practice skills for the physical dysfunction* (8th ed., p. 1129). St. Louis, MO: Mosby Elsevier.

NBCOT® Study Guide for the OTR Certification Examination

NOTES

36. A client is in the early stages of a slow, progressive upper motor neuron disease. Mild intention tremors and fatigue interfere with completion of typical daily tasks and ability to work a full day as an accountant. Currently, the client ambulates with a cane in the home and uses a wheelchair for community mobility. The client's goal is to remain working as long as possible. Which work accommodation meets the employer's obligation for this client as required by the Americans with Disabilities Act?

A. Consideration for modifying the client's current work schedule

B. Employee review to change the essential elements of the job description

C. Modification of doorways throughout the workplace for maximal accessibility

Correct Answer: A

RATIONALE:
Modifying the client's current work schedule is a reasonable accommodation as outlined by the Americans with Disabilities Act.

Reference:
Pendleton, H. M., & Schultz-Krohn, W. (Eds.). (2018). *Pedretti's occupational therapy: Practice skills for the physical dysfunction* (8th ed., pp. 379-380). St. Louis, MO: Mosby Elsevier.

37. Which federal law in the United States regulates the provision of early intervention, special education, and related services to children with disabilities from birth to two years of age?

    A. Individuals with Disabilities Education Act (IDEA) Part C

    B. Section 504 of the Vocational Rehabilitation Act

    C. Individuals with Disabilities Education Act (IDEA) Part B

Correct Answer: A

RATIONALE:
The Individuals with Disabilities Education Act (IDEA) Part C regulates the provision of early intervention, special education, and related services to children with disabilities from birth to 2 years of age.

References:
Case-Smith, J., & O'Brien, J. C. (2015). *Occupational therapy for children and adolescents* (7th ed., pp. 665-666). St. Louis, MO: Mosby Elsevier.

Mulligan, S. (2014). *Occupational therapy evaluation for children: A pocket guide* (2nd ed., pp. 29-34). Philadelphia, PA: Lippincott Williams & Wilkins.

NBCOT® Study Guide for the OTR Certification Examination

NOTES

38. An OTR is a contract employee at a preschool and works 2-3 shifts each month. During a scheduled shift, the OTR receives a call from a student's physician asking for a progress update for a student. The therapist locates the student's file but is unsure of the school's confidentiality policy. What action should the OTR take **NEXT**?

   A. Provide the physician with a summary of functional gains made by the student.

   B. Consult with the therapy supervisor to understand the privacy restrictions.

   C. Request that the family provide written consent for consultation with team members.

Correct Answer: B

RATIONALE:
In this situation, the OTR should first consult with the therapy supervisor to understand the privacy restrictions prior to taking any additional actions.

Reference:
Hinojosa, J., & Kramer, P. (Eds.). (2014). *Evaluation in occupational therapy: Obtaining and interpreting data* (4th ed., p. 59). Bethesda, MD: AOTA Press.

Domain 4: Multiple Choice Answers, Rationales, and References

39. An OTR working in a home health setting receives a phone call about a new referral for a patient who has Parkinson's disease and whose primary insurance is Medicare Part A. The physician has only requested OT services on the referral. What action **MUST** the OTR take prior to scheduling a home visit with this patient?

   A. Determine how many visits are authorized based on the diagnosis.

   B. Ensure the appropriate disciplines have opened the case.

   C. Identify which procedural codes will be reimbursed by the payer.

Correct Answer: B

RATIONALE:
The Medicare Part A home health benefit only covers occupational therapy services after the case has been opened by an appropriate discipline.

Reference:
Jacobs, K., & McCormack, G. L. (Eds.). (2011). *The occupational therapy manager* (5th ed., pp. 390-391). Bethesda, MD: AOTA Press.

NBCOT® Study Guide for the OTR Certification Examination

NOTES

40. A rheumatologist has prescribed bilateral nighttime resting hand orthotics for a child who has early stage juvenile rheumatoid arthritis. The parents ask the OTR who works at the child's school to fabricate the orthotics. Despite having this condition, the child is functioning at grade-level and is not on the OT caseload. What action should the OTR take in response to the parents' request?

A. Schedule a time after school hours to fabricate the orthotics for the child.

B. Initiate an IEP indicating the child's needs for school-based OT.

C. **Inform the parents to schedule an appointment at an outpatient OT clinic.**

D. Provide the parents with catalog information for ordering pre-fabricated orthotics.

Correct Answer: C

RATIONALE:

School-based OT must relate to curriculum-based activities. These orthotics are typically preventive positioning orthotics for nighttime use. Since this intervention is not directly related to curriculum-based activities and the orthotics will not be worn during the school day, the OTR should refer the child to an outpatient OT clinic for the orthotics.

Reference:
Case-Smith, J., & O'Brien, J. C. (2015). *Occupational therapy for children and adolescents* (7th ed., p. 668). St. Louis, MO: Mosby Elsevier.

Domain 4: Multiple Choice Answers, Rationales, and References

41. An OTR is leading a community-based class for self-referred clients who have rheumatoid arthritis. Through class discussion and observation, the OTR determines that one of the clients in the class would benefit from bilateral hand orthotics. After discussing this observation with the client and determining the client intends to pay for services using insurance benefits, what action should the OTR take **NEXT** to address the client's needs?

   A. Contact the insurance company to obtain reimbursement authorization for the orthotics.

   B. Arrange a clinic appointment time to fabricate the orthotics for the client.

   C. Understand the state regulatory requirements for direct access to OT services.

   D. Complete a comprehensive evaluation to justify the need for the orthotics to the primary care physician.

Correct Answer: C

RATIONALE:
The OTR must understand the state regulatory requirements for direct access to OT services within the jurisdiction where services will be provided.

Reference:
Pendleton, H. M., & Schultz-Krohn, W. (Eds.). (2018). *Pedretti's occupational therapy: Practice skills for the physical dysfunction* (8th ed., pp. 25-26). St. Louis, MO: Mosby Elsevier.

NBCOT® Study Guide for the OTR Certification Examination

NOTES

42. A patient who has global aphasia and flaccid hemiplegia secondary to a CVA has been participating in OT. During an employee safety in-service, a customer service employee, who is a distant relative of this patient, asks the OTR about the patient's progress in OT. Which statement represents an appropriate response for the OTR to provide to this inquiry?

   A. "Based on the recent evaluation, the patient has a long way to go."

   B. **"I can't talk about the patient without the patient's approval."**

   C. "The patient seems to be satisfied with the overall progress."

   D. "I think the patient will have a difficult time returning home."

Correct Answer: B

RATIONALE:
Although the co-worker is the patient's relative, there is no evidence that the patient has given signed consent to provide this relative with personal health information. The OTR should advise the co-worker of the need for patient approval.

Reference:
Jacobs, K., & McCormack, G. L. (Eds.). (2011). *The occupational therapy manager* (5th ed., pp. 610-611). Bethesda, MD: AOTA Press.

322

Domain 4: Multiple Choice Answers, Rationales, and References

43. A client who is recovering from a severe hand injury uses Medicaid as the primary source of reimbursement for OT services provided at a hand therapy clinic. The client plans to relocate to an adult child's home in another state even though the client requires continuation of OT services. Upon learning this information, what recommendation regarding transitional services should the OTR make to the client?

    A. Determine the Medicaid benefits that will be authorized based on the new address.

    B. Notify the current Medicaid provider to transfer benefits based on the new address.

    C. Have a family member locate a comparable hand therapy clinic near the new address.

Correct Answer: A

RATIONALE:
Medicaid benefits are a state-regulated program and eligibility requirements vary by state. The OTR should advise the client to determine the Medicaid benefits based on the new residential address.

Reference:
Schell, B. A. B., Gillen, G., & Scaffa, M. E. (2014). *Willard & Spackman's occupational therapy* (12th ed., pp. 1062-1063). Philadelphia, PA: Lippincott Williams & Wilkins.

323

NBCOT® Study Guide for the OTR Certification Examination

NOTES

44. A third-party payer has denied reimbursement of pre-authorized occupational therapy services based on "insufficient information to substantiate payment." The OTR is writing a letter to appeal the denial. What type of client-related information is **MOST IMPORTANT** to include to increase the likelihood of reimbursement?

   A. Outline of functional tasks used during each intervention session

   B. **Summary of progress based on functional goals and medical necessity**

   C. Annotated reference list indicating evidence-based best practice guidelines

   D. Rate of progress compared to other clients who have the same diagnosis

Correct Answer: B

RATIONALE:
The letter of appeal for a pre-authorized visit should include evidence of functional outcomes and medical necessity.

Reference:
Sames, K. M. (2015). *Documenting occupational therapy practice* (3rd ed., pp. 243-248). Upper Saddle River, NJ: Pearson Education, Inc.

Domain 4: Multiple Choice Answers, Rationales, and References

45. An inpatient in a Medicare funded rehabilitation facility recently had transtibial amputations of both legs. The patient participates in 3 hours of therapy per day and is currently scheduled for discharge in 2 weeks. During the weekly interprofessional meeting the OTR reports the patient has met the OT intervention goals. The physical therapist reports the patient will continue to require physical therapy 2 hours per day until discharge from the facility in 2 weeks. The prosthetist will also be working with the patient during this time. What action should the OTR take based on the meeting reports?

NOTES

A. Complete a discharge summary and discontinue the patient from OT services.

B. Determine if there are any other activities in which the patient would like to participate.

C. Schedule the patient for at least one hour of OT per day to meet the 3-hour therapy rule.

D. Continue to schedule OT sessions to maintain the progress the patient has made thus far.

Correct Answer: A

RATIONALE:

The 3-hour rule is a touchstone the Centers for Medicare and Medicaid use for making an initial finding of medical necessity. The patient can continue to participate in PT for 2 hours per day despite being discharged from OT and receive services from the prosthetist. All intervention goals must result in improvements in the patient's level of performance.

Reference:
Schell, B. A. B., Gillen, G., & Scaffa, M. E. (2014). *Willard & Spackman's occupational therapy* (12th ed., pp. 1055-1062). Philadelphia, PA: Lippincott Williams & Wilkins.

325

NBCOT® Study Guide for the OTR Certification Examination

NOTES

46. An OTR who works in a Medicare-funded inpatient rehabilitation unit is completing an evaluation of a patient who had bilateral total knee arthroplasties 3 days ago. The patient is in generally good health, plans to live independently at home, and wants to resume volunteer work in the community. The patient currently requires OT services to increase independence in bathing, dressing, and toileting. What **MUST** the OTR consider when scheduling the patient for OT?

A. Availability of caregivers to participate in daily sessions for caregiver education and training

B. Impact of the patient's prior level of function on frequency and duration of sessions

C. **Minimum number of therapy hours required for reimbursement by the third-party payer**

D. Patient's physical endurance for completing activities according to a clinical pathway

Correct Answer: C

RATIONALE:
The OTR has the responsibility of understanding policies and procedures related to reimbursement when establishing the intervention plan.

Reference:
Schell, B. A. B., Gillen, G., & Scaffa, M. E. (2014). *Willard & Spackman's occupational therapy* (12th ed., pp. 1053-1062). Philadelphia, PA: Lippincott Williams & Wilkins.

326

Domain 4: Multiple Choice Answers, Rationales, and References

47. A client sustained a hand injury 8 weeks ago and has been participating in an outpatient OT program several times a week for the past 3 weeks. The OTR has just fabricated a dynamic orthotic to correct a PIP joint contracture. What information is **MOST IMPORTANT** to include in the contact note for this visit?

    A. Results of a sensory evaluation of the affected hand

    B. Goniometric measurements of the affected hand

    C. Thickness and type of material used for the orthotic

    D. Orthotic construction methods and care instructions

Correct Answer: B

RATIONALE:
Goniometric measurements provide objective baseline information for tracking efficacy of the orthotic.

References:
Cooper, C. (2014). *Fundamentals of hand therapy: Clinical reasoning and treatment guidelines for common diagnoses of the upper extremity* (2nd ed., pp. 371-374). St. Louis, MO: Mosby Elsevier.

Coppard, B. M., & Lohman, H. (2015). *Introduction to orthotics: A clinical reasoning and problem-solving approach* (4th ed., pp. 45-46, 107-108). St. Louis, MO: Mosby Elsevier.

NBCOT® Study Guide for the OTR Certification Examination

NOTES

48. An OTR has completed the initial evaluation of an inpatient who has leukemia. The OTR plans to work with the patient on a daily basis prior to the patient's planned discharge to home in one week. What information is **MOST IMPORTANT** to include in the initial evaluation report?

    A. Summary data as it relates to the occupational profile

    B. Details about interventions for promoting goal attainment

    C. Descriptions of community support services available

    D. Recommendations for post-discharge OT services

Correct Answer: A

RATIONALE:
Initial reports should include evaluation results as they relate to a patient's overall occupational profile.

Reference:
Gateley, C. A., & Borcherding, S. (2017). *Documentation manual for occupational therapy: Writing SOAP notes* (4th ed., pp. 4, 170-171). Thorofare, NJ: SLACK, Inc.

Domain 4: Multiple Choice Answers, Rationales, and References

49. An inpatient has been participating in ADL, social skills, and prevocational groups as part of a multidisciplinary program for the treatment of anorexia. What information about the patient's participation should be documented in the "A" section of the SOAP note to provide the **MOST BENEFICIAL** information about the patient's progress?

    A. Patient reports of compliance with caloric intake requirements

    B. Evidence of specific decision-making skills the patient uses during assigned group tasks

    C. Examples of patient's conformity with strict limits set on personal behavior

    D. Impressions about the patient's ability to use appropriate judgment related to own skills and assets

Correct Answer: D

RATIONALE:
The 'A' section of the note includes professional impressions that the OTR forms about the client's status or progress based on clinical data.

Reference:
Gateley, C. A., & Borcherding, S. (2017). *Documentation manual for occupational therapy: Writing SOAP notes* (4th ed., pp. 89-95). Thorofare, NJ: SLACK, Inc.

NBCOT® Study Guide for the OTR Certification Examination

NOTES

50. A client who sustained a Colles' fracture of the dominant extremity has been participating in OT. Reevaluation results indicate that the client's active wrist extension and supination increased by 5°, grip strength increased by 5 lbs (2.27kg), and pinch strength improved by 1 lb (0.45kg). The client is able to touch fingertips to palm, but stiffness and swelling limit tight gripping. Pain interferes with the client's ability to complete typical work tasks using the affected hand, but the client compensates for most tasks, except writing, by using the non-dominant hand. Which statement is **BEST** to include in the assessment section of the client's weekly progress note?

A. **"Improvements are noted in ROM and strength, but persistent stiffness, swelling, and pain interfere with full functional use of the affected hand for completion of daily tasks."**

B. "ROM and strength of the affected hand and wrist are improved slightly compared to previous evaluation. Pain and swelling interferes with ability to make a full fist."

C. "Client is able to complete work tasks by using the non-dominant extremity. Recommend continuation of OT for pain management and to improve ROM and strength of the dominant hand."

D. "Decreased ROM and strength interfere with client's ability to write at work. Client would benefit from training activities to improve fine motor skills."

Correct Answer: A

RATIONALE:
This statement accurately states the assessment of the client's progress in relation to meaningful daily occupations.

Reference:
Gateley, C. A., & Borcherding, S. (2017). *Documentation manual for occupational therapy: Writing SOAP notes* (4th ed., pp. 93-95). Thorofare, NJ: SLACK, Inc.

330

Section 4
Appendices

NBCOT® Study Guide for the OTR Certification Examination

Appendix A

Content Outline for the OTR Examination

	OTR DOMAIN DESCRIPTIONS	% OF EXAM
DOMAIN 01	**EVALUATION AND ASSESSMENT** Acquire information regarding factors that influence occupational performance on an ongoing basis throughout the occupational therapy process.	25%
DOMAIN 02	**ANALYSIS AND INTERPRETATION** Formulate conclusions regarding client needs and priorities to develop and monitor an intervention plan throughout the occupational therapy process.	23%
DOMAIN 03	**INTERVENTION MANAGEMENT** Select interventions for managing a client-centered plan throughout the occupational therapy process.	37%
DOMAIN 04	**COMPETENCY AND PRACTICE MANAGEMENT** Manage professional activities of self and relevant others as guided by evidence, regulatory compliance, and standards of practice to promote quality care.	15%

Appendix A • Content Outline for the OTR Examination

Validated Domain, Task, Knowledge Statements for the OTR Examination

DOMAIN 01	EVALUATION AND ASSESSMENT **Acquire information regarding factors that influence occupational performance on an ongoing basis throughout the occupational therapy process.**

Task 0101	**Identify the influence of development; body functions and body structures; and values, beliefs, and spirituality on a client's occupational performance.**

	KNOWLEDGE OF:	
	010101	Impact of typical development and aging on occupational performance, health, and wellness across the life span
	010102	Expected patterns, progressions, and prognoses associated with conditions that limit occupational performance
	010103	Impact of body functions, body structures, and values, beliefs, and spirituality on occupational performance

Task 0102	**Acquire information specific to a client's functional skills, roles, culture, performance context, and prioritized needs through the use of standardized and non-standardized assessments and other available resources in order to develop and update the occupational profile.**

	KNOWLEDGE OF:	
	010201	Resources for acquiring information about the client's current condition and occupational performance
	010202	Administration, purpose, indications, advantages, and limitations of standardized and non-standardized screening and assessment tools
	010203	Internal and external factors influencing a client's meaningful engagement in occupation related to typical habits, roles, routines, and rituals, and the level and type of assistance required

333

NBCOT® Study Guide for the OTR Certification Examination

Task 0103	Determine the influence of task demands and contexts on occupational performance through the application of theoretical constructs within the practice setting.

KNOWLEDGE OF:	
010301	Therapeutic application of theoretical approaches, models of practice, and frames of reference that guide intervention in a variety of practice contexts and environments
010302	Task analysis in relation to a client's performance skills, the occupational profile, practice setting, stage of occupational therapy process, areas of occupation, and activity demands

Appendix A • Content Outline for the OTR Examination

DOMAIN	**ANALYSIS AND INTERPRETATION**
02	Formulate conclusions regarding client needs and priorities to develop and monitor an intervention plan throughout the occupational therapy process.

Task 0201	**Synthesize assessment results and information obtained about the client's current condition and context with client needs and priorities to determine eligibility for services consistent with the objectives of the initial referral to develop a client-centered intervention plan.**

KNOWLEDGE OF:	
020101	Interpretation and analysis of quantitative assessments designed to measure specific client factors and performance skills
020102	Integration of qualitative data collected from interviews, observation, and assessment of the social and physical environments, valued activities, necessary occupations, and priorities
020103	Integration of screening and assessment results with the client occupational profile, client condition, expected outcomes, and level of service delivery to guide critical decision-making for determining eligibility for services, prioritizing needs, and identifying a targeted intervention plan

335

NBCOT® Study Guide for the OTR Certification Examination

Task 0202	Collaborate with the client, the client's relevant others, occupational therapy colleagues, and other professionals and staff by using a culturally sensitive, client-centered approach and therapeutic use of self to manage occupational therapy services guided by evidence and principles of best practice.

	KNOWLEDGE OF:
020201	Characteristics and functions of interprofessional teams for coordinating client care and providing efficient and effective programs and services consistent with specific core competencies, expertise, unique contributions, team roles, and context of the organization
020202	Management of collaborative client-centered intervention plans, Individualized Education Program plans, and transition plans based on client skills, abilities, and expected outcomes in relation to available resources, level of service delivery, and frequency and duration of intervention
020203	Prioritization of intervention goals and activities based on client needs, wants, developmental skills, abilities, progress, and expected outcomes in relation to level of service delivery as well as frequency and duration of intervention
020204	Strategies used for assessing and addressing health literacy to enhance non-verbal and verbal interactions with a client and relevant others in order to promote positive health behaviors, enable informed decisions, maximize safety of care delivery, and promote carry-over of the intervention to support positive intervention outcomes

Appendix A • Content Outline for the OTR Examination

Task 0203	Manage the intervention plan by using clinical reasoning, therapeutic use of self, and cultural sensitivity to identify, monitor, and modify the intervention approach, context, or goals based on client needs, priorities, response to intervention, changes in condition, reevaluation results, and targeted outcomes.

	KNOWLEDGE OF:	
	020301	Factors used for determining and managing the context and type of individual and group activities for effectively supporting intervention goals and objectives
	020302	Methods for monitoring the effectiveness of individual and group intervention in order to make decisions about continuation of the intervention or modifications to the intervention approach, context, or goals
	020303	Clinical decision-making for adapting or modifying the intervention plan and prioritizing goals in response to physiological changes, behavioral reaction, emotion regulation, and developmental needs of the client

NBCOT® Study Guide for the OTR Certification Examination

DOMAIN 03	INTERVENTION MANAGEMENT
	Select interventions for managing a client-centered plan throughout the occupational therapy process.

Task 0301	**Incorporate methods and techniques as an adjunct to interventions in order to facilitate healing and enhance engagement in occupation-based activities.**

KNOWLEDGE OF:

030101	Methods and techniques for selecting and preparing the environment to support optimal engagement in the intervention and promote goal achievement
030102	Indications, contraindications, and precautions associated with wound management, considering the characteristics of a wound, the stage of wound healing, and the influence of the wound on engagement in occupation as guided by evidence, best practice standards, scope of practice, and state licensure practice acts in order to support functional outcomes
030103	Indications, contraindications, precautions, and appropriate clinical application of superficial thermal agents as guided by evidence, best practice standards, scope of practice, and state licensure practice acts
030104	Indications, contraindications, precautions, and appropriate clinical application of deep thermal, mechanical, and electrotherapeutic physical agent modalities as guided by evidence, best practice standards, scope of practice, and state licensure practice acts

338

Appendix A • Content Outline for the OTR Examination

Task 0302	Implement occupation-based strategies to support participation in activities of daily living (ADL), instrumental activities of daily living (IADL), rest and sleep, education, work, play, leisure, and social participation across the life span.

KNOWLEDGE OF:

030201	Interventions for supporting leisure and play-based exploration and participation consistent with client interests, needs, goals, and context
030202	Methods for grading an activity, task, or technique based on level of development, client status, response to intervention, and client needs
030203	Methods for facilitating individual and group participation in shared tasks or activities consistent with the type, function, format, context, goals, and stage of the group
030204	Interventions to support optimal sensory arousal, and visual motor, cognitive, or perceptual processing for supporting engagement in meaningful occupations consistent with developmental level, neuromotor status, mental health, cognitive level, psychosocial skills and abilities, task characteristics, context, and environmental demands
030205	Compensatory and remedial strategies for managing cognitive and perceptual deficits or intellectual disabilities
030206	Adaptive and preventive strategies for optimal engagement in occupation consistent with developmental level, neuromotor status, and condition
030207	Intervention strategies and techniques used to facilitate oral motor skills for drinking, eating, and swallowing consistent with developmental level, client condition, caregiver interaction, and mealtime environment and context
030208	Prevocational, vocational, and transitional services, options, and resources for supporting strengths, interests, employment, and lifestyle goals of the adolescent, middle-aged, and older adult client

Task 0303	Manage interventions for improving range of motion, strength, activity tolerance, sensation, postural control, and balance based on neuromotor status, cardiopulmonary response, and current stage of recovery or condition in order to support occupational performance.

KNOWLEDGE OF:	
030301	Methods for grading various types of therapeutic exercise and conditioning programs consistent with indications and precautions for strengthening muscles, increasing endurance, improving range of motion and coordination, and increasing joint flexibility in relation to task demands
030302	Methods and strategies used to develop, implement, and manage sensory and motor reeducation, pain management, desensitization, edema reduction, and scar management programs
030303	Techniques and activities for promoting or improving postural stability, facilitating dynamic balance, and teaching proper body mechanics and efficient breathing patterns during functional tasks to support engagement in occupation

Task 0304	Apply anatomical, physiological, biomechanical, and healing principles to select or fabricate orthotic devices, and provide training in the use of orthotic and prosthetic devices by using critical thinking and problem-solving as related to a specific congenital anomaly or type of injury, current condition, or disease process in order to support functional outcomes.

KNOWLEDGE OF:	
030401	Types and functions of immobilization, mobilization, restriction, and non-articular orthoses for managing specific conditions
030402	Influence of anatomical, physiological, biomechanical, and healing principles on orthotic selection, design, fabrication, and modification
030403	Methods and techniques for training in the safe and effective use of orthotic and prosthetic devices consistent with prioritized needs, goals, and task demands in order to optimize or enhance function

Appendix A • Content Outline for the OTR Examination

Task 0305	Select assistive technology options, adaptive devices, mobility aids, and other durable medical equipment, considering the client's developmental, physical, functional, cognitive, and mental health status; prioritized needs; task demands; and context to enable participation in meaningful occupation.

KNOWLEDGE OF:

030501	Factors related to measuring, selecting, monitoring fit of, and recommending modifications to seating systems, positioning devices, and mobility aids
030502	Characteristics and features of high- and low-tech assistive technology for supporting engagement in meaningful occupation
030503	Mobility options, vehicle adaptations, and alternative devices for supporting participation in community mobility
030504	Training methods and other factors influencing successful use and maintenance of commonly used assistive technology options, adaptive devices, and durable medical equipment

Task 0306	Recommend environmental modifications guided by an occupation-based model, disability discrimination legislation, and accessibility guidelines and standards to support participation in occupation consistent with a client's physical needs, emotion regulation, cognitive and developmental status, context, and task demands.

KNOWLEDGE OF:

030601	Principles of ergonomics and universal design for identifying, recommending, and implementing reasonable accommodations and features in the workplace, home, and public spaces in order to optimize accessibility and usability
030602	Processes and procedures for identifying, recommending, and implementing modifications in the workplace, home, and public spaces, considering the interaction among client factors, contexts, roles, task demands, and resources

341

NBCOT® Study Guide for the OTR Certification Examination

DOMAIN 04	COMPETENCY AND PRACTICE MANAGEMENT
	Manage professional activities of self and relevant others as guided by evidence, regulatory compliance, and standards of practice to promote quality care.

Task 0401	Manage professional development activities and competency assessment tasks by using evidence-based strategies and approaches in order to provide safe, effective, and efficient programs and services.

KNOWLEDGE OF:	
040101	Methods for defining a clinical question and performing a critical appraisal to support evidence-based practice
040102	Methods for applying continuous quality improvement processes and procedures to occupational therapy service delivery
040103	Methods for evaluating, monitoring, and documenting service competency and professional development needs of self and assigned personnel based on scope of practice and certification standards for occupational therapy
040104	Methods for developing, analyzing, and applying evidence that supports occupation-based programming to advance positive health outcomes for individuals, groups, and specific populations
040105	Application of ethical decision-making and professional behaviors guided by the NBCOT standards of practice and Code of Conduct

342

Appendix A • Content Outline for the OTR Examination

Task 0402	Incorporate risk management techniques at an individual and service-setting level to protect clients, self, staff, and others from injury or harm during interventions.

KNOWLEDGE OF:	
040201	Precautions or contraindications associated with a client condition or stage of recovery
040202	Infection control procedures and universal precautions for reducing transmission of contaminants
040203	Basic first aid in response to minor injuries and adverse reactions
040204	Safety procedures to implement during interventions
040205	Preventive measures for minimizing risk in the intervention environment

Task 0403	Manage occupational therapy service provision in accordance with laws, regulations, state occupational therapy practice acts, and accreditation guidelines in order to protect consumers and meet applicable reimbursement requirements in relation to the service delivery setting.

KNOWLEDGE OF:	
040301	Methods for identifying, locating, and integrating federal regulations, facility policies, and accreditation guidelines related to service delivery across occupational therapy practice settings
040302	Influence of reimbursement policies and guidelines on occupational therapy service delivery
040303	Accountability processes and procedures using relevant practice terminology, abbreviations, information technology, and reporting mechanisms for justifying, tracking, and monitoring sentinel events and outcomes related to occupational therapy service delivery

Using this resource alone or with other resources does not guarantee a passing score on the certification examination.

NBCOT® Study Guide for the OTR Certification Examination

Appendix B

An Illustrated Description of Entry-Level OTR® Practice

The *Illustrated Description of Entry-Level OTR® Practice* brings to life the results from the 2017 NBCOT practice analysis study. Practice analysis is the method used to establish a clearly delineated set of domains, tasks, and associated knowledge necessary for the entry-level certified occupational therapist to provide safe and effective services to clients. The results of the practice analysis study are used to develop the content outline for the OTR certification examination.

Much like looking through the clinic window, the NBCOT's *Illustrated Description of Entry-Level OTR® Practice* presents sample scenarios across a variety of practice settings that depict the tasks OTRs complete in practice. Alongside each scenario* is a description of how the knowledge required to competently perform a task is applied throughout the occupational therapy process. Occupational therapy students may use the sample **scenarios** and associated **application to practice** to support their understanding of entry-level practice, as described in the practice analysis study, and as a tool to prepare for the national certification examination.

344

Appendix B • An Illustrated Description of Entry-Level OTR® Practice

The following is an extract from the Illustrated Description of Entry-Level OTR® Practice that shows the related knowledge, scenario, and application to practice for the class code presented:

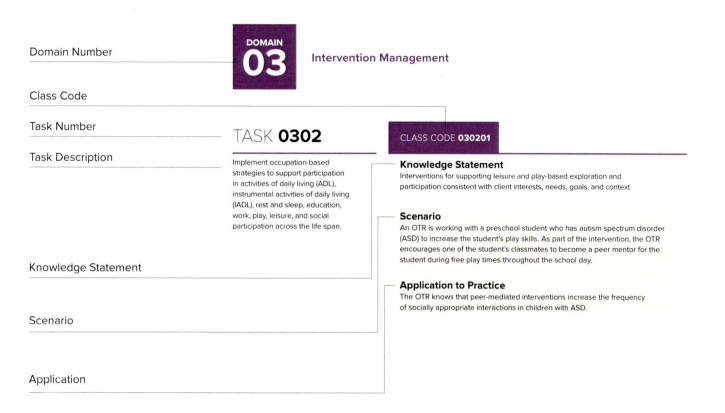

- **Domain Number** — DOMAIN 03 — Intervention Management
- **Class Code** — CLASS CODE 030201
- **Task Number** — TASK 0302
- **Task Description** — Implement occupation-based strategies to support participation in activities of daily living (ADL), instrumental activities of daily living (IADL), rest and sleep, education, work, play, leisure, and social participation across the life span.
- **Knowledge Statement** — Interventions for supporting leisure and play-based exploration and participation consistent with client interests, needs, goals, and context
- **Scenario** — An OTR is working with a preschool student who has autism spectrum disorder (ASD) to increase the student's play skills. As part of the intervention, the OTR encourages one of the student's classmates to become a peer mentor for the student during free play times throughout the school day.
- **Application to Practice** — The OTR knows that peer-mediated interventions increase the frequency of socially appropriate interactions in children with ASD.

*The content contained in the Illustrated Guide was developed to support your certification examination preparation activities. Please note, the scenarios presented in this document are single examples. They are condensed in focus and NOT intended to be inclusive of all the practice situations where you may use this knowledge or all of the knowledge you may be assessed on during the NBCOT certification examination. Using this resource alone or with other resources does not guarantee a passing score on your certification examination.

NBCOT® Study Guide for the OTR Certification Examination

DOMAIN 01

Evaluation and Assessment

Acquire information regarding factors that influence occupational performance on an ongoing basis throughout the occupational therapy process.

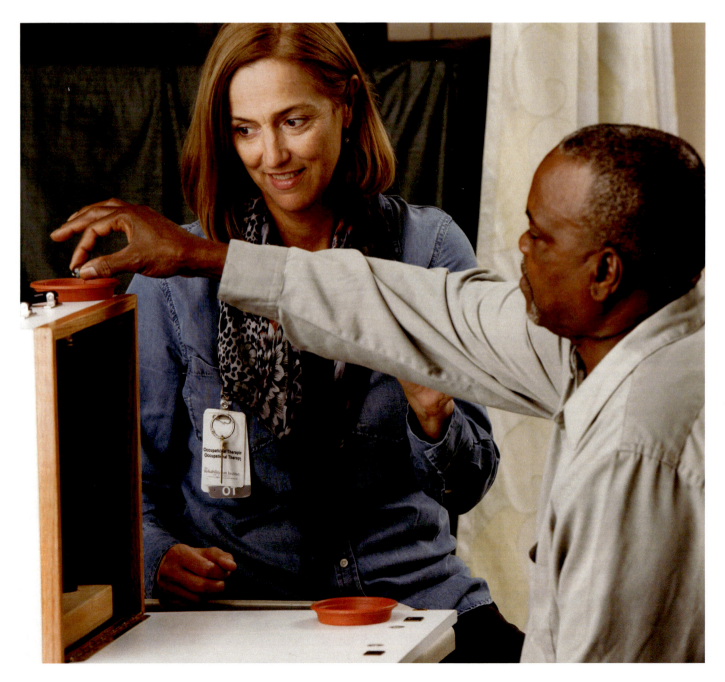

Appendix B • An Illustrated Description of Entry-Level OTR® Practice

DOMAIN 01 — Evaluation and Assessment

TASK 0101

Identify the influence of development; body functions and body structures; and values, beliefs, and spirituality on a client's occupational performance.

CLASS CODE 010101

Knowledge Statement
Impact of typical development and aging on occupational performance, health, and wellness across the life span

Scenario
An OTR working in early intervention is evaluating an 18-month-old child who has a developmental delay. During a feeding session, the OTR observes the child use a lateral pincer grasp to hold the bottle.

Application to Practice
The OTR knows that in normal development, lateral pincer grasp is replaced by inferior pincer grasp at approximately 10 months of age and superior pincer grasp at approximately 12 months of age.

CLASS CODE 010102

Knowledge Statement
Expected patterns, progressions, and prognoses associated with conditions that limit occupational performance

Scenario
An OTR is evaluating a client who has Parkinson's disease. As part of the initial screening, the OTR asks the client about incidences of coughing while eating.

Application to Practice
The OTR knows that movement dysfunction impacting swallowing can occur as Parkinson's disease progresses to Stage 4.

Domain 01: Evaluation and Assessment

TASK 0101

CLASS CODE 010103

Knowledge Statement
Impact of body functions, body structures, and values, beliefs, and spirituality on occupational performance

Scenario
A school-based OTR is observing the behavior of an 8-year-old student who has ADHD. While working on a written assignment, the student is in constant motion, fidgeting with clothing and looking around the classroom.

Application to Practice
The OTR knows that attention is a cognitive process associated with being able to focus on relevant information when performing a task.

TASK 0102

Acquire information specific to a client's functional skills, roles, culture, performance context, and prioritized needs through the use of standardized and non-standardized assessments and other available resources in order to develop and update the occupational profile.

CLASS CODE 010201

Knowledge Statement
Resources for acquiring information about the client's current condition and occupational performance

Scenario
An OTR is reviewing the medical record of an inpatient who has acute Guillain-Barré syndrome. The patient was admitted to the intensive care unit 3 days ago after waking up with flu-like symptoms that progressed to tetraplegia over the course of 12 hours. The patient requires mechanical ventilation for respiratory support.

Application to Practice
The OTR knows that symptoms at the initial stage of Guillain-Barré syndrome progress quickly and that understanding information in the patient's medical record will guide safe and effective clinical elements to include in the initial evaluation.

DOMAIN 01
Evaluation and Assessment

TASK 0102

CLASS CODE 010202

Knowledge Statement
Administration, purpose, indications, advantages, and limitations of standardized and non-standardized screening and assessment tools

Scenario
An outpatient OTR is evaluating a client who has diabetes mellitus and a history of major depression. During an initial interview, the client reports independence with ADL tasks but is unable to identify preferred leisure activities or plans for the future. The OTR administers the Canadian Occupational Performance Measure (COPM).

Application to Practice
The OTR knows that the COPM includes having the client self-identify and prioritize meaningful goals and that these results can be used by the OTR to guide the intervention planning process.

CLASS CODE 010203

Knowledge Statement
Internal and external factors influencing a client's meaningful engagement in occupation related to typical habits, roles, routines, and rituals, and the level and type of assistance required

Scenario
An OTR is interviewing a client, who has mild cognitive impairment secondary to Alzheimer's disease, and the caregiver. The OTR learns that the client bathes infrequently and only brushes teeth and combs hair when provided with verbal cues. The OTR plans to work with the client and the caregiver to establish a visual checklist for a self-care routine to be performed daily.

Application to Practice
The OTR knows to introduce compensatory strategies to support effective habits and routines for a client in the early stages of Alzheimer's disease.

DOMAIN 01 — Evaluation and Assessment

TASK 0103
Determine the influence of task demands and contexts on occupational performance through the application of theoretical constructs within the practice setting.

CLASS CODE 010301

Knowledge Statement
Therapeutic application of theoretical approaches, models of practice, and frames of reference that guide intervention in a variety of practice contexts and environments

Scenario
An OTR is using the Model of Human Occupation (MOHO) to guide the evaluation process for a client who has schizophrenia and is participating in a residential treatment program. The OTR administers the Occupational Performance History Interview (OPHI) and uses the results from the assessment and the tenets of MOHO to establish goals with the client and guide intervention planning.

Application to Practice
The OTR knows that volitional impairment is a key symptom of schizophrenia and that using the Model of Human Occupation to frame treatment will address the client's motivation and support progress toward the intended intervention outcome.

CLASS CODE 010302

Knowledge Statement
Task analysis in relation to a client's performance skills, the occupational profile, practice setting, stage of occupational therapy process, areas of occupation, and activity demands

Scenario
A client who has dystonia in both upper extremities wants to resume playing the violin with a local orchestra. During the evaluation process, the OTR analyzes the quality of the client's available upper extremity movement, the size and style of the instrument, and the position the client typically sits in to play the violin. From the results, the OTR develops a list of recommendations to assist the client in attaining their goal.

Application to Practice
The OTR knows to analyze and integrate the demands of the activity, client factors, and features of the environment to develop specific, client-centered recommendations.

Appendix B • An Illustrated Description of Entry-Level OTR® Practice

DOMAIN 02

Analysis and Interpretation

Formulate conclusions regarding client needs and priorities to develop and monitor an intervention plan throughout the occupational therapy process.

351

DOMAIN 02: Analysis and Interpretation

TASK 0201

Synthesize assessment results and information obtained about the client's current condition and context with client needs and priorities to determine eligibility for services consistent with the objectives of the initial referral to develop a client-centered intervention plan.

CLASS CODE 020101

Knowledge Statement
Interpretation and analysis of quantitative assessments designed to measure specific client factors and performance skills

Scenario
An OTR is interpreting the results of the Peabody Developmental Motor Scales administered to a child. The fine motor quotient is 76, placing the child in the fifth percentile for age. The OTR further analyzes the results to understand the child's strengths and relative weaknesses in fine motor skills based on the test scores.

Application to Practice
The OTR knows how to interpret and analyze the results of the child's fine motor quotient on the Peabody Developmental Motor Scales and use the results to contribute to the overall understanding of the child's performance in everyday activities.

CLASS CODE 020102

Knowledge Statement
Integration of qualitative data collected from interviews, observation, and assessment of the social and physical environments, valued activities, necessary occupations, and priorities

Scenario
An OTR who works in early intervention is evaluating the self-feeding skills of a 2-year-old child who has cerebral palsy. In addition to measuring the child's fine and gross motor skills, the OTR interviews the parents to understand typical mealtime routines, assesses the setup of the dining room, and observes the child's self-feeding ability during a mealtime activity.

Application to Practice
The OTR knows to integrate qualitative information obtained during the interview and observations made during mealtime with quantitative test results to guide the development of a client-centered intervention plan.

Appendix B • An Illustrated Description of Entry-Level OTR® Practice

Analysis and Interpretation

TASK 0201

CLASS CODE 020103

Knowledge Statement
Integration of screening and assessment results with the client occupational profile, client condition, expected outcomes, and level of service delivery to guide critical decision-making for determining eligibility for services, prioritizing needs, and identifying a targeted intervention plan

Scenario
An OTR is screening a resident of a skilled nursing facility who had an exacerbation of COPD and wants to regain independence. Prior to this episode, the resident completed ADL with setup and supervision but now requires 50% assistance to complete the same activities. The OTR schedules a time to complete a comprehensive OT evaluation.

Application to Practice
The OTR knows to gather information about a resident who has a recent change in function to determine the need for an evaluation.

TASK 0202

Collaborate with the client, the client's relevant others, occupational therapy colleagues, and other professionals and staff by using a culturally sensitive, client-centered approach and therapeutic use of self to manage occupational therapy services guided by evidence and principles of best practice.

CLASS CODE 020201

Knowledge Statement
Characteristics and functions of interprofessional teams for coordinating client care and providing efficient and effective programs and services consistent with specific core competencies, expertise, unique contributions, team roles, and context of the organization

Scenario
An outpatient OTR is working with a client who has post-concussive syndrome. The client wants to resume working as a medical transcriptionist but has intermittent diplopia that interferes with reading information on the computer monitor. The OTR provides the client with strategies to address double vision and refers the client to a neuro-ophthalmologist for further evaluation.

Application to Practice
The OTR knows that a neuro-ophthalmologist is a medical doctor who is trained to evaluate and provide intervention on visual problems caused by neurological conditions and is a member of the interprofessional team for a client who has diplopia.

Analysis and Interpretation

TASK 0202

CLASS CODE 020202

Knowledge Statement
Management of collaborative client-centered intervention plans, Individualized Education Program plans, and transition plans based on client skills, abilities, and expected outcomes in relation to available resources, level of service delivery, and frequency and duration of intervention

Scenario
An OTR is attending a transition planning meeting for a high-school student with autism spectrum disorder who wants to find a meaningful job after graduation. The OTR collaborates with the student, the resource teacher, and the school counselor to facilitate a series of peer-mentored volunteer opportunities for the student to trial throughout the school year.

Application to Practice
The OTR knows to collaborate with school-based team members to provide a variety of volunteer experiences that will promote the student's self-determination and self-advocacy for a desired career path.

CLASS CODE 020203

Knowledge Statement
Prioritization of intervention goals and activities based on client needs, wants, developmental skills, abilities, progress, and expected outcomes in relation to level of service delivery as well as frequency and duration of intervention

Scenario
An OTR is developing an intervention plan for an outpatient client who had cardiac surgery 8 days ago and currently performs ADL with assistance from a caregiver. The client wants to resume working as an in-home day-care provider. The OTR collaborates with the client to establish short-term goals for independence in ADL and long-term goals to support progress toward the client's return to work.

Application to Practice
The OTR knows to prioritize short-term goals based on the client's current level of function and preferences and to modify the intervention plan as tolerated by the client to support progress toward long-term goals.

Appendix B • An Illustrated Description of Entry-Level OTR® Practice

DOMAIN 02 — Analysis and Interpretation

TASK 0202

CLASS CODE 020204

Knowledge Statement
Strategies used for assessing and addressing health literacy to enhance non-verbal and verbal interactions with a client and relevant others in order to promote positive health behaviors, enable informed decisions, maximize safety of care delivery, and promote carry-over of the intervention to support positive intervention outcomes

Scenario
An OTR is teaching pain management strategies to an outpatient client with complex regional pain syndrome. The OTR teaches the client each strategy separately, provides an opportunity for the client to trial each strategy, and modifies the intervention approach based on the client's understanding of the instructions. At the end of the session, the OTR asks the client to summarize preferred strategies learned during the session, provides the client with a written handout, and allows time for the client to ask questions.

Application to Practice
The OTR knows the principles of health literacy and continually evaluates the client's understanding of the information provided to promote carry-over of learning into the client's everyday routines.

TASK 0203

Manage the intervention plan by using clinical reasoning, therapeutic use of self, and cultural sensitivity to identify, monitor, and modify the intervention approach, context, or goals based on client needs, priorities, response to intervention, changes in condition, reevaluation results, and targeted outcomes.

CLASS CODE 020301

Knowledge Statement
Factors used for determining and managing the context and type of individual and group activities for effectively supporting intervention goals and objectives

Scenario
An outpatient OTR is assisting a client, who has mild cognitive impairment, in completing an accounting task that simulates the client's work demands. The client is distracted by the noise and activity in the busy therapy clinic, which causes the client to make errors and abandon the task before completion. The OTR reserves a private room for the next scheduled therapy session.

Application to Practice
The OTR knows to assess the influence of contextual demands on the client's level of occupational performance and to modify the intervention environment to support the client's current level of function.

Analysis and Interpretation

TASK 0203

CLASS CODE 020302

Knowledge Statement
Methods for monitoring the effectiveness of individual and group intervention in order to make decisions about continuation of the intervention or modifications to the intervention approach, context, or goals

Scenario
An OTR who works in an inpatient program for patients with eating disorders is leading a social skills group. One of the group members attends all the scheduled group sessions but does not participate in the large group discussions. For the next scheduled group session, the OTR plans activities to be completed in teams of two.

Application to Practice
The OTR knows to continually reassess the patients' response to intervention and to modify the level of difficulty of the therapeutic approach for each client in the group to achieve a positive and successful outcome.

CLASS CODE 020303

Knowledge Statement
Clinical decision-making for adapting or modifying the intervention plan and prioritizing goals in response to physiological changes, behavioral reaction, emotion regulation, and developmental needs of the client

Scenario
A client who had a CVA 2 months ago identifies driving as an intervention goal. Prior to goal achievement, the client has an additional CVA resulting in a significant decline in function. The OTR collaborates with the client to develop alternative community mobility goals that include accessing a curb-to-curb community transportation service.

Application to Practice
The OTR knows to reevaluate the client's functional status following a change in medical condition and to modify intervention goals to address the client's current level of function and abilities.

Appendix B • An Illustrated Description of Entry-Level OTR® Practice

DOMAIN 03

Intervention Management

Select interventions for managing a client-centered plan throughout the occupational therapy process.

Domain 03: Intervention Management

TASK 0301

Incorporate methods and techniques as an adjunct to interventions in order to facilitate healing and enhance engagement in occupation-based activities.

CLASS CODE 030101

Knowledge Statement
Methods and techniques for selecting and preparing the environment to support optimal engagement in the intervention and promote goal achievement

Scenario
An OTR is preparing to provide recommendations to an inpatient who recently had spinal surgery and must follow precautions for 6 weeks. The OTR prepares for the session by gathering the materials and equipment needed to demonstrate the recommendations and develops a printed handout to provide to the patient.

Application to Practice
The OTR knows that gathering necessary equipment and planning the intervention session appropriately are essential factors in facilitating optimal patient engagement and carry-over of care.

CLASS CODE 030102

Knowledge Statement
Indications, contraindications, and precautions associated with wound management, considering the characteristics of a wound, the stage of wound healing, and the influence of the wound on engagement in occupation as guided by evidence, best practice standards, scope of practice, and state licensure practice acts in order to support functional outcomes

Scenario
An OTR who works in an acute-care setting is working with an inpatient who is deconditioned and is recovering from pneumonia. While the patient is participating in lower body dressing, the OTR notices redness on both heels. The OTR informs the primary care nurse and teaches the patient to routinely check skin on the heels and to relieve pressure with positioning options when in bed.

Application to Practice
The OTR knows that an integral part of preventing skin breakdown is for the patient to routinely perform skin checks of the at-risk areas of the body and to instruct the patient to use pressure-relieving positioning methods when in bed.

DOMAIN 03
Intervention Management

TASK 0301

CLASS CODE 030103

Knowledge Statement
Indications, contraindications, precautions, and appropriate clinical application of superficial thermal agents as guided by evidence, best practice standards, scope of practice, and state licensure practice acts

Scenario
A client who has chronic rheumatoid arthritis has pain, stiffness, weakness, and decreased ROM in both hands that interfere with the client's goal of independent meal preparation. The OTR adheres to the OT clinic's physical agent modality protocols by administering a paraffin wax treatment at the start of the intervention session prior to engaging the client in a kitchen-related task.

Application to Practice
The OTR knows that paraffin wax provides an even distribution of heat to the affected joints, which effectively reduces the client's stiffness and pain caused by arthritis. Completing this at the beginning of the intervention enables the client to successfully engage in the kitchen task.

CLASS CODE 030104

Knowledge Statement
Indications, contraindications, precautions, and appropriate clinical application of deep thermal, mechanical, and electrotherapeutic physical agent modalities as guided by evidence, best practice standards, scope of practice, and state licensure practice acts

Scenario
A service competent OTR, who has met local state regulatory requirements, is using functional electrical stimulation (FES) as part of the intervention plan to facilitate voluntary grasp and release in a client who has hemiparesis. The OTR applies electrodes to the muscles of the forearm and assists the client to pick up items from the table.

Application to Practice
The OTR knows that using neuromuscular electrical stimulation, as part of the intervention plan, supports muscle reeducation and strengthening while completing a meaningful task.

DOMAIN 03 — Intervention Management

TASK 0302

Implement occupation-based strategies to support participation in activities of daily living (ADL), instrumental activities of daily living (IADL), rest and sleep, education, work, play, leisure, and social participation across the life span.

CLASS CODE 030201

Knowledge Statement
Interventions for supporting leisure and play-based exploration and participation consistent with client interests, needs, goals, and context

Scenario
An OTR is working with a preschool student who has autism spectrum disorder (ASD) to increase the student's play skills. As part of the intervention, the OTR encourages one of the student's classmates to become a peer mentor for the student during free play times throughout the school day.

Application to Practice
The OTR knows that peer-mediated interventions increase the frequency of socially appropriate interactions in children with ASD.

CLASS CODE 030202

Knowledge Statement
Methods for grading an activity, task, or technique based on level of development, client status, response to intervention, and client needs

Scenario
A school-based OTR is working with a preschool student who has hypotonic cerebral palsy. The OTR positions the student prone on an incline wedge to complete a wooden puzzle with pegs. At first, the OTR places the puzzle close to the student; but as the session progresses, the OTR increases the challenge by repositioning the puzzle further away from the student to encourage greater upper extremity reach and trunk and neck extension.

Application to Practice
The OTR knows to start the activity with a just-right challenge and to grade or increase the level of difficulty of the activity to support goal achievement.

DOMAIN 03: Intervention Management

TASK 0302

CLASS CODE 030203

Knowledge Statement
Methods for facilitating individual and group participation in shared tasks or activities consistent with the type, function, format, context, goals, and stage of the group

Scenario
An OTR is facilitating a social skills group for clients who have severe and enduring mental illness. The OTR plans a session for the clients to practice appropriate skills for returning an item to a store. The OTR first encourages the group to discuss the scenario, then demonstrates appropriate communication skills to the group before instructing the clients to role-play the scenario with a partner.

Application to Practice
The OTR knows that role-playing in a group setting is an effective technique for clients to learn, practice, and receive feedback on appropriate social skills.

CLASS CODE 030204

Knowledge Statement
Interventions to support optimal sensory arousal, and visual motor, cognitive, or perceptual processing for supporting engagement in meaningful occupations consistent with developmental level, neuromotor status, mental health, cognitive level, psychosocial skills and abilities, task characteristics, context, and environmental demands

Scenario
An OTR is teaching self-regulation strategies to a student in the third grade who has difficulty paying attention in class. During a math class, the OTR observes the student moving constantly around the room and frequently falling and bumping into objects and furniture. The OTR begins the intervention by teaching the student to self-assess energy level to determine if calming or energizing strategies would assist the student in focusing in class.

Application to Practice
The OTR knows the importance of teaching the student methods to self-assess energy level and to identify an appropriate self-regulation strategy to support increased focus for learning in the classroom.

DOMAIN 03: Intervention Management

TASK 0302

CLASS CODE 030205

Knowledge Statement
Compensatory and remedial strategies for managing cognitive and perceptual deficits or intellectual disabilities

Scenario
A young adult client with an intellectual disability is attending a prevocational program. As part of the intervention, the OTR first collaborates with the client to record role-playing situations that demonstrate positive communication skills in a work setting. The OTR and the client watch the video together several times to discuss key skills and strategies prior to practicing at a jobsite.

Application to Practice
The OTR knows that video-based interventions can promote imitation of specific behaviors in clients who have intellectual disabilities and support the development of foundational skills for vocational success.

CLASS CODE 030206

Knowledge Statement
Adaptive and preventive strategies for optimal engagement in occupation consistent with developmental level, neuromotor status, and condition

Scenario
A client with flaccid hemiplegia wants to independently put on a front fastening shirt. The OTR teaches the client to first put the affected arm into the sleeve and pull it over the affected shoulder, then swing the shirt around the back and put the unaffected arm into the remaining sleeve.

Application to Practice
The OTR knows the appropriate sequence of steps to support progress toward independent dressing using one-handed techniques.

DOMAIN 03 — Intervention Management

TASK 0302

CLASS CODE 030207

Knowledge Statement
Intervention strategies and techniques used to facilitate oral motor skills for drinking, eating, and swallowing consistent with developmental level, client condition, caregiver interaction, and mealtime environment and context

Scenario
A 3-year-old child with cerebral palsy pockets food in the cheeks and has poor tongue lateralization that interferes with nutritional intake. As part of the intervention, the OTR uses a vibrating brush to stimulate tongue movements prior to offering the child food on a spoon. The OTR also teaches the child play activities that facilitate tongue movements from side-to-side.

Application to Practice
The OTR knows appropriate oral-motor techniques to facilitate tongue lateralization needed to support the child's effective eating and swallowing.

CLASS CODE 030208

Knowledge Statement
Prevocational, vocational, and transitional services, options, and resources for supporting strengths, interests, employment, and lifestyle goals of the adolescent, middle-aged, and older adult client

Scenario
An OTR is working with a client who has executive dysfunction. One of the client's goals is to improve organization of morning routines to prepare for obtaining future employment. The OTR assists the client in identifying and prioritizing key tasks. Together, they develop an activity schedule that the OTR posts in a prominent place in the client's home.

Application to Practice
The OTR knows that cognitive compensatory strategies support the integration of effective habits in the client's daily routines enabling the client to effectively prepare for the work day.

DOMAIN 03

Intervention Management

TASK 0303

Manage interventions for improving range of motion, strength, activity tolerance, sensation, postural control, and balance based on neuromotor status, cardiopulmonary response, and current stage of recovery or condition in order to support occupational performance.

CLASS CODE 030301

Knowledge Statement
Methods for grading various types of therapeutic exercise and conditioning programs consistent with indications and precautions for strengthening muscles, increasing endurance, improving range of motion and coordination, and increasing joint flexibility in relation to task demands

Scenario
A client who is recovering from Guillain-Barré syndrome has Fair plus (3+/5) muscle strength of the upper extremity. One of the client's goals is to resume laundry activities. As part of an intervention session, the OTR removes 10 large bath towels from the dryer and instructs the client to fold 5 of them, take a break, and fold 5 more. When the client's upper extremity strength has increased, the OTR instructs the client to remove 10 pieces of wet clothing from the washer and place them in the dryer, take a break, and repeat.

Application to Practice
The OTR knows that it is important to develop a strengthening program based on meaningful occupation. The OTR begins with the client completing resistance-based tasks during a laundry activity suited to the client's current muscle strength. In subsequent interventions, the OTR increases the intensity of the tasks to support the client in progressing toward goal attainment.

CLASS CODE 030302

Knowledge Statement
Methods and strategies used to develop, implement, and manage sensory and motor reeducation, pain management, desensitization, edema reduction, and scar management programs

Scenario
An inpatient who has hemiparesis has significant edema in the affected hand limiting range of motion and use of available movement for ADL. As part of the intervention plan, the OTR recommends to the patient a compression glove to be worn at all times except during hygiene tasks.

Application to Practice
The OTR knows that compression is an edema reduction technique that restricts the accumulation of fluid in the subcutaneous tissue through application of external pressure. By wearing this glove, the patient's edema will reduce, enabling the patient to reengage with ADL tasks.

Appendix B • An Illustrated Description of Entry-Level OTR® Practice

DOMAIN 03

Intervention Management

TASK 0303

CLASS CODE 030303

Knowledge Statement
Techniques and activities for promoting or improving postural stability, facilitating dynamic balance, and teaching proper body mechanics and efficient breathing patterns during functional tasks to support engagement in occupation

Scenario
A client who has COPD wants to be independent in ADL but is often short of breath during the morning routine. As part of the intervention plan, the OTR teaches the client energy conservation strategies, including sitting on the edge of the bed for dressing tasks and using pursed lip breathing techniques during activity.

Application to Practice
The OTR knows that using the pursed lip breathing technique will help the airway stay open during exhalation, decrease the rate of respiration, and reduce symptoms of breathlessness and anxiety. In addition, completing some tasks in a sitting position causes less energy expenditure and can assist the client in pacing activities throughout the day.

TASK 0304

Apply anatomical, physiological, biomechanical, and healing principles to select or fabricate orthotic devices, and provide training in the use of orthotic and prosthetic devices by using critical thinking and problem-solving as related to a specific congenital anomaly or type of injury, current condition, or disease process in order to support functional outcomes.

CLASS CODE 030401

Knowledge Statement
Types and functions of immobilization, mobilization, restriction, and non-articular orthoses for managing specific conditions

Scenario
A client with chronic rheumatoid arthritis has painful joints of the hands and wrists that interfere with functional activities during the day. Based on the evaluation results, the OTR plans to provide prefabricated static resting hand orthoses for the client to wear at night.

Application to Practice
The OTR knows that wearing resting hand orthoses at night positions the client's hands in anatomical alignment to reduce stress on joint capsules and decreases symptoms of pain, which will enable the client to engage in functional tasks during the day.

365

Intervention Management

TASK 0304

CLASS CODE 030402

Knowledge Statement
Influence of anatomical, physiological, biomechanical, and healing principles on orthotic selection, design, fabrication, and modification

Scenario
An OTR is checking the fit of a short thumb spica orthosis for an outpatient client who has a distal median nerve injury.

Application to Practice
The OTR knows the importance of checking the fit of a hand-based thumb-positioning orthosis to ensure it maintains the web space and positions the thumb for function.

CLASS CODE 030403

Knowledge Statement
Methods and techniques for training in the safe and effective use of orthotic and prosthetic devices consistent with prioritized needs, goals, and task demands in order to optimize or enhance function

Scenario
A client, who has carpal tunnel syndrome, is learning the wear and care instructions for a custom thermoplastic volar wrist extension orthosis. In addition to providing the client with written information, the OTR teaches the client how to remove and reapply the orthosis, then asks the client to demonstrate the skill.

Application to Practice
The OTR knows that providing effective client education will enhance compliance with the wearing schedule and positively influence the overall outcome for the client.

DOMAIN 03

Intervention Management

TASK 0305

Select assistive technology options, adaptive devices, mobility aids, and other durable medical equipment, considering the client's developmental, physical, functional, cognitive, and mental health status; prioritized needs; task demands; and context to enable participation in meaningful occupation.

CLASS CODE 030501

Knowledge Statement
Factors related to measuring, selecting, monitoring fit of, and recommending modifications to seating systems, positioning devices, and mobility aids

Scenario
An outpatient OTR is recommending a power-assist wheelchair for a child who has cerebral palsy. The child is independent in self-propulsion for short distances but is not able to propel a manual chair around the community at the same speed as friends who are ambulatory.

Application to Practice
The OTR knows the appropriate wheelchair to select for the child to support successful participation in the community.

CLASS CODE 030502

Knowledge Statement
Characteristics and features of high- and low-tech assistive technology for supporting engagement in meaningful occupation

Scenario
An OTR is recommending an environmental control device for a client who has minimal movement capabilities and wants to independently operate the lights and the television. After reviewing the evaluation results, the OTR selects a programmable tablet with a point activation system for the client to use in the home.

Application to Practice
The OTR knows which high-technology assistive device is most beneficial to support the client's limited physical capacities and achieve occupational performance goals.

DOMAIN 03: Intervention Management

TASK 0305

CLASS CODE 030503

Knowledge Statement
Mobility options, vehicle adaptations, and alternative devices for supporting participation in community mobility

Scenario
An OTR is working with a student who has low vision and wants to be independent in taking public transportation to and from college. The OTR teaches the student to use interactive software to plan the route and GPS tracking to find the location. As part of the intervention, the OTR accompanies the student to a local train station and demonstrates how to use the audible output device on the ticket vending machine.

Application to Practice
The OTR knows that practicing the learned skills at the train station with the student will improve the student's ability to use public transportation and participate in the community.

CLASS CODE 030504

Knowledge Statement
Training methods and other factors influencing successful use and maintenance of commonly used assistive technology options, adaptive devices, and durable medical equipment

Scenario
An OTR recommends a half bed rail for a client who has limb-girdle muscular dystrophy and difficulty transferring in and out of bed. After the bed rail is secured on the client's bed, the OTR teaches the client how to use the rail to provide leverage assistance when transferring from sitting on the edge of the bed to standing up.

Application to Practice
The OTR knows that in addition to making recommendations for durable medical equipment, it is necessary to teach the client how to use the equipment in the home to support performance outcomes.

Appendix B • An Illustrated Description of Entry-Level OTR® Practice

DOMAIN 03: Intervention Management

TASK 0306

Recommend environmental modifications guided by an occupation-based model, disability discrimination legislation, and accessibility guidelines and standards to support participation in occupation consistent with a client's physical needs, emotion regulation, cognitive and developmental status, context, and task demands.

CLASS CODE 030601

Knowledge Statement
Principles of ergonomics and universal design for identifying, recommending, and implementing reasonable accommodations and features in the workplace, home, and public spaces in order to optimize accessibility and usability

Scenario
An OTR is working with a school-based team to promote universal access to outdoor play equipment for students of all abilities. As part of the recommendations for a new play structure, the OTR includes ramps and bridges with double rails, activity panels at varying levels, and a poured-in synthetic surface for the playground.

Application to Practice
The OTR knows the tenets of universal design and the accessibility features that would enhance playful spaces for all students who use the outdoor play equipment.

CLASS CODE 030602

Knowledge Statement
Processes and procedures for identifying, recommending, and implementing modifications in the workplace, home, and public spaces, considering the interaction among client factors, contexts, roles, task demands, and resources

Scenario
An OTR is making worksite recommendations for a client who has a low back injury and is participating in a work-hardening program to prepare to return to work as a shipping clerk. After completing the job analysis and worksite evaluation, the OTR meets with the client and the supervisor to negotiate a graduated return-to-work plan. The OTR recommends that the client use a cart to transport mail around the facility and schedule regular rest breaks throughout the work day.

Application to Practice
The OTR knows to integrate the needs of the employer and the client in the work plan to develop job-specific accommodations and recommendations that support a safe and successful return to work.

369

DOMAIN 04

Competency and Practice Management

Manage professional activities of self and relevant others as guided by evidence, regulatory compliance, and standards of practice to promote quality care.

DOMAIN 04

Competency and Practice Management

TASK 0401

Manage professional development activities and competency assessment tasks by using evidence-based strategies and approaches in order to provide safe, effective, and efficient programs and services.

CLASS CODE 040101

Knowledge Statement
Methods for defining a clinical question and performing a critical appraisal to support evidence-based practice

Scenario
An outpatient who had a CVA 3 months ago asks if playing stimulating computer-based games would help improve cognitive function in everyday life activities. The OTR uses the PICO method to gather information about this intervention activity to respond to the client's query.

Application to Practice
The OTR knows that the PICO method is an efficient way to frame an evidence-based literature search. By using this method, the OTR will appraise articles for validity and quality to help determine whether to support the use of this intervention strategy with the client.

CLASS CODE 040102

Knowledge Statement
Methods for applying continuous quality improvement processes and procedures to occupational therapy service delivery

Scenario
An OTR who works in a skilled nursing facility has been asked to develop a fall management program. The OTR begins by designing a tracking form to record the frequency of falls and the environmental and client-centered risk factors associated with the occurrence of a fall at the facility.

Application to Practice
The OTR knows that the first step in the continuous quality improvement process is to develop an effective data collection tool to gather facts. The results from this can be used to determine if a fall management program is warranted at the facility.

Competency and Practice Management

TASK 0401

CLASS CODE 040103

Knowledge Statement
Methods for evaluating, monitoring, and documenting service competency and professional development needs of self and assigned personnel based on scope of practice and certification standards for occupational therapy

Scenario
A school-based OTR is transitioning to a new job in an adult rehabilitation setting. To prepare, the OTR accesses the NBCOT Navigator, completes the self-reflection tool, and takes several of the tools related to rehabilitation practice. After completing the tools, the OTR reads the evidence-based articles provided in the feedback report.

Application to Practice
The OTR knows that the NBCOT Navigator is a competency assessment platform designed to support certificants in identifying practice knowledge and skills. By using the tools in the NBCOT Navigator, the OTR can determine professional development needs to support the transition to a new work setting.

CLASS CODE 040104

Knowledge Statement
Methods for developing, analyzing, and applying evidence that supports occupation-based programming to advance positive health outcomes for individuals, groups, and specific populations

Scenario
An OTR is using a population-based approach to develop a health and wellness program for community-dwelling adults who have multiple sclerosis. The OTR convenes a client focus group and collects information on factors that support a healthy lifestyle.

Application to Practice
The OTR knows that conducting a focus group is an effective method for obtaining qualitative data from clients to guide outcome-driven community-based programming.

Appendix B • An Illustrated Description of Entry-Level OTR® Practice

DOMAIN 04
Competency and Practice Management

TASK 0401

CLASS CODE 040105

Knowledge Statement
Application of ethical decision-making and professional behaviors guided by the NBCOT standards of practice and Code of Conduct

Scenario
An OT student is preparing to post information in an online study group about car transfer techniques for clients with spinal cord injuries. The post includes photographs of a client completing a transfer during a recent intervention session. The supervising OTR immediately stops the student from posting the pictures and explains the principles of HIPAA and the NBCOT Code of Conduct.

Application to Practice
The OTR knows that posting photographs of the client is a violation of HIPAA and Principle 8 of the NBCOT Code of Conduct, which states: Certificants shall not electronically post personal health information or anything, including photos, that may reveal a patient's/client's identity or personal or therapeutic relationship.

TASK 0402

Incorporate risk management techniques at an individual and service-setting level to protect clients, self, staff, and others from injury or harm during interventions.

CLASS CODE 040201

Knowledge Statement
Precautions or contraindications associated with a client condition or stage of recovery

Scenario
An outpatient client had a metacarpal fracture of the second digit 7 weeks ago that was immobilized in a cast for 6 weeks. One of the client's goals is to resume independent meal preparation. The client has joint capsule tightness limiting ROM and functional use of the hand. The OTR is teaching the client gentle finger flexion and stretching exercises and use of joint mobilization techniques.

Application to Practice
The OTR knows that it is important to initiate a gentle ROM program at this stage of recovery to prevent the client from experiencing an increase in pain, inflammation, and edema and to enable the client to begin using the affected hand to resume everyday activities.

Competency and Practice Management

TASK 0402

CLASS CODE 040202

Knowledge Statement
Infection control procedures and universal precautions for reducing transmission of contaminants

Scenario
An OTR, who works in a hospital, is preparing to evaluate a patient who has respiratory failure, a tracheostomy, and was tested positive for pseudomonas. A sign posted on the patient's door indicates droplet precautions are to be followed. Before entering the patient's room, the OTR puts on a custom-fit N95 respirator, gloves, and gown.

Application to Practice
The OTR knows that wearing the protective equipment during all contact with the patient reduces the risk of cross-contamination and supports the safety and wellbeing of all patients and personnel at the facility.

CLASS CODE 040203

Knowledge Statement
Basic first aid in response to minor injuries and adverse reactions

Scenario
An OTR is teaching a client, who has peripheral neuropathy and diabetes mellitus, to use a tub transfer bench. After performing the transfer several times, the client reports feeling shaky, weak, and clammy. The OTR has the client check blood glucose levels and, based on the low blood sugar reading, gives the client a glass of orange juice to drink.

Application to Practice
The OTR knows that the exertion from the transfer training session places the client at risk of experiencing hypoglycemic symptoms and responds by assessing the situation and providing the client with a quickly absorbing high carbohydrate beverage.

DOMAIN 04
Competency and Practice Management

TASK 0402

CLASS CODE 040204

Knowledge Statement
Safety procedures to implement during interventions

Scenario
An OTR is teaching a primary caregiver how to transfer a client from a wheelchair to the bed. After demonstrating the transfer, the OTR asks the caregiver and the client to practice the transfer. While observing the return demonstration, the OTR notices that the caregiver forgot to lock both wheels on the wheelchair and quickly intervenes to provide additional instruction before the demonstration proceeds.

Application to Practice
The OTR knows that both the client and caregiver are at risk during the transfer if proper safety procedures are not followed.

CLASS CODE 040205

Knowledge Statement
Preventive measures for minimizing risk in the intervention environment

Scenario
An OTR is orienting an OT student to facility-specific procedures for fabricating custom-made orthoses. The OTR reviews with the student the information on the Safety Data Sheet (SDS) for the cooling spray and shows the student where the SDS is located for future reference.

Application to Practice
The OTR knows that the cooling spray is a hazardous material and that it is essential for all personnel to know where the SDS is stored, understand the information written on the SDS, and know how to apply it.

Domain 04: Competency and Practice Management

TASK 0403

Manage occupational therapy service provision in accordance with laws, regulations, state occupational therapy practice acts, and accreditation guidelines in order to protect consumers and meet applicable reimbursement requirements in relation to the service delivery setting.

CLASS CODE 040301

Knowledge Statement
Methods for identifying, locating, and integrating federal regulations, facility policies, and accreditation guidelines related to service delivery across occupational therapy practice settings

Scenario
An OTR is participating in an annual hospital-wide competency assessment. The OTR reads written information and watches a video on proper hand hygiene techniques before demonstrating the techniques to a supervisor and successfully completing a written test.

Application to Practice
The OTR knows that effective hand hygiene is one method for preventing the spread of infection and that hand hygiene guidelines is part of the accreditation survey conducted by The Joint Commission.

CLASS CODE 040302

Knowledge Statement
Influence of reimbursement policies and guidelines on occupational therapy service delivery

Scenario
An OTR who works in an outpatient pediatric setting is entering billing information for a client who has ataxic cerebral palsy. The OTR uses the ICD-10-CM Official Guidelines for Coding and Reporting to determine that the correct ICD-10 code is G80.4.

Application to Practice
The OTR knows that using the 10th revision of the International Statistical Classification of Diseases and Related Health Problems (ICD-10-CM) to accurately select the diagnosis code for ataxic cerebral palsy will facilitate reimbursement for OT services and reduce the possibility of reimbursement denial.

DOMAIN 04: Competency and Practice Management

TASK 0403

CLASS CODE 040303

Knowledge Statement
Accountability processes and procedures using relevant practice terminology, abbreviations, information technology, and reporting mechanisms for justifying, tracking, and monitoring sentinel events and outcomes related to occupational therapy service delivery

Scenario
An outpatient OTR is conducting an evaluation of a new pain management program. As part of the evaluation, the OTR uses data stored in the electronic health record (EHR), to review scores from standardized outcome measures administered to clients before and after completing the program.

Application to Practice
The OTR knows that analyzing health information in the EHR will provide effective data to guide program development that may contribute to improved performance outcomes for clients participating in the pain management program.

Bibliography

Asher, I. E. (2014). *Asher's occupational therapy assessment tools: An annotated index* (4th ed.). Bethesda, MD: American Occupational Therapy Association, Inc.

Braveman, B. (2016). *Leading and managing occupational therapy services: An evidence-based approach* (2nd ed.). Philadelphia, PA: F.A. Davis Company.

Bracciano, A.G. (2008). *Physical agent modalities: Theory and application for the occupational therapist* (2nd ed.). Thorofare, NJ: SLACK, Inc.

Brown, C., & Stoffel V.C. (2011). *Occupational therapy in mental health: A vision for participation.* Philadelphia, PA: F.A. Davis Company.

Case-Smith, J., & O'Brien, J. (2015). *Occupational therapy for children and adolescents* (7th ed.). St. Louis, MO: Elsevier Mosby, Inc.

Cooper, C. (2014). *Fundamentals of hand therapy: Clinical reasoning and treatment guidelines for common diagnoses of the upper extremity* (2nd ed.). St. Louis, MO: Mosby Elsevier.

Gillen, G. (2016). *Stroke rehabilitation: A function-based approach* (4th ed.). St. Louis, MO: Elsevier Mosby.

Haertl, K. (Ed.). (2014). *Adults with intellectual and developmental disabilities: Strategies for occupational therapy.* Bethesda, MD: American Occupational Therapy Association, Inc.

Jacobs, K., MacRae, N., & Sladyk, K. (2014). *Occupational therapy essentials for clinical competence* (2nd ed.). Thorofare, NJ: SLACK, Inc.

Lane, S.J., & Bundy A.C. (2012). *KIDS can be kids: A childhood occupations approach.* Philadelphia, PA: F.A. Davis Company.

Law, M., & MacDermid, J. (2014). Evidenced-based rehabilitation: A guide to practice (3rd ed.). Thorofare, NJ: SLACK, Inc.

Miller Kuhaneck, H., & Watling, R. (Eds.). (2010). *Autism: A comprehensive occupational therapy approach* (3rd ed.). Bethesda, MD: American Occupational Therapy Association, Inc.

O'Brien, J.C., Solomon, J.W. (2013). *Occupational analysis group process.* St. Louis, MO: Elsevier Mosby.

Pendleton, H.M., & Schultz-Krohn, W. (Eds.). (2018). *Pedretti's occupational therapy practice skills for the physical dysfunction* (8th ed.). St. Louis, MO: Elsevier Mosby.

Radomski, M.V., & Trombly Latham, C.A. (2014). *Occupational therapy for physical dysfunction* (7th ed.). Philadelphia, PA: Lippincott Williams & Wilkins.

Sames, K.M. (2015). *Documenting occupational therapy practice* (3rd ed.). Upper Saddle River, NJ: Pearson Education, Inc.

Scaffa, M.E., Reitz, S.M., & Pizzi, M.A. (2010). *Occupational therapy in the promotion of health and wellness*. Philadelphia, PA: F.A. Davis Company.

Smith-Gabai, H. (2017). *Occupational therapy in acute care* (2nd ed.). Bethesda, MD: American Occupational Therapy Association, Inc.

Appendix C

Worksheet: Illustrated Guide

Use the sample scenarios in each domain area to brainstorm your own examples of situations where you have seen an OTR use this knowledge in practice. From this, jot down your own list of study topics.

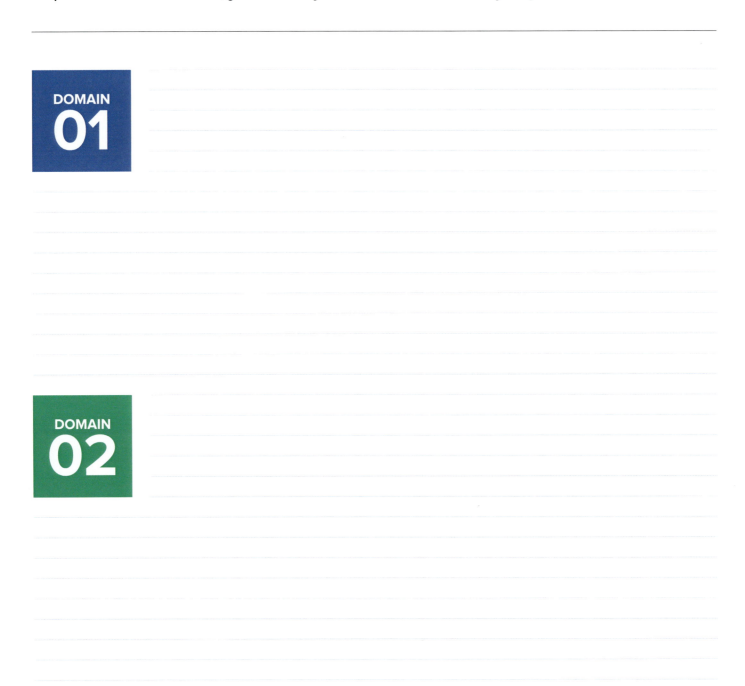

DOMAIN 03

DOMAIN 04

Appendix D

NBCOT OTR® Entry-Level Self-Assessment

DOMAIN 01

Evaluation and Assessment

Acquire information regarding factors that influence occupational performance on an ongoing basis throughout the occupational therapy process.

Task 1: Identify the influence of development; body functions and body structures; and values, beliefs, and spirituality on a client's occupational performance.

When thinking about your knowledge and experience related to the following entry-level OTR skills, how would you rate your current level of competence?	
Impact of typical development and aging on occupational performance, health, and wellness across the life span	○ 0 ○ 1 ○ 2 ○ 3
Expected patterns, progressions, and prognoses associated with conditions that limit occupational performance	○ 0 ○ 1 ○ 2 ○ 3
Impact of body functions, body structures, and values, beliefs, and spirituality on occupational performance	○ 0 ○ 1 ○ 2 ○ 3

Appendix D • Self Assessment

Task 2: Acquire information specific to a client's functional skills, roles, culture, performance context, and prioritized needs through the use of standardized and non-standardized assessments and other available resources in order to develop and update the occupational profile.

When thinking about your knowledge and experience related to the following entry-level OTR skills, how would you rate your current level of competence?

Resources for acquiring information about the client's current condition and occupational performance	○ 0	○ 1	○ 2	○ 3
Administration, purpose, indications, advantages, and limitations of standardized and non-standardized screening and assessment tools	○ 0	○ 1	○ 2	○ 3
Internal and external factors influencing a client's meaningful engagement in occupation related to typical habits, roles, routines, and rituals, and the level and type of assistance require	○ 0	○ 1	○ 2	○ 3

Task 3: Determine the influence of task demands and contexts on occupational performance through the application of theoretical constructs within the practice setting.

When thinking about your knowledge and experience related to the following entry-level OTR skills, how would you rate your current level of competence?

Therapeutic application of theoretical approaches, models of practice, and frames of reference that guide intervention in a variety of practice contexts and environments	○ 0	○ 1	○ 2	○ 3
Task analysis in relation to a client's performance skills, the occupational profile, practice setting, stage of occupational therapy process, areas of occupation, and activity demands	○ 0	○ 1	○ 2	○ 3

383

Analysis and Interpretation

Formulate conclusions regarding client needs and priorities to develop and monitor an intervention plan throughout the occupational therapy process.

Task 1: Synthesize assessment results and information obtained about the client's current condition and context with client needs and priorities to determine eligibility for services consistent with the objectives of the initial referral to develop a client-centered intervention plan.

When thinking about your knowledge and experience related to the following entry-level OTR skills, how would you rate your current level of competence?

Interpretation and analysis of quantitative assessments designed to measure specific client factors and performance skills	○ 0 ○ 1 ○ 2 ○ 3
Integration of qualitative data collected from interviews, observation, and assessment of the social and physical environments, valued activities, necessary occupations, and priorities	○ 0 ○ 1 ○ 2 ○ 3
Integration of screening and assessment results with the client occupational profile, client condition, expected outcomes, and level of service delivery to guide critical decision-making for determining eligibility for services, prioritizing needs, and identifying a targeted intervention plan	○ 0 ○ 1 ○ 2 ○ 3

Appendix D • Self Assessment

Task 2: Collaborate with the client, the client's relevant others, occupational therapy colleagues, and other professionals and staff by using a culturally sensitive, client-centered approach and therapeutic use of self to manage occupational therapy services guided by evidence and principles of best practice.

When thinking about your knowledge and experience related to the following entry-level OTR skills, how would you rate your current level of competence?

Characteristics and functions of interprofessional teams for coordinating client care and providing efficient and effective programs and services consistent with specific core competencies, expertise, unique contributions, team roles, and context of the organization	○ **0** ○ **1** ○ **2** ○ **3**
Management of collaborative client-centered intervention plans, Individualized Education Program plans, and transition plans based on client skills, abilities, and expected outcomes in relation to available resources, level of service delivery, and frequency and duration of intervention	○ **0** ○ **1** ○ **2** ○ **3**
Prioritization of intervention goals and activities based on client needs, wants, developmental skills, abilities, progress, and expected outcomes in relation to level of service delivery as well as frequency and duration of intervention	○ **0** ○ **1** ○ **2** ○ **3**
Strategies used for assessing and addressing health literacy to enhance non-verbal and verbal interactions with a client and relevant others in order to promote positive health behaviors, enable informed decisions, maximize safety of care delivery, and promote carry-over of the intervention to support positive intervention outcomes	○ **0** ○ **1** ○ **2** ○ **3**

NBCOT® Study Guide for the OTR Certification Examination

Task 3: Manage the intervention plan by using clinical reasoning, therapeutic use of self, and cultural sensitivity to identify, monitor, and modify the intervention approach, context, or goals based on client needs, priorities, response to intervention, changes in condition, reevaluation results, and targeted outcomes.

When thinking about your knowledge and experience related to the following entry-level OTR skills, how would you rate your current level of competence?

Factors used for determining and managing the context and type of individual and group activities for effectively supporting intervention goals and objectives	○ **0** ○ **1** ○ **2** ○ **3**
Methods for monitoring the effectiveness of individual and group intervention in order to make decisions about continuation of the intervention or modifications to the intervention approach, context, or goals	○ **0** ○ **1** ○ **2** ○ **3**
Clinical decision-making for adapting or modifying the intervention plan and prioritizing goals in response to physiological changes, behavioral reaction, emotion regulation, and developmental needs of the client	○ **0** ○ **1** ○ **2** ○ **3**

386

Appendix D • Self Assessment

Intervention Management

Select interventions for managing a client-centered plan throughout the occupational therapy process.

Task 1: Incorporate methods and techniques as an adjunct to interventions in order to facilitate healing and enhance engagement in occupation-based activities.

When thinking about your knowledge and experience related to the following entry-level OTR skills, how would you rate your current level of competence?

Methods and techniques for selecting and preparing the environment to support optimal engagement in the intervention and promote goal achievement	○ 0 ○ 1 ○ 2 ○ 3
Indications, contraindications, and precautions associated with wound management, considering the characteristics of a wound, the stage of wound healing, and the influence of the wound on engagement in occupation as guided by evidence, best practice standards, scope of practice, and state licensure practice acts in order to support functional outcomes	○ 0 ○ 1 ○ 2 ○ 3
Indications, contraindications, precautions, and appropriate clinical application of superficial thermal agents as guided by evidence, best practice standards, scope of practice, and state licensure practice act	○ 0 ○ 1 ○ 2 ○ 3
Indications, contraindications, precautions, and appropriate clinical application of deep thermal, mechanical, and electrotherapeutic physical agent modalities as guided by evidence, best practice standards, scope of practice, and state licensure practice acts	○ 0 ○ 1 ○ 2 ○ 3

NBCOT® Study Guide for the OTR Certification Examination

Task 2: Implement occupation-based strategies to support participation in activities of daily living (ADL), instrumental activities of daily living (IADL), rest and sleep, education, work, play, leisure, and social participation across the life span.

When thinking about your knowledge and experience related to the following entry-level OTR skills, how would you rate your current level of competence?

Interventions for supporting leisure and play-based exploration and participation consistent with client interests, needs, goals, and context	○0 ○1 ○2 ○3
Methods for grading an activity, task, or technique based on level of development, client status, response to intervention, and client needs	○0 ○1 ○2 ○3
Methods for facilitating individual and group participation in shared tasks or activities consistent with the type, function, format, context, goals, and stage of the group	○0 ○1 ○2 ○3
Interventions to support optimal sensory arousal, and visual motor, cognitive, or perceptual processing for supporting engagement in meaningful occupations consistent with developmental level, neuromotor status, mental health, cognitive level, psychosocial skills and abilities, task characteristics, context, and environmental demands	○0 ○1 ○2 ○3
Compensatory and remedial strategies for managing cognitive and perceptual deficits or intellectual disabilities	○0 ○1 ○2 ○3
Adaptive and preventive strategies for optimal engagement in occupation consistent with developmental level, neuromotor status, and condition	○0 ○1 ○2 ○3
Intervention strategies and techniques used to facilitate oral motor skills for drinking, eating, and swallowing consistent with developmental level, client condition, caregiver interaction, and mealtime environment and context	○0 ○1 ○2 ○3
Prevocational, vocational, and transitional services, options, and resources for supporting strengths, interests, employment, and lifestyle goals of the adolescent, middle-aged, and older adult client	○0 ○1 ○2 ○3

Appendix D • Self Assessment

Task 3: Manage interventions for improving range of motion, strength, activity tolerance, sensation, postural control, and balance based on neuromotor status, cardiopulmonary response, and current stage of recovery or condition in order to support occupational performance.

When thinking about your knowledge and experience related to the following entry-level OTR skills, how would you rate your current level of competence?

Methods for grading various types of therapeutic exercise and conditioning programs consistent with indications and precautions for strengthening muscles, increasing endurance, improving range of motion and coordination, and increasing joint flexibility in relation to task demands	○ 0　○ 1　○ 2　○ 3
Methods and strategies used to develop, implement, and manage sensory and motor reeducation, pain management, desensitization, edema reduction, and scar management programs	○ 0　○ 1　○ 2　○ 3
Techniques and activities for promoting or improving postural stability, facilitating dynamic balance, and teaching proper body mechanics and efficient breathing patterns during functional tasks to support engagement in occupation	○ 0　○ 1　○ 2　○ 3

Task 4: Apply anatomical, physiological, biomechanical, and healing principles to select or fabricate orthotic devices, and provide training in the use of orthotic and prosthetic devices by using critical thinking and problem-solving as related to a specific congenital anomaly or type of injury, current condition, or disease process in order to support functional outcomes.

When thinking about your knowledge and experience related to the following entry-level OTR skills, how would you rate your current level of competence?

Types and functions of immobilization, mobilization, restriction, and non-articular orthoses for managing specific conditions	○ 0　○ 1　○ 2　○ 3
Influence of anatomical, physiological, biomechanical, and healing principles on orthotic selection, design, fabrication, and modification	○ 0　○ 1　○ 2　○ 3
Methods and techniques for training in the safe and effective use of orthotic and prosthetic devices consistent with prioritized needs, goals, and task demands in order to optimize or enhance function	○ 0　○ 1　○ 2　○ 3

NBCOT® Study Guide for the OTR Certification Examination

Task 5: Select assistive technology options, adaptive devices, mobility aids, and other durable medical equipment, considering the client's developmental, physical, functional, cognitive, and mental health status; prioritized needs; task demands; and context to enable participation in meaningful occupation.

When thinking about your knowledge and experience related to the following entry-level OTR skills, how would you rate your current level of competence?

Factors related to measuring, selecting, monitoring fit of, and recommending modifications to seating systems, positioning devices, and mobility aid	○0 ○1 ○2 ○3
Characteristics and features of high- and low-tech assistive technology for supporting engagement in meaningful occupation	○0 ○1 ○2 ○3
Mobility options, vehicle adaptations, and alternative devices for supporting participation in community mobility	○0 ○1 ○2 ○3
Training methods and other factors influencing successful use and maintenance of commonly used assistive technology options, adaptive devices, and durable medical equipment	○0 ○1 ○2 ○3

Task 6: Recommend environmental modifications guided by an occupation-based model, disability discrimination legislation, and accessibility guidelines and standards to support participation in occupation consistent with a client's physical needs, emotion regulation, cognitive and developmental status, context, and task demands.

When thinking about your knowledge and experience related to the following entry-level OTR skills, how would you rate your current level of competence?

Principles of ergonomics and universal design for identifying, recommending, and implementing reasonable accommodations and features in the workplace, home, and public spaces in order to optimize accessibility and usability	○0 ○1 ○2 ○3
Processes and procedures for identifying, recommending, and implementing modifications in the workplace, home, and public spaces, considering the interaction among client factors, contexts, roles, task demands, and resources	○0 ○1 ○2 ○3

390

Appendix D • Self Assessment

Competency and Practice Management

Manage professional activities of self and relevant others as guided by evidence, regulatory compliance, and standards of practice to promote quality care.

Task 1: Manage professional development activities and competency assessment tasks by using evidence-based strategies and approaches in order to provide safe, effective, and efficient programs and services.

When thinking about your knowledge and experience related to the following entry-level OTR skills, how would you rate your current level of competence?	
Methods for defining a clinical question and performing a critical appraisal to support evidence-based practice	○0 ○1 ○2 ○3
Methods for applying continuous quality improvement processes and procedures to occupational therapy service delivery	○0 ○1 ○2 ○3
Methods for evaluating, monitoring, and documenting service competency and professional development needs of self and assigned personnel based on scope of practice and certification standards for occupational therapy	○0 ○1 ○2 ○3
Methods for developing, analyzing, and applying evidence that supports occupation-based programming to advance positive health outcomes for individuals, groups, and specific populations	○0 ○1 ○2 ○3
Application of ethical decision-making and professional behaviors guided by the NBCOT standards of practice and Code of Conduct	○0 ○1 ○2 ○3

NBCOT® Study Guide for the OTR Certification Examination

Task 2: Incorporate risk management techniques at an individual and service-setting level to protect clients, self, staff, and others from injury or harm during interventions.

When thinking about your knowledge and experience related to the following entry-level OTR skills, how would you rate your current level of competence?

Precautions or contraindications associated with a client condition or stage of recovery	○0 ○1 ○2 ○3
Infection control procedures and universal precautions for reducing transmission of contaminants	○0 ○1 ○2 ○3
Basic first aid in response to minor injuries and adverse reactions	○0 ○1 ○2 ○3
Safety procedures to implement during interventions	○0 ○1 ○2 ○3
Preventive measures for minimizing risk in the intervention environment	○0 ○1 ○2 ○3

Task 3: Manage occupational therapy service provision in accordance with laws, regulations, state occupational therapy practice acts, and accreditation guidelines in order to protect consumers and meet applicable reimbursement requirements in relation to the service delivery setting.

When thinking about your knowledge and experience related to the following entry-level OTR skills, how would you rate your current level of competence?

Methods for identifying, locating, and integrating federal regulations, facility policies, and accreditation guidelines related to service delivery across occupational therapy practice settings	○0 ○1 ○2 ○3
Influence of reimbursement policies and guidelines on occupational therapy service delivery	○0 ○1 ○2 ○3
Accountability processes and procedures using relevant practice terminology, abbreviations, information technology, and reporting mechanisms for justifying, tracking, and monitoring sentinel events and outcomes related to occupational therapy service delivery	○0 ○1 ○2 ○3

Appendix E

References

Ainsworth, E., & de Jonge, D. (2011). *An occupational therapist's guide to home modification practice.* Thorofare, NJ: SLACK, Inc.

Asher, I. E. (Ed.). (2014). *Asher's occupational therapy assessment tools: An annotated index* (4th ed.). Bethesda, MD: AOTA Press.

Bonder, B. R. (2015). *Psychopathology and function* (5th ed.). Thorofare, NJ: SLACK, Inc.

Brown, C., & Stoffel V. C. (2011). *Occupational therapy in mental health: A vision for participation.* Philadelphia, PA: F.A. Davis Company.

Braveman, B. (2016). *Leading and managing occupational therapy services: An evidence-based approach* (2nd ed.). Philadelphia, PA: F.A. Davis Company.

Cara, E., & MacRae, A. (2013). *Psychosocial occupational therapy: An evolving practice* (3rd ed.). Clifton Park, NY: Delmar Cengage Learning.

Case-Smith, J., & O'Brien, J. C. (2015). *Occupational therapy for children and adolescents* (7th ed.). St. Louis, MO: Mosby Elsevier.

Cole, M. B. (2018). *Group dynamics in occupational therapy: The theoretical basis and practice application of group intervention* (5th ed., p. 202). Thorofare, NJ: SLACK, Inc.

Cook, A. M., & Polgar, J. M. (2015). *Assistive technologies: Principles & practice* (4th ed.). St. Louis, MO: Mosby Elsevier.

Cooper, C. (2014). *Fundamentals of hand therapy: Clinical reasoning and treatment guidelines for common diagnoses of the upper extremity* (2nd ed.). St. Louis, MO: Mosby Elsevier.

Coppard, B. M., & Lohman, H. (2015). *Introduction to orthotics: A clinical reasoning and problem-solving approach* (4th ed.). St. Louis, MO: Mosby Elsevier.

DePoy, E., & Gitlin, L. N. (2016). *Introduction to research: Understanding and applying multiple strategies* (5th ed.). St. Louis, MO: Mosby Elsevier.

Fazio, L. S. (2017). *Developing occupation-centered programs with the community* (3rd ed.). Upper Saddle River, NJ: Pearson Education, Inc.

Gateley, C. A., & Borcherding, S. (2017). *Documentation manual for occupational therapy: Writing SOAP notes* (4th ed.). Thorofare, NJ: SLACK, Inc.

Gillen, G. (2016). *Stroke rehabilitation: A function-based approach* (4th ed.). St. Louis, MO: Elsevier.

Greene, D. P., & Roberts, S. L. (2017). *Kinesiology: Movement in the context of activity* (3rd ed.). St. Louis, MO: Mosby Elsevier.

Gutman, S. A., & Schonfeld, A. B. (2009). *Screening adult neurologic populations: A step-by-step instruction manual* (2nd ed.). Bethesda, MD: AOTA Press.

Hinojosa, J., & Kramer, P. (Eds.). (2014). *Evaluation in occupational therapy: Obtaining and interpreting data* (4th ed.). Bethesda, MD: AOTA Press.

Jacobs, K., & McCormack, G. L. (Eds.). (2011). *The occupational therapy manager* (5th ed.). Bethesda, MD: AOTA Press.

Kuhaneck, H. M., & Watling, R. (2010). *Autism: A comprehensive occupational therapy approach* (3rd ed.). Bethesda: AOTA Press.

Law, M., & MacDermid, J. (Eds.). (2014). *Evidence-based rehabilitation: A guide to practice* (3rd ed.). Thorofare, NJ: SLACK, Inc.

Lundy-Ekman, L. (2013). *Neuroscience: Fundamentals for rehabilitation* (4th ed.). St. Louis, MO: Saunders Elsevier.

Mulligan, S. (2014). *Occupational therapy evaluation for children: A pocket guide* (2nd ed.). Philadelphia, PA: Lippincott Williams & Wilkins.

Pendleton, H. M., & Schultz-Krohn, W. (Eds.). (2018). *Pedretti's occupational therapy: Practice skills for the physical dysfunction* (8th ed.). St. Louis, MO: Mosby Elsevier.

Radomski, M. V., & Trombly Latham, C. A. (Eds.). (2014). *Occupational therapy for physical dysfunction* (7th ed.). Philadelphia, PA: Lippincott Williams & Wilkins.

Rybski, M. F. (2012). *Kinesiology for occupational therapy* (2nd ed.). Thorofare, NJ: SLACK, Inc.

Sames, K. M. (2015). *Documenting occupational therapy practice* (3rd ed.). Upper Saddle River, NJ: Pearson Education, Inc.

Scaffa, M. E., Reitz, S. M., & Pizzi, M. A. (2010). *Occupational therapy in the promotion of health and wellness.* Philadelphia, PA: F.A. Davis Company.

Smith-Gabai, H., & Holm, S. (Eds.). (2017). *Occupational therapy in acute care* (2nd ed.). Bethesda, MD: AOTA Press.

Schell, B. A. B., Gillen, G., & Scaffa, M. E. (2014). *Willard & Spackman's occupational therapy* (12th ed.). Philadelphia, PA: Lippincott Williams & Wilkins.

Zoltan, B. (2007). *Vision, perception, and cognition: A manual for the evaluation and treatment of the adult with acquired brain injury* (4th ed.). Thorofare, NJ: SLACK, Inc.